HV 6721 .R62 J46 1998

Jensen, Katherine, 1946-

The last gamble

DATE DUE

THE
LAST
GAMBLE

THE LAST GAMBLE

Betting on the Future in Four Rocky Mountain Mining Towns

Katherine Jensen and Audie Blevins

The University of Arizona Press   Tucson

The University of Arizona Press

© 1998 The Arizona Board of Regents

First printing

Manufactured in the United States of America

03   02   01   00   99   98   6   5   4   3   2   1

Library of Congress Cataloging-in-Publication Data

Jensen, Katherine, 1946–
The last gamble : betting on the future in four Rocky Mountain
mining towns / Katherine Jensen and Audie Blevins.
p. cm.
Includes index.
ISBN 0-8165-1854-8 (acid-free paper)
1. Gambling—Economic aspects—Rocky Mountains Region.
2. Gambling—Economic aspects—West (U.S.) 3. Community
development—Rocky Mountains Region. 4. Community development—
West (U.S.) 5. Tourist trade—Rocky Mountains Region. 6. Tourist
trade—West (U.S.) I. Blevins, Audie L. II. Title.
HV6721.R62 J46 1998
363.4'2'0978—dc21
98-8962
CIP

British Library Cataloguing-in-Publication Data

A catalogue record for this book is available from the British Library.

CONTENTS

List of Illustrations   vii

Acknowledgments   ix

Introduction   3

1   The Drive for the Legalization of Gambling   9

2   Race, Gender, and Class in the Legacy of the Gamble   27

3   Stagnation and Decay in Retrospect   54

4   Gold Rush Returns   74

5   Historic Preservation, Facadism, and the Fast Buck   105

6   Community Transformation in the Gamble   132

7   Mining Quarters: Settler Camps to Gambler Traps   166

8   Legalized Gambling as a Community Development
      Quick Fix   182

Notes   197
Index   217

ILLUSTRATIONS

Lace House in Black Hawk   67

The Gillmore Hotel in Deadwood   110

The Adams House in Deadwood   112

New "period" construction for Silver Hawk Casino in Black Hawk   124

Creekside "mill" construction for Harvey's Casino in Central City   125

Historic facades that front Harrah's Casino in Central City   126

Slot machines in Deckers Food Center in Deadwood   140

Cripple Creek Market, closed and for sale   150

Bullwhackers, which replaced the Kwik Mart in Black Hawk   151

Bennett Avenue in Cripple Creek   167

ACKNOWLEDGMENTS

We want first to thank whoever made us think we could be academics, instead of a baseball player and whatever a "teaching credential as insurance policy" was protection against. As much as we both enjoy teaching students, administering departments and programs, and participating in a huge range of committee assignments, the opportunity to do extended research and writing on issues that have social implications still has to be one of the great rewards of the professorial life.

As we pursued this historical, regional, and now national topic, people in a large number of libraries were very generous with their time and helpful with our questions. We must acknowledge especially the Hearst Public Library in Lead, the Denver Public Library Western History Collection, the Colorado Springs Public Library, the Colorado College Library, the Leland Case Collection at Black Hills State University, and the Coe Library of the University of Wyoming. We also learned much in the Adams Museum in Deadwood and the Cripple Creek and Central City museums.

We relied heavily on data sent us monthly from both the Colorado Division of Gaming and the South Dakota Commission on Gaming. But we also have to thank the many people who willingly gave us personal interviews and allowed us to tape them for accuracy. While the transcription process is long and tedious, it also produced some of our best insights into the experiences of local residents and business people.

In addition to our own extensive files of local and regional newspaper articles on gambling and our bibliographic search of scholarly publications, we have to thank our unpaid research assistants who took on particular assignments. They include especially Frances Cushing, who made sure we didn't miss anything in the *New York Times, Wall Street Journal,* or southwestern gambling news; Georgia Jensen and Celia Jensen, who sent us South Dakota news because of their own interest in community and economic change; and Ludie Blevins, who kept us up with Mississippi and Red River casino boats and politics.

We had cooperative colleagues and administrators who granted us teaching schedules that would allow long weekend forays to our research sites with some frequency. We also had support from a National Endowment for the Humanities Summer Fellowship (NEH Grant FT-38528), a Charles Redd Foundation Grant, and a research leave apiece. We also thank the University of Wyoming Institute for Environmental and Natural Resource Research and Policy and the Office of the Vice-President for Research for their interest in and support of this publication.

We also want to thank the anonymous reviewers who gave us organizational and stylistic suggestions; Joanne O'Hare, who sponsored the project at the University of Arizona Press; Al Schroder, Anne Keyl, and especially Mary Hill and Evelyn VandenDolder, all of whom helped make this study available for public consideration; and Jane Reverand, who prepared the index.

And we have to thank each other for making this a project that was almost always interesting and enjoyable and almost never, even in its most tedious moments, very tension producing. While we developed an informal division of labor, both of us have conjectured, documented, drafted, and edited every observation we make here and have taken all of the photographs. The order of authorship is quite arbitrary. Other than launching four offspring into adulthood, this must be our largest collaborative adventure.

THE
LAST
GAMBLE

INTRODUCTION

On November 1, 1989, thirty-four businesses in Deadwood, South Dakota, with cautious celebration, opened their doors for legal low stakes gambling, including nickel, dime, quarter, and dollar slot machines and black jack and poker tables with five-dollar bet limits. The event marked Deadwood as the first local government in the United States to permit casino gambling since Atlantic City, New Jersey, went into the casino business in 1976 and made the infamous nineteenth-century gold rush settlement in the Black Hills the only town with legal casino gambling between the Atlantic coast and the state of Nevada.

Almost two years later, two more nineteenth-century mining camps in Colorado followed suit with the conviction that legalized gambling might turn around the long decline they, like Deadwood, had been suffering. Gambling initiatives in Central City and the adjacent municipality of Black Hawk, up Clear Creek Canyon west of Denver, and Cripple Creek, on the slopes of Pikes Peak west of Colorado Springs, had survived legislation and state and local votes to allow casinos with limited stakes gambling to begin operation on October 1, 1991. Twenty-one gaming halls in the three towns were ready for an opening day that would draw regional and national attention.

But the move to gambling cannot be bracketed by those dates. All four towns have been transformed, not simply by an economic boom but by differing notions of what their communities would be. From the first day, gaming revenues exceeded expectations by a factor of ten in Deadwood. The Colorado towns, which had been witnesses to the rush to Deadwood, found it difficult to hold to their intentions of "going slow" in the opening of their casinos. And the transformation is far from complete, even after the initial "shakedown" of entrepreneurial ventures produced losers as well as phenomenal success stories.

Nor can the introduction of gambling be understood simply by tracing the local boosters, the legislative campaigns, the local voting margins, or even property speculation, although those political and economic ingredients all factor into the story. Deadwood, Cripple Creek, and Central City/Black Hawk all reflect their longer heritage as Rocky Mountain gold-mining towns and, more generally, as speculative gathering points for exploiting the rich resources of the American West. Their geopolitical situations seem significant, not only because of the Wild West themes the towns employ to lure visitors to drop their quarters in the slots and their dollars on the bar but because of the commencement of gambling in these particular places and the community reactions to it as well.

This study is intentionally limited in its appraisal of the current gambling explosion in late-twentieth-century American culture. Although our focus is Rocky Mountain towns that were among the first civic entities to turn to gambling in the last decade of the twentieth century, their transformation and prognosis must now be examined within the general circumstances of the expansion of riverboat gambling, state lotteries, the most recent developments of theme entertainment in the meccas of Las Vegas and Atlantic City, and especially Indian gaming, which is nationwide, expansive, and also proximate. Likewise, our project does not examine the personal issues of "problem gambling," except as it is reflected as a community concern.

The project does explore the ways in which gambling comes as no surprise as an economic venture in these once prosperous mining locales. It also investigates the ways that the "preservation" of their histories as western bonanzas became both a rationale and the chief metaphor of their new incarnations. And it delineates the differences among the towns, in historical legacy and contemporary legislation, to explain how their individual fortunes might vary from each other, as well as to speculate on their chances in the context of the larger gambling boom. This study of the process of transforming mining and "family tourist" towns into gambling towns is intended to have a narrow focus while recognizing the wide angle, both historically and nationally.

Our pursuit of this project came from some of the same sources as our analysis of it. They are geographical, historical, and professional. As sociologists at the University of Wyoming, we sit literally between Deadwood, South Dakota, and the Colorado gambling towns. Not only the surrounding media but the political interests of our own state have been fascinated with the newest regional economic boom. Audie Blevins started a file of news stories and documents sometime after we returned from Europe in 1989, and soon Katherine Jensen's mother was contributing to the clipping file. Eventually friends, relatives, and colleagues from all over the country were sending us gambling-related materials they thought we should know about.

The family connection provided another stimulus. Jensen was born in Deadwood and grew up in Lawrence County, of which Deadwood is the county seat. Like her parents, she graduated from Lead High School, just three miles up the gulch from Deadwood, and spent much of her early life traversing the length of the town going back and forth from the family ranch at the northern end of the county. The dramatic changes taking place in Deadwood (and in adjacent Lead) provided a social laboratory almost impossible for a sociologist to resist. Thirty years' residence away from Lawrence County made the analysis less invested in old suppositions while still offering enough memory of local culture to provide a comfortable entrée with most residents. Blevins had the advantage of the more disinterested social scientist who had extensive experience researching the Wyoming energy resource booms of the 1970s. He could observe the changes taking place in Deadwood and Colorado without the nostalgia for "the way things used to be."

But like most scholarly endeavors, this work springs not simply from the training, interests, or position of the authors but also from the prior work of colleagues in the academic community. As sociologists, we would begin with Jerome H. Skolnick's *House of Cards: Legalization and Control of Casino Gambling*. Skolnick started with the question of whether gambling was a pathology, a social problem, but moved to an analysis of the "political economy of a vice," that is, the economic and regulatory issues connected to legal gambling. Ultimately he argued that the control of legal casino gambling was an uncertain, even precarious, enterprise. This was an important starting point. Yet the fit wasn't perfect. Skolnick's focus on Nevada and Great Britain was on large-scale casino gambling, and our project was specifically limited stakes. Moreover, we were looking at "gaming" both before and after the mid-twentieth-century legalization of gambling and the concern for control of organized crime associated with it.

The Business of Risk: Commercial Gambling in Mainstream America, by Vicki Abt, James F. Smith, and Eugene Martin Christiansen, seemed from the beginning closer to our project, in which communities instituted gambling for economic redevelopment and even the lofty goals of historic preservation. Abt, Smith, and Christiansen distinguished between gambling at games of equal chance and commercial gambling games that by definition ensure collective player losses and guarantee commercial and state advantage. While a good portion of this work looked at gambling behaviors under these circumstances, the last chapters focused on gambling as a social institution and the relation of gambling to American values. The cultural and institutional view spoke more directly to our interest in the legacy of gambling in western mining towns, the somewhat contradictory history of tolerance and condemnation of vice, and the growing arguments in favor of individual "rights to recreation."

That led us to a broader historical analysis of gambling in America, especially as detailed in John M. Findlay's *People of Chance: Gambling in American Society from Jamestown to Las Vegas*. Findlay's social history of gambling explored the affinity between gambling and frontiers, from the first permanent English settlements in North America to the transformation of Las Vegas casinos into "embodiments of Southern California culture" and, as such, "stunning new landmarks of United States civilization." Findlay saw casino games, as opposed to other forms of gambling, as ideally suited to frontier shaping, with the speed and relative portability catering to the preferences of a fluid and impatient society. That nexus, of gambling as a frontier entertainment or enterprise, and Nevada gambling as coming to represent Southern California's particular modern frontier, launched our undertaking chronologically both forward and backward. We had noted some local objections to the vices of gambling and prostitution but very little to drinking in these mining towns during the Progressive Era. But if Americans were lamenting the loss of their national innocence, as Ruth Rosen argued in chapter 1, "From Necessary to Social Evil," in *The Lost Sisterhood,* the gold-mining towns of the West had never been innocent places nor even made much attempt to be. Drinking, gambling, and prostitution had continued unabated, except for the strictures of Prohibition, which drove them underground. More puzzling were the dramatic raids on gambling and prostitution in both South Dakota and Colorado in the late forties and fifties. In a real sense, our study begins where Findlay's leaves off. If Las Vegas was coming to represent not only Southern California but the images of Orientalism in its transformation to a mecca of gambling, prostitution, and quick marriage and quick divorce, the Rocky Mountain states would no longer be so tolerant of those vices in their old mining towns. They would abruptly shut down operations that had been open secrets for sixty to eighty years.

Meanwhile, what had become of these mining communities? To focus on communities themselves in this broader historical milieu, we have referred to the work of a broad range of rural sociologists, from Cornelia and Jan Flora, who look at the legacy of rural communities, to Gene Summers, Calvin Beale, and others who have traced the decline of rural communities in the second half of the twentieth century. That led us to an analysis of federal programs aimed at a "rural turnaround" and efforts to stem urban migration through the revitalization of smaller communities in the face of social, economic, and technological forces working in the opposite direction. The decline of the Rocky Mountain mining communities magnified national trends because of their dependence on a single industry, mining, and their shift, for lack of other opportunities, increasingly to tourism. The particular scheme for economic redevelopment seemed to colleagues with whom we spoke to resemble Peter Eisinger's model in *The Rise of the Entrepreneurial State*. Yet we came to realize that while government would play an essential role in this form of development, rather than "jump-starting" an increase in private investment, government would in these places first authorize, then regulate, but ultimately become a dependent partner in the business of gambling.

Concurrently with efforts toward a rural turnaround, another federal mandate, the preservation of historic landmarks and sites, gave the old frontier mining towns a new romance and a more positive identity. The field of historic preservation was newer to us than political economy, sociology of public policy, social history, or rural sociology. Nevertheless, since gambling as a means to community redevelopment had succeeded in Deadwood, Central City, Black Hawk, and Cripple Creek only when the legal authorization was specifically linked to historic preservation, we immersed ourselves in documents of historic preservation across the country. Moreover, the analyses of William J. Murtagh in *Keeping Time: The History and Theory of Preservation in America* and Michael Wallace, "Reflections on the History of Historic Preservation," in *Presenting the Past: Essays on History and the Public,* edited by Susan Porter Benson, Stephen Brier, and Roy Rosenzweig, provided essential conceptual groundwork for understanding what we saw happening in the gambling towns, which would now accumulate abundant resources for historic preservation. "Adaptive reuse" and "facadism" flashed before our eyes each time we visited them. That image from historic preservation led us back to the concept of the "decorated shed," from Robert Venturi, Denise Scott Brown, and Steven Izenour's celebrated study, *Learning from Las Vegas: The Forgotten Symbolism of Architectural Form,* which we had looked at early on but really had not appreciated very much until we started enumerating how many ironies the project encompassed.

That insight, generally of narrative ironies, suggests the position we believe we have occupied in this pursuit, reflecting work in the new social history of the West. This enterprise recognizes the power that a mythology of the rugged individualist in a particularly challenging environment has had while questioning that mythology at every turn. Several essays in the volume edited by Patricia Limerick, Clyde Milnar, and Charles

Parker called *Trails: Toward a New Western History,* from the Santa Fe conference with the same name that we attended in 1989, and especially Richard White's essay on "Trashing the Trails," spoke to our pursuit of placing the standardized electronic slot machine within the context of gold mining on the "American frontier."

Finally, in the last chapters of the book we rely on our general critical perspectives on social change and assess differential impacts on various groups and institutions, giving particular attention to gender, age, and class. Here we examine the gains and losses from local option, limited stakes gambling that developed in this particular historical and cultural setting. Informing this work is our understanding of conflict over scarce resources. Contrary to the local arguments that this venture provides "new money from outside sources," with a consequent greater good for everyone, in fact, the communities and the states as governmental entities still face myriad questions about distribution of resources. Especially as gambling expands within the communities themselves and across the nation, there are necessarily as many losers as winners, and those with fewer resources to begin with, whether citizens or entrepreneurs or local governments, are the most likely losers.

From the initial moments of legalized gambling in the Rocky Mountains we have collected economic data; walked around looking at people and their activities; interviewed officials and citizens singly and in groups, sometimes repeatedly; shot videotape and still photos; read old newspapers and recent ones; discovered secondary sources of scholarly merit; and perused countless local amateur historical accounts. All of these efforts are directed at an understanding of the dramatic community transformation imposed by the choice of gambling as a means to stimulate economic development. The towns had all deteriorated physically and economically. Their citizens thought gambling would complement their mining histories and tourist industries. But they failed to comprehend that "a little gambling" would become the sole industry and one that was entirely adult based. The obvious new economic prosperity belied the fundamental changes in the social fabric of the communities.

Our gamble is that what we have to say here speaks clearly to the issue of community development through gaming and the long-term prospects of a recreational resource more problematic and volatile than the nonrenewable precious metals responsible for the founding of these western mining towns.

CHAPTER 1

The Drive for the Legalization of Gambling

When local option, limited stakes gambling was initiated in Deadwood, South Dakota, in the fall of 1989 and in three Colorado mining towns almost two years later, most residents imagined providing an additional tourist attraction to bolster the somewhat tawdry Main Streets of each of these "Old West" mining towns. Instead, it transformed employment, physical space, and revenues to become the dominant industry in all four towns. Soon retailers from car dealers to ladies' ready-to-wear would sell out or convert to casino operations. The citizens who had voted for gambling with the vision that restaurants and bars, maybe even the bakery, might each have a few slot machines in the fronts of their businesses would soon find that businesses necessarily accommodated slot machines first, and only services that supported the playing of slot machines would survive. Everywhere, mostly run-down buildings that had been previously valued at a few thousand dollars were selling for a few hundred thousand. Not only buildings but streets and sewer and water lines would be renovated or, where possible, simply torn down for a new structure. And all of this was happening as roughly four times as many visitors were coming to town to check out the possibilities of getting rich quickly or at least to be able to have fun in ways previously impermissible.

But it was hardly the first time that locals and visitors would take risks to make a fast buck in Deadwood, Cripple Creek, Central City, or Black Hawk. All four towns had been founded by individuals, mostly white men, who had figured on an opportunity too good to pass up, regardless of its apparent dangers and questionable ethics. The willingness to take chances has always been an attractive attribute in the United States, whether in business or in recreation. Taking risks also implies a resource to invest, whether one's life or livelihood or capital, and over the last century and a half the citizens of western mining towns have taken chances with all of these assets. If risk taking figures prominently in descriptions of American character generally, then speculators and entrepreneurs on the frontier are endowed with especially large doses of venturesome behaviors, at least in the mythology of the American West. Each of these towns had its share of risk takers in its beginnings, just as its citizens made the decision for risk taking a century or more later.

The Black Hills Gold and Gambling Rush

Deadwood, South Dakota, was the focal point of the Black Hills gold rush of 1876 that abrogated the 1868 Treaty of Fort Laramie, which had preserved that land as part of the Great Sioux Reservation for the most recent of native peoples to occupy the vicinity.[1] It would become famous as the place where U.S. Marshal James Butler ("Wild Bill") Hickok was shot and where the also legendary Calamity Jane Canary was buried (at her request, next to Wild Bill). Deadwood was, however, not the locale of the first gold strike, which was at the southern end of the Hills near Custer in 1874. It was also not the biggest: this proved to be the Homestake, discovered in 1877, which fostered the Hearst company town of Lead, three miles up the gulch. But the gold strikes in Deadwood Gulch in 1875 spawned placer and lode mines all over the creeks and steep slopes of the Northern Hills and nearly thirty different mining camp communities. By early March 1876, six hundred miners were working Deadwood, Whitewood, Gold Run, Blacktail, Whitetail, and Grizzly gulches, all in what would become Lawrence County.[2] Deadwood, from the beginning, would be the milling and commercial center of the eleven mining districts surrounding Deadwood Gulch. Stamp mills, amalgamation and chlorination refining processes, and pyritic matte smelters were the real mining business of Deadwood. Deadwood, increasingly the downstream refining area of the burgeoning Homestake mine, would be demarcated with a "slime plant" on the hill at one end and a "slag pile" marking the other. Both are now being renamed in the interest of public image.[3] But if those unglamorous enterprises fail as tourist attractions in the late twentieth century, the businesses where miners celebrated their successes and paid their bills in gold dust have certain appeal.

With the miners came merchants, doctors, lawyers, ministers, and bankers, "all of whom helped provide a civilizing influence in the midst of the chaotic search for gold."[4] More conspicuously, Main Street featured, much as it would a century later, a preponderance of boarding houses, saloons, and gambling halls. Deadwood had seventy-five saloons in 1877, many of them operating in tents, and sixty-three were listed in the 1880 city directory. Virtually all offered gambling of some kind, if only in the form of card games.[5] Generally, gambling was so commonplace as to be a matter of comment more by writers and activists in the distance than by locals. By 1907, Edith Eudora Kohl, a homesteader in the central part of South Dakota, reported on the reform efforts of newspaperman E. L. Senn, who described "gambling halls, operated as openly as grocery stores, running twenty-four hours a day."[6] Most of these establishments provided opportunities for miners to part with some of their gold dust directly on the scales that sat behind the bar. Professionals and amateurs wagered large and small amounts, unfettered by regulations or even expectations of honesty. According to Seth Bullock, early marshal and long-time resident, now celebrated with a casino and hotel named for him, "That rare avis, the square gambler, and his associate, the law abiding saloon keeper, were not much in evidence in any of the towns."[7]

Retrospective discussions of gambling in Deadwood often refer to 1947 as the year that gambling became illegal. In fact, gambling had been illegal in Dakota Territory since 1881; 1947 is the year that South Dakota Attorney General (later Governor) Sigurd Anderson forced the Lawrence County sheriff and state's attorney to enforce the state gambling law. Sixteen "raiders" simultaneously struck five Deadwood bars during a busy Saturday night, although the Lawrence County state's attorney, Larry McDonald, said that all operators in Deadwood had been warned by letter that they could expect an investigation at any time. The gambling places had just reopened three weeks earlier after being closed a year and a half in the wake of an antigambling campaign by former Lawrence County State's Attorney Clinton Richards.[8]

It is fair to say that gambling operators merely became more circumspect after that time, for one of Deadwood's current casino managers reported having been "trained as a card dealer" for one of the most prominent saloons in town in 1954. Local establishments continued to open for short periods of time, and as long as business ran smoothly and no one lost too much money, gambling continued informally, with "troubleshooters" cutting off big losers and occasionally returning money to families hurt by gambling losses. The Lead-Deadwood Chamber of Commerce manager who helped to form the local initiative to legalize gambling argued that across the state in the 1950s people talked about "bringing gambling back to Deadwood to try and re-create what we had here in the days when gaming was a common thing."[9]

The brothels had been closed down in 1980, with a similar raid orchestrated by the state attorney general's office that included local law enforcement officers only at the last moment. The Old Style Saloon No. 10, across the street on the lower end of Main Street near the brothels, had reported a long history of getting as many as thirty requests per night for directions to "the houses," and their closure had hurt the Main Street economy, especially in the fall.[10] Hunters had long sustained the community between the summer tourist season and the beginning of ski season, but a well-known town joke tells of the hunter who returns from Deadwood and berates his wife for not packing his underwear. She replies that she had "put them in his gun case." Businessman and former priest Bill Walsh had sounded a note of desperate optimism. "Look, I'm opposed to prostitution, but there is no question that we've been hurt economically. The challenge for us is not to rely on the romance of the past. We need to be creative, reemphasize winter sports, do whatever it takes to attract people to the area."[11]

But perhaps the first organized effort to legalize Deadwood's old vices took place in 1984, with the initiative of Lew Keen, long-time owner of the locally famous Old Style Saloon No. 10. He suggested to Dan Schenkein of the Chamber of Commerce that it was time to take action and bring gambling back to Deadwood. Keen and Schenkein met with Deadwood Mayor Tom Blair; they joined Bill Walsh, an owner of the Franklin Hotel and Durty Nelly's Saloon; music and arcade vendor Mike Trucano; and Dakota Territory Saloon owner Jerry Apa at a lunch meeting to explore the process of legalizing gambling in Deadwood.[12] But a ballot measure for local option gambling anywhere in the state failed that year.

Meanwhile, a "Save the Courthouse" group began to meet in the wake of the condemnation of the Lawrence County Courthouse, declared unsafe and set for demolition. Paul Putz, director of the South Dakota Historical Preservation Center, gave a passionate talk about the meaning of the courthouse to the community and warned of the danger that Deadwood might lose its National Historic Landmark designation. Schenkein made the connection and called Mayor Tom Blair and the rest of the progambling group, and the strategy became apparent.

Blair recalled, "It was a natural fit. We were trying to save the town. The issue of gaming was a part of our past and of our culture. The goal there was to re-create the 'Deadwood Experience,' as we came to call it. We also knew of how hard it was for our local building owners to try and save the culture they were caretakers for by the fact of owning these old buildings. The plan was the right plan, and the issue of preservation was a real and pressing need. It just all came together."[13]

In a culture that thrives on storytelling, the formation of the citizens' group to promote gambling yields a short and universally accepted tale. When Lew Keen approached Dan Schenkein about the need to get people fired up about gaming, he said they ought to have buttons made to distribute the message to the public. Schenkein responded, "You bet." Deciding that was the perfect slogan, he immediately ordered five hundred "Deadwood You Bet" buttons.

Melodee Nelson, who had just made an unsuccessful bid for an appointment to a vacant seat on the Deadwood City Commission, was called by Mayor Blair to join the Deadwood You Bet Committee, which she would chair. Nelson was joined by Blair, Schenkein, Trucano (as vice chairperson, secretary, and treasurer, respectively), City Commissioner and bar owner Mary Dunne, Deadwood Historic Preservation Commissioner Dave Larson, hotel owner Bill Walsh, and Betty Wittington. Blair and Schenkein registered as lobbyists for the 1987 session of the legislature to get the issue on the 1988 ballot. Meanwhile the Northern Hills Mayors voted to endorse the creation of a gaming "oasis" in Deadwood, with the notion that the cities of Sturgis, Whitewood, Spearfish, Lead, and Deadwood would work as a loose confederacy for northern Black Hills interests.[14]

The committee focused a well-organized effort to promote a proposal for limited gambling, making certain that members of the group argued consistently for a limit of fifteen (a number that would be doubled before implementation) gaming machines per business establishment and five-dollar bet limits. Despite the emphasis on keeping Deadwood's "small town" character and providing additional recreation ("one more thing . . . to do" and "selling our history to those who come to find it"), persuading the legislature proved unsuccessful. The proposal to put the issue on the ballot failed by one vote on the floor of the House. While working to have the measure reconsidered, a busload of Deadwood citizens in period costumes descended on the legislature, but the bill was defeated a second time.[15]

Undaunted, the committee set out to collect the 29,000 signatures needed to put the measure on the November 1988 ballot by petition, a task that some members thought initially would be an easy one. But by early August of 1987, only 7,000 people had signed the petitions due in the capitol in November. At the state fair, committee members managed four clipboards at a time and collected 10,000 more signatures. At the Sioux Empire Fair, committee members were taken by surprise by the turnout and interest of 60,000 people (they thought then because of the free food being served), but they must have wondered later how many plans for Indian gaming were laid during their initial campaign.

Having eventually collected the necessary signatures to call for a constitutional amendment to allow limited gambling in Deadwood, the committee intensified its efforts to sell the idea to South Dakota voters. With a five-member central board and ten committee members, now including Linda Blair, wife of the mayor, and still chaired by Melodee Nelson, Deadwood You Bet received an initial $20,000 from the city of Deadwood to continue the campaign.

Nelson pointed to polls showing statewide support for limited gambling, with a Lead-Deadwood Chamber of Commerce poll showing 70 percent in favor in nearby Rapid City. The committee had also employed Michael Madden, an economist with the University of South Dakota extension at Ellsworth Air Base, to prepare a study of the impact of limited gambling on Deadwood, Lawrence County, and the state of South Dakota in terms of tax revenues and tourism development. Madden began with the premise that South Dakota was unable to meet the "needs and expectations" of young adults and older travelers in the $60,000 and over annual income category; he argued additionally that of the five Old West Trail states, South Dakota ranked fourth in quality of entertainment and night life activities.[16] It was no great surprise, then, that Madden would see gambling as an appropriate means of economic development for the town and for the state. His projections also fit the hopes of Deadwood businesses that gaming would merely bring an addition to the retail and entertainment opportunities that Deadwood already offered.

But Nelson was also mindful that despite Deadwood's seeming comfort with gambling for more than a century, some citizens of the state were apprehensive about the social impacts of gambling. She took the position that city officials would maintain steadfastly, pointing to a 1983 speech by Walter Read, chairman of the Casino Control Commission of Atlantic City. Nelson stated:

> Critics have pointed to an increase in criminal activity associated with the legalization of gambling. It is true that with an increase in the number of people in any one location, you can logically expect an equal increase in the individual incidences of criminal activity. The crime rate [in Atlantic City] is not much worse than it was a year ago on a per capita basis. You can't bring millions of people into a city and not expect to see some increase in the amount of crime. It has been pointed out to me that the crime rate in Atlantic City is not any greater than that in Disney World.[17]

Nelson emphasized that some forms of gambling had been proven successful in North Dakota and Montana and that the limitations on the number of available games and the bet limit would control gaming, so that Deadwood had everything to gain and nothing to lose. By the November election, the committee had spent $110,000, $80,000 in direct contributions and $30,000 in loans from the Twin City Development Corporation and the Deadwood Economic Development Corporation. Nearly all of the funds were used for brochures, radio, TV and newspaper advertising, and legislative lobbyists.[18]

The effort was successful, as South Dakota as a whole voted 64 percent in favor of the constitutional amendment to allow limited legalized gambling in Deadwood. In March the 1989 legislature passed enabling legislation, which included a required vote of the Deadwood citizenry in April. Deadwood voters approved the measure with 75 percent (690 to 230) voting yes and with more than 60 percent of the registered voters turning out. Ironically, in the mayoral race, Tom Blair received 2 percent fewer votes than printshop owner Bruce Oberlander, whose position at the time was opposed to gambling and who beat Blair in a runoff election two weeks later. Despite his position, at the high noon opening on November 1, 1989, when the gunshots and fire sirens had died down, Mayor Oberlander noted the historical significance of the occasion positively. "It's not very often small towns . . . get to do something really great [noting that many of the significant dates from Deadwood's history were of devastating fires]. Hopefully with this effort November 1 will be the day we started to rebuild Deadwood."[19]

Blair, however, was the master of ceremonies for the day. Among the official speakers were the South Dakota attorney general and former Lawrence County State's Attorney Roger Tellinghuisen, who warned the crowd, "Know when to hold 'em; know when to fold 'em. Know when to walk away, and know when to run." State Treasurer David Volk, who, along with then–Attorney General Mark Meierhenry, had been caught gambling illegally two years before, explained that they had merely been ahead of their time. An executive proclamation from Governor George Mickelson declared November 1, 1989, as Deadwood Gambling Day.[20]

On the day before, the South Dakota Gaming Commission had held a special meeting to approve 120 additional licenses for gambling parlor employees, including cashiers and dealers for the thirty-four businesses approved for gambling. Ninety dealers had been licensed previously, but the businesses (none permitted by statute to call themselves casinos) were still short of dealers, signs, and finishing construction. In an effort to restrict gambling according to gaming regulations, Deadwood "gaming parlors" were to be limited to thirty "gaming devices" (slot machines or card tables) per building, and each machine would have a maximum hold of 20 percent. Community stability was intended in the initial requirement that at least 50 percent of the ownership of each establishment be held by local residents.

To safeguard against the possibility of organized crime the South Dakota Gaming Commission was granted tsarist powers to regulate, license, and enforce gaming rules, and the commission's Deadwood employees were ensconced in a second-floor office looking out over the main intersection in town. South Dakota decided to levy an 8 percent tax on adjusted gaming revenues. Of those revenues the South Dakota Gaming Commission was to receive 50 percent; the South Dakota general fund, 40 percent; and Lawrence County, only 10 percent. The Deadwood Historic Preservation fund would receive a two-thousand-dollar annual licensing fee on each gaming device, plus unspent monies allocated to the gaming commission. The lion's share of gaming revenues, in fact, beyond profits to owners of establishments, was returned to the local Historic Preservation Commission. Only a small number of nickel slot machines controlled by the city of Deadwood were exempt from the tax and licensing fees. Thus, South Dakota's emphasis was on the historic revitalization of Deadwood. While the impact of this decision could not be fully foreseen on November 1, hopes ran high in Deadwood when the slot machines started their incessant jangle at high noon.

Learning from Deadwood

By summer 1990, three separate gambling initiatives had been proposed in Colorado, and proponents of each were touring sporting events, shopping malls, and concerts in search of 50,668 valid signatures due in the secretary of state's office by August 6. Advocates made explicit references to Deadwood, saying that since limited stakes gambling had been launched eight months earlier, some locals had become millionaires. They touted South Dakota Gaming Commission reports that $14 million in revenues had been reported, that the state had collected $1.1 million in taxes on that money as of June 30. Deadwood itself had received $11,600 for historic preservation in the first six months.[21]

Foremost among the Coloradans interested in Deadwood were representatives of a petition drive to give the historic mining camps of Central City, Black Hawk, and Cripple Creek a place on the ballot for limited stakes casinos. Historically preceding the Black Hills gold rush by more than fifteen years was the gold strike in Russell Gulch of 1859 that led to the development of Central City and Black Hawk in Colorado. Then, approximately a decade and a half after the establishment of Deadwood/Lead, another gold strike of significant proportions occurred in southern Colorado, resulting in the development of the Cripple Creek gold district in 1890.

The discovery of gold in western Kansas Territory, to become the state of Colorado, like the discovery and development of gold mining in the Black Hills, led to the extraordinarily rapid growth of cities that were among the largest in the region. Their economies depended on the extraction of rich ore from the earth and the extraction of revenues from miners in exchange for a range of entertainments and services. Yet the same exploitation of mineral resources that contributed to the rapid growth of rather isolated gulches and mountaintops led to the almost equally rapid decline with their depletion, so that by 1990 some of these communities were subsisting on summer tourism while others had become part of the ghost town lore of the West. While they each reflect a combination of unique historical, environmental, technological, and social factors, the communities that grew up around the first of these discoveries and the last great strike were remarkably similar, even a century later.

But it would be a mistake to think of Colorado's gambling legalization effort as mere copycat behavior of Deadwood's recent success or even a recollection of a distant memory of mining boomtown gambling. If gambling in Deadwood had gone mostly underground or become more informal after the 1947 raid, Central City, at least, had exhibited outright defiance for a time. The confrontation may have begun with a newspaper article in the February 5, 1948, *Rocky Mountain News* that surveyed Internal Revenue Service records and listed 1,503 slot machines on which federal taxes of $150,300 had been paid for the 1947–48 tax year, despite the fact that slot machines were not legal in Colorado. While Denver had the largest number of machines operating, with a total of 148, the much smaller town of Pueblo had 111. Operators avoiding confrontation with the federal government included a state representative from Fort Collins and the Englewood Volunteer Fire Department, whose device was located in the city hall. Altogether, 676 establishments in 146 Colorado towns paid taxes on slot machines of which the state was officially "unaware." Of the towns that would legalize gambling in the 1990s, Central City residents declared sixty-seven slot machines, Black Hawk only six, Cripple Creek four.[22]

In July both Denver newspapers reported wide-open gambling in Central City in connection with the opera festival. The *Rocky Mountain News* described blackjack, "roulet," and craps operating in two establishments in plain view from the street. The *Denver Post* not only named three businesses in which roulette, blackjack, craps, and bingo were being played while *Così fan tutte* played in the Opera House but quoted Sheriff Oscar Williams as explaining, "Why sure, that's it. Right there in plain sight. We have nine months of hard winter up here. This is summertime in Central City. The Chamber of Commerce likes it. The community is going to benefit. We're going to get our streets fixed out of it."[23] The story described the event as the "resumption of gambling . . . to fill a great need," that being principally a large hole in the pavement on one of the main approaches to the Opera House, and the general consensus among townspeople was that Central City would garner a ten-thousand-dollar "gift" when the festival season ended. Although vague in his identifications, the sheriff thought the games were being run by "local boys," somebody from Craig and somebody named Tommy, but not the "Denver bunch," who with a contingent from Pueblo had tried to set up shop earlier in the month but were run out of town with minor gunfire on July 4. District Attorney Richard Simon also passed the buck: "There is [*sic*] a sheriff and two deputies up there. There is a townful of respectable people who, I am sure, would complain if they had reason to complain. I have heard no complaints concerning gambling. If I receive a complaint on gambling I shall investigate it, of course."[24]

Meanwhile, Cripple Creek in Teller County continued a long history of handing out small fines for vice that required some official form of objection but was in no danger of being eliminated. On November 30, 1948, six residents paid fines ranging from $60 to $300 for possession of slot machines. Previous pleas of "not guilty" under a statute calling for a mandatory prison term were permitted to be changed to "guilty" under a statue making such imprisonment optional. Many citizens hoped that the new pari-mutuel bill that legalized betting on horse and dog racing would encourage the authorities to take a liberal view of other forms of gambling.[25]

But it was the following opera season in Central City that saw the elite collectively thumbing their noses at Colorado law. As the year before, gambling was unveiled for the gala opening of the opera festival at the beginning of July 1949. The *Denver Post* devoted major stories on pages 1, 2, and 3 to descriptions of the gambling devices, their delivery within feet of the governor's car, the fourteenth season of the festival opening with Strauss's *Die Fledermaus*, and the Saturday evening first-nighter parties that would draw Denver's and Colorado's socialites, including the Boettchers, the Phipps, and Governor Knous.[26]

But by Thursday of the same week, the highbrow celebration of opera and gambling in Central City would be threatened. District Attorney Clement Hackenthal of the first judicial district announced, "It's all over. The operators are shutting down. Slot machines have been pulled in Gilpin and Jefferson Counties, and they will be pulled everywhere else in my district. The gambling tables have shut down. If those activities don't remain closed I'll take action to see that they are shut and kept shut."[27]

The announcement came after a day on which Mayor John C. Jenkins

Jr. had headed a delegation of business owners in a meeting with Attorney General John W. Metzger during which he asked that the state not interfere with Central City gambling during the opera festival, arguing that the games had remained free of gang violence and contributed to the "Old West" atmosphere of the town. But during the same meeting Mayor Jenkins revealed that all Central City gambling, except play at slot machines, was operated by Clyde Smaldone, a Denver underworld figure of the Prohibition Era. The year before, Smaldone, described as a "good, clean gambler," had contributed $7,000 to the Central City welfare fund. Slot machine profits, on the other hand, were divided between the machine owners and the local businesses housing them, with about 15 percent held back for a "youth fund." Smaldone's police record, in fact, included thirty-three arrests, and his most recent parole had come in 1943 after serving six years on convictions for grand larceny, assault to commit murder, and assault to commit a felony. Arguing, however, that there had been no breakdown in law enforcement, as one local justice of the peace had charged, the mayor's delegation and another group of Jefferson County tavern owners asked for three weeks to regulate the gambling situation while continuing to operate the slot machines "necessary to maintain the festival atmosphere in Central City."[28]

A month later, local Justice of the Peace Lowell Griffith secured complaints from five local citizens (whom he swore in as special constables), issued warrants to thirty-nine local proprietors of eighteen Central City establishments, and proceeded to round up trucks to haul away confiscated gaming machines. As word leaked out that the "1949 Carrie Nations" were on the march, Marshal Tom Jacobsen and his own phalanx of constables confronted Griffith and ordered him away from the barred door at a drugstore, against which he had a warrant. A blackjack, a hammer, then a bigger sledge hammer were brandished by the principals, but only verbal blows were struck as Main Street citizens flocked to the scene, which lasted long enough for the contested slot machines to vanish.[29]

This would not be the most sustained confrontation. On August 11, Gilpin County Sheriff Kenneth Mckinzie began serving Justice of the Peace Lowell Griffith's warrants, the first of which was delivered to rival Justice of the Peace Earl Person. The second arrest was of J. W. Martin, manager of the Teller House and faculty member of the University of Denver, which owned the Teller House and the Central City Opera House. Also arrested were Mayor John C. Jenkins Jr., owner of Ye Olde Fashioned Eating House; Mona Robb, who ran the museum store; and Emily Wilson, owner of the Glory Hole, one of the most famous taverns in town.[30] At least seven of the arrested were women, the most notable of whom was Alice C. Ramstetter, age sixty-eight, co-owner of Ramstetter's Restaurant and church organist for both the Catholic and Episcopal churches. Even though no bail money was demanded, Mrs. Ramstetter refused to sign a personal recognizance bond to obtain her release, pending an August 25 hearing.[31] Ramstetter found the air in the jail stale and the cot uncomfortable, so a few nights later she had her own bed moved into the jail and was pictured on the front page of the *Denver Post* with her husband tucking her in.[32] She was also permitted to take two meals a day in her own restaurant across the street and was photographed, as usual in her calico apron, holding an angel food cake that neighbors had delivered with a saw sticking out one side and a file protruding from the other.[33] On Saturday night, the sheriff escorted her to the big annual dance for Central City locals at a nearby ranch, and he deputized his daughter, a choir member at St. Mary's Catholic Church, to accompany Mrs. Ramstetter to church so she could play for mass the next morning.[34]

The Ramstetter saga may have signaled the ultimate outcome of this particular antigambling campaign, but a physical confrontation between two other women precipitated its demise. After having been served with her arrest warrant, museum store operator Mona Robb had encountered Faye Shobert on her rounds as mail carrier, and words and blows were exchanged. Three days later, Faye Shobert was one of three of the five witnesses who said in sworn statements that Lowell Griffith had misrepresented what she was signing, ending his antigambling campaign.[35]

The legal process included not only fisticuffs and sitdowns, for the county judge himself announced on August 15 that attorneys for the accused were studying the 1864 territorial charter granted to Central City, which permitted gambling, to see if it might supersede state law. By August 20, a group of prominent business people were proposing an ordinance that would allow Central City to license and regulate gambling games. Denver lawyer and former Colorado public utilities commissioner Leroy Williams argued that previous legal decisions had held that the state couldn't supersede charters drawn in advance of the state constitution and that "every time Central City wants to change its charter we have to go to the State Legislature and have a state law enacted. The charter says the city has a right to regulate gambling. Until the Legislature changes the law, we have that right."[36] Additonally, Williams proposed licensing games at various rates: $1,500 per year for a craps table; $1,200 for a roulette wheel; $500 for a blackjack table; a poker, stud, or low ball table at $400; slot machines at $120 each; and beat the dealer or over-and-under games at $200 each.

That suggestion provoked an editorial response pointing out forty years before its eventuation that with this move the state would not only be regulating gambling but would itself be going into the gambling business.[37] It also charged that gambling in one community and not in another would not work, because while one community had embraced "gambling elements," other communities would battle to keep them out. It concluded by saying that Central City was the last city in the state that should seek to legalize gambling, inasmuch as the Opera Association ("created by Denver people"), which was responsible for Gilpin County's prosperity, might consider shutting down the festival or moving it someplace else because of the "petty chiseling" growing out of the existing gambling.[38]

Lowell Griffith also petitioned Governor Knous for intervention in the "gangster operation," but Knous declared that he had "no first-hand knowledge whatsoever of the conditions with respect to gambling in Central City" and stated that he had neither legal authority nor any intention of influencing the pending litigation.[39] By the end of the second week after Griffith's gambling raid, the district attorneys from across the state of Colorado had been polled by the *Denver Post,* with the overwhelming response that they were enforcing the present gambling laws and were opposed to any changes in the law. District attorneys in only two districts argued that gambling problems should be handled at the local level.[40] And Alice Ramstetter, Central City's "martyr," finally signed the personal recognizance bond and left jail after the case was transferred from the jurisdiction of Lowell Griffith to Justice Charles Everitt of Rollinsville.[41]

But the issue did not die down completely in Colorado during the 1950s. Both Georgetown and Central City attempted to license slot machines, using the argument that the charters granted them by the territorial legislature empowered the city councils to "license, restrain, regulate, prohibit and suppress gambling houses."[42] A Georgetown court case from 1936 was also cited. However, the question of whether Central City had the right to pass ordinances that were not in accord with the general laws of the state of Colorado was obviated by City Attorney Henry Toll's discovery that on March 2, 1864, nine days before the territorial legislature granted Central City its special charter, it had passed an act to suppress gambling. A year later the legislature passed a law to exempt Denver from the operation of the antigambling law but did not exempt Central City. Denver's exemption was repealed in 1866, so gambling had never, in effect, been legal in the state of Colorado.[43]

Nevertheless, gambling remained a hot political issue: gambling proposals continued to surface in the Colorado legislature in 1951;[44] a district attorney named George Priest ordered the shutdown of games of chance at church bazaars and sent sheriffs to two Denver metropolitan area churches to close the games in 1953;[45] and a major raid at a "fishing" lodge near Black Hawk resulted in the arrest of twelve members of a nationwide crime syndicate in 1959. The worst fears (or hopes) of anti-gambling forces were confirmed with the identities of the operators and the discoveries of table-rigging devices, loaded dice, and poker chips good for $1,000 each. But the intended publicity was clear as well, for District Attorney Barney O'Kane himself conducted the sting in the company of two *Denver Post* reporters and a blond female stockbroker in a rented white Cadillac, posing as "vacationing Californians looking for some action," at the plush hideaway casino that had reportedly opened for the tourist season.[46]

The "sting" may have been a symbol of the postwar concern about gambling in the late 1940s and the 1950s in the Rocky Mountain West. The episodic efforts to close down gambling that had been going on for seventy-five to a hundred years in these towns is otherwise puzzling, unless one wants to attribute the moves to some amorphous tribute to the idealized version of midcentury "family values." But the connection is probably much more specific and threatening. Las Vegas had legalized gambling in 1931, first as a Hoover Dam construction boomtown, then as a waystation to Southern California, and finally as a divorce and marriage mecca that sustained it through the Great Depression. It eventually became the home of licensed brothels. The clubs of the 1930s had evolved from late-nineteenth-century saloons dependent on the mining industry and celebrating the Old West in decor and atmosphere. But after 1940, the Strip developed its luxury hotels, and Fremont Avenue became "Glitter Gulch," marrying the Old West with Hollywood.

The development of Las Vegas had depended on illicit gamblers as investors, bringing them above ground in order to use their expertise and skills. It had also appealed to wartime social patterns, where conventional moral standards shrank as servicemen prepared to face tremendous risks, war industry workers labored in oppressive conditions, and thousands of people were removed from homes and families. If the Old West that was celebrated by the surviving Rocky Mountain mining towns symbolized American values of tolerance and risk taking, the new Las Vegas represented a "whole new style of living," that of freedom, luxury, and mobility. It was an extension of Southern California.[47] Gambling had become something law enforcement in South Dakota and Colorado wanted nothing to do with. And so they tried for a time to root it out.

Nevertheless, the Internal Revenue Service continued to collect taxes on coin-operated gaming devices by issuing gambling revenue stamps at

$250 each. In 1965, 213 machines in 20 Colorado counties produced $53,250 in tax revenue. Most were in private fraternal or veterans' club-houses, but some were in service stations, cafes, and taverns, although the Colorado state liquor code forbade gambling devices of any kind at liquor outlets.[48] So clearly, while slot machines were widespread if not ubiq-uitous in Colorado at midcentury, what Colorado and particularly the old gold-mining towns considered "gambling" was not slot machines but high stakes card and dice games tied to tourism and high rollers.

This history provided the setting for Colorado's response to Dead-wood's successful initiation of legalized gambling. One of the Colorado petitions circulated in 1990 called for a Nevada-style development called Highland City, labeled by some the "Disneyland of casinos," to be built on the eastern plains. Promoters argued that an alternative to Las Vegas or Atlantic City could save much of the estimated $30 million in gambling money that left the state and would provide jobs to 24,000 people. Ac-cording to Phil Avello, development resource manager for Highland City, his ambitious project included an eight-hundred-million-dollar payroll and promised 10 percent of the take toward a state health insurance plan, education, and historic preservation. The group printed petitions with space for 86,000 names but never divulged how many signatures they secured.

A second ballot initiative would have let voters from six south and central Colorado communities have the right to operate limited stakes casinos. Lou Vezzani, the Democratic Party chair in Huerfano County who coordinated the petition drive for Walsenburg, La Vetta, Silver Cliff, Lake City, Silverton, and Fairplay, became both pessimistic and irritated at Colorado Governor Roy Romer for his lack of support. "I'm so mad at those legislators and Governor Romer," he said. "Romer ran on the plat-form that we should all help ourselves. We're doing just that, and he's not supporting us. And there are those worthless legislators." Even though his occupation as owner of a highway paving company allowed him to walk from car to car while traffic was stopped for highway repairs on Highway 160 east of Trinidad, he doubted that the group would get 30,000 signa-tures but vowed to come back with a proposal for the 1992 ballot.[49]

The third proposal was to give the historic mining camps of Central City, Black Hawk, and Cripple Creek a place on the ballot for limited stakes casinos. Central City stretched a banner across Main Street, en-couraging opera patrons and other visitors to sign petitions, and coordi-nator Lary Brown worried more about the November vote than about the success of the petition drive. Indeed, this audience proved more sympa-thetic than the stalled traffic on the state highway, for the proposal that most closely resembled the Deadwood plan was the only one to reach the ballot in 1990.

To secure the second successful round the Preservation Initiation Committee in Colorado hired Freda Poundstone (always identified by the press as "controversial lobbyist") for a twenty-five-thousand-dollar retainer and a promised additional $200,000 to make Amendment 4 a successful statewide campaign.[50] In 1974 Poundstone had spearheaded the state law that prevented Denver from annexing property without voter approval. Later, her fees from dog track interests and the liquor industry had earned her a widespread reputation as a powerful lobbyist.

Poundstone, Amendment 4 author Lary Brown, and Central City Mayor Bruce Schmalz, however, painted a low-key image of the campaign, despite the fact that Poundstone's fee represented $200 for every citizen of the three small mining towns. They described their focus on a brochure for the "Always Bet Colorado" campaign, which emphasized that "LIMITED gambling would help preserve our heritage and restore Colorado's economy." The 750,000 brochures promised hundreds of new jobs and a major fund for historic preservation throughout Colorado. Their "poor man's" approach to billboards included five tandem trailers placed in strategic spots to tell motorists in five-foot-tall letters "Vote Yes on 4." Neither newspaper nor television advertising was planned "unless our opponents come out strong against us. So far we haven't heard a thing."[51]

Besides having the example of Deadwood's eventual success, Colorado gambling proponents may have had the advantage of distraction by a measure with much more widespread implications, a proposed amendment to require voter approval of any tax increases and a ceiling on property tax increases. While not only Governor Romer but former Governor Dick Lamm had campaigned actively to defeat a Pueblo initiative for gambling in 1984, opponents of gambling also complained that Romer gave them too little help. June Sylvain of Cripple Creek claimed that she and two other town council members were ousted in a recall election because they opposed gambling, and Donna Melson and fellow opponents called for a fact-finding meeting at the Gilpin County High School, claiming they had tried to reach the governor for weeks without response. Nevertheless, as governor, Romer opposed the Colorado lottery and also criticized Amendment 4 when it was before the legislature in the spring of 1989. In September he said:

> I think it's a mistake. I will vote against it and urge others to vote against it for the following reasons: If adopted, it will be expanded beyond three

towns. I think it will be expanded to higher limits, and I think it's another step that could lead to casino gambling. I think it will hurt the environment by overdeveloping the towns where it's located, and I think it will change the historic character of the towns in an adverse way. I do not believe Colorado needs to expand gambling to have a healthy economy.[52]

In both South Dakota and Colorado, part of the opposition to legalized gambling came from church groups. Two previous unsuccessful attempts in South Dakota in the 1980s had drawn fairly organized opposition from the Black Hills Ministerial Association. But as Dick Salmonson, minister of United Methodist Church of Lead, said, "The population was told gaming was not a moral issue but an economic one. Now ministers try to help people to use discretion in the use of their leisure time and money."[53] Not all churches held the same views on gambling either, and it was difficult to take a clear position when some of the major churches had fairly permissive histories of gambling themselves. In Colorado, Reverend Gil Horn, executive director of the Colorado Council of Churches, vowed "to support the request of our sister churches" in the three mountain towns to oppose gambling in their communities. But church officials in Gilpin and Teller Counties claimed never to have requested the council's help because their congregations had decided to remain politically neutral. Kathryn Eccer, a trustee of St. James Methodist Church in Central City, Mona Hawkins of St. Paul's Episcopal, and Dolores Spellmen of St. Mary's Catholic Church all said their congregations were divided over the gambling initiative.[54] Only the Rocky Mountain Evangelical Free Church in Black Hawk, which was not a member of the church council, had asked the group to oppose Amendment 4.

In the November 1990 election, Amendment 4 was approved by a 57 percent to 43 percent vote at the state level, but citizens of the affected communities were far less certain about the project than Deadwood people had been, with 499 voting in favor and 461 opposed in Black Hawk, Central City, and Cripple Creek combined. Enabling legislation was introduced in the Colorado Senate by Sally Hopper of Golden, the Denver suburb closest to Central City and Black Hawk, and by Ken Chlouber of Leadville. The bill allowed up to 40 percent of the gross proceeds to be taxed, with half of the taxes going to the state, 12 percent to Gilpin and Teller Counties, 10 percent to the affected towns, and 28 percent to historic preservation in Colorado. Counties adjacent to those where gambling was legal could tap state funds to offset costs attributable to gambling, including increased road maintenance or social service costs. The original House bill also restricted gambling to historic structures restored to their pre–World War I condition and allowed 35 percent of a building's total square footage to be used for gambling. It maintained the provision added by a Denver Democrat to bar local elected officials, local judges, and state and local law enforcement officials from owning interests in gambling establishments.[55]

By October 1, 1991, nearly a year after the passage of the constitutional amendment, only twenty-one casinos were ready to open in Cripple Creek, Black Hawk, and Central City. Despite notable construction bustle before the onset of winter in these mountain towns at altitudes of 8,000 to 10,000 feet, their citizenry had vowed to learn from Deadwood and not rush headlong into gambling, despite their concerted effort to gain its approval. In Colorado more revenues would return directly to local governments, and historic preservation mandates would be less stringent and more widespread.

Similarities in settings and general proposals disguise what would eventually contribute to major differences in city operations, size of gambling establishments, and distribution of revenues. On the other hand, Colorado's determination to do some things differently from Deadwood, including "going slow" with the gambling business, proved to be a futile effort. Within weeks, property speculation in both Gilpin and Teller Counties was as frenzied as anything Deadwood had encountered. Within four months of Colorado's opening day of gambling, Deadwood was insisting that the bet limits and allowable number of slot machines must be increased in order to compete, not only with Colorado but with midwestern riverboat and reservation casinos. The restriction in Deadwood of thirty slot machines per building began slipping in creative ways early on, and by 1994 establishments needed relatively little rationale or construction to be declared "multiple buildings." Reminiscent of the gold rushes that had spawned these and hundreds of other nineteenth-century mining camps, additional Colorado towns would continue to bid for their chance to offer gambling as well. The dream of low stakes, limited gambling turned out to be so good that communities could no longer settle for either low stakes or limits.

CHAPTER 2

Race, Gender, and Class
in the Legacy of the Gamble

The founding of Deadwood in 1876 was itself an illegal activity, for the Black Hills were officially part of the Great Sioux Reservation. In the first of a series of poor choices, it was General George Armstrong Custer who had sent word back to the War Department in 1874 that on French Creek in the Southern Hills "gold was obtained in numerous localities in what are termed gulches. . . . It has not required an expert to find gold in the Black Hills, as men without former experience in mining have discovered it at an expense of but little time or labor."[1] General Crook was sent to try to keep the miners out but would be defeated at Rosebud in 1876, as was General Custer. Somewhere between thirty-five and a hundred white settlers were killed by Indians in 1876, prompting the Lawrence County Commission to vote in July 1876 for a reward of $25 for Indians brought in dead or alive. Sheriff Seth Bullock reported that the offer went to $50, payable "in clean merchantable gold dust" to anybody bringing in an Indian's head, and by 1877 the county board had raised the bounty to $250 for Indians taken dead or alive.[2]

Yet despite being interlopers, Deadwood citizens expected the federal government to provide military assistance, only to be reminded by the acting secretary of the interior that "white inhabitants of the Black Hills are there not only without authority of law, but in actual violation of law."[3] But in 1877 soldiers began protecting miners in the Hills, and by 1878 General Sheridan had sent officers to the Hills to hunt for a site on which to build a military post to guard the miners. Just north of the Hills they would found Fort Meade, which became the longest lasting cavalry unit in the country and remains as a Veterans Administration Hospital. By 1882 legislation had been introduced in Congress to exempt the Black Hills from the Great Sioux Reservation.[4]

This legacy of Anglo/Native relations and competing land claims left little room for celebration in Deadwood lore, except for a contingent of ceremonially dressed Lakotas in the annual Days of '76 parade. Other groups, however, would contribute to a persistent and elaborate mythology on which the town could capitalize. From the 1870s through the 1890s Deadwood was literally a mining camp, providing temporary living quarters and recreation for the men who exploited the mineral resources of the Hills. In describing the entertainments of prostitution, opium dens, and gambling, narratives linked women and Chinese to the general atmosphere of vice in Deadwood, even though there were apparently no saloons in Chinatown itself. "The first places visited were the opium joints of Chinatown, where the modus operandi of 'hitting the pipe' was explained to the uninitiated, and demonstrated to them to their satisfaction a practical way. . . . From Chinatown to the dance halls and inmates of the Green Front—the Gem was visited next, then to Colonel Allen's Saloon—games of chance, faro, roulette, stud poker, and dice."[5]

The Gem Theatre provided not only such entertainment as stage performances and dancing but also the services of prostitutes, many of whom were recruited by deceptive means, as illustrated in the September 5, 1884, edition of the *Black Hills Daily Times*. Front page headlines blared out the news—"A Den of Unsuspecting and Innocent Girls—Engaged through Misrepresentation by Its Bestial Proprietor . . . Narrow Escape."

Deadwood boasted in the *Black Hills Times* in 1883 of having "the largest colony of Chinese outside of San Francisco," numbering five hundred,[6] although the 1880 census showed 217 Chinese in western Dakota and 108 in Deadwood. Not all Chinese businesses provided prostitution or opium by any means, although the most celebrated entrepreneur was the "Yellow Doll," a singer and barroom dancer remembered as much for her murder as her entertaining talents. But most of the Chinese were men who ran restaurants, laundries, and groceries.

Wong Wing Tsu rose to a position of high status in the white community, not only as a merchant who sold groceries, novelties, chinaware, and herbal medicine but as a family man. After nearly twenty years in the United States, Wong returned to Guangzhou in 1882, came back with a wife and maid, and had nine children, the first eight born and raised in Deadwood, where they also attended public school. That Wong would not only be a leader in Chinatown but a prominent merchant who sold silk and porcelain to Deadwood's wealthiest citizens at the time the Chinese Exclusion Act was being passed reflected some level of tolerance. Indeed, contemporaneous accounts exist both of Wong and family members visiting in prestigious Anglo family homes and of return visits to the Wong home.[7]

Nevertheless, one very prominent attorney, Henry Frawley, defended a white client who had murdered a Chinese man by alleging that there was no law against such an act. He urged the judge to fine the murderer $25 for "cruelty to animals" instead, and the judge agreed. In 1878 a "Caucasian League" was organized to "protect the interest of the white miners" and "to prevent the employment of the Celestials"; four Chinese houses were burned and one blown up that year.[8] When Wong Wing Tsu left Deadwood in 1919 three years before he would die an old man back in Guangzhou, Deadwood's Chinatown was in decline, although the last Chinese janitor was bid farewell by a large crowd when he boarded the train in 1931, reflecting the continued ambivalence Deadwood exhibited toward its most distinctive ethnic group. In 1994 Miss Kitty's Chinatown Restaurant sponsored a celebration of the Chinese New Year complete with a dragon, a lion dance, and martial arts demonstrations.[9]

Deadwood's women have been assessed with similar ambivalence. The complexity of attitudes on gender goes beyond distinctions between "good" women and "notorious" ones. Their rarity may have been their most important characteristic at first. The 1880 census showed a nine to one ratio of men to women for Lawrence County's counted population of 13,248; the total population of Deadwood was 3,777. Dora Defraun, one of Deadwood's early madams, may have been self-serving with her estimates when she claimed that of the population of three thousand, a thousand were sporting types and five hundred were ladies of the evening.[10] But Deadwood became famous early on for its brothels and prostitutes, unsuspecting or opportunistic. Although the lower Main Street "badlands" may have made the city "unpleasantly famous," it can also be said that only on rare occasions in the past 120 years has the town made much attempt to eliminate the prostitutes or their businesses. When Edward Senn, the editor of the *Deadwood Telegraph* in 1910, took up an anti-prostitution campaign, he concluded that a third of the population drew their income from one form of decadence or another and gave up the effort. Indeed, after the last raids staged by the state in 1980 and the arrest of well-known madam Pam Holladay, townspeople staged a parade in support of Pam and her girls.[11]

There were well-known proper women as well, and some of them made public contributions. Annie Tallent, the first white woman to have entered the Hills with the Gordon party, who first mined French Creek, would publish a notable history, *The Black Hills, or The Last Hunting*

Grounds of the Dakotahs, in 1899; Estelline Bennett, daughter of founding Judge Granville Bennett, wrote an account of the early years in *Old Deadwood Days,* which may have done more to shape Deadwood's conception of itself than any other piece of history.[12] Given the lack of institutionalization in a frontier community, even one of the Victorian period, women found it possible not only to engage in a variety of occupations but to be forthright about them as well. The 1898 city directory listed women who identified themselves as midwives, artists, seamstresses, and teachers. Women were among the earliest hourly tutors in Deadwood, and when the first formal school was opened in the fall of 1880, it was run by a "professor" (as any male in an academic or artistic occupation seemed to have been called) and three female teachers. Marital status was apparently no barrier to women's employment in the earliest days. While some women who worked as prostitutes avoided the label by calling themselves "boarders," several women who ran brothels listed themselves as "proprietress" in the local directories.

Deadwood ritually claims embarrassment about the women in its past. Yet it made a historical counterpart to Wild Bill Hickok of Martha ("Calamity") Jane Canary Burke, who arrived with Colonel Dodge's soldiers in the summer of 1875, and local historians have only recently attempted to disclaim any romantic relationship or perhaps any relationship at all between the two, save their final resting place. Much is made of Calamity Jane's hard drinking, loud talking, poor mothering, yet generous demeanor, including her nursing of smallpox victims in an outbreak among miners in 1876, as she is celebrated nightly in the summer productions of *The Trial of Jack McCall.*

Deadwood even identifies Poker Alice Tubbs, who was a madam in Sturgis twenty miles away in Meade County, as their character. She was famous in Sturgis for her openness in getting bank loans to expand her business to serve the army encampment at Fort Meade. But Deadwood has always claimed her, for it was there she came to deal poker and either chew on a dead cigar or smoke lighted ones, depending on the account.

Deadwood: Metropolis of the Black Hills

The Deadwood Board of Trade adopted the motto "the Metropolis of the Black Hills, South Dakota," as early as 1892, announcing its intentions to be something other than the typical agricultural or resource-extracting community of the early century. More than a mining town, Deadwood was in fact better characterized by production, or what we would now call "value-added" business. It had acquired seven large mills and smelters as its basic industry, including prominently the Golden Reward Mining

Company, which in 1877 consolidated thirteen small mines and had opened a two-hundred-ton mill and a five-hundred-ton smelter by 1899. The mining itself moved increasingly from prospecting in the gulches to consolidated Homestake Mining Company holdings in Lead.[13]

In addition, Deadwood became something of a wholesale distribution center. Half a dozen businesses, some started in the first year of the gold strike and some in the first twenty years of the following century, increasingly turned to wholesale business to carry them to 1980. They included Adams-Webster Wholesale Grocers, Paxton and Gallagher, Pioneer Fruit, P. A. Gushurst—Wholesale and Retail Grocer, Fish and Hunter Hardware and Wholesale, and Black Hills Mercantile.[14] Of these P. A. Gushurst was the first, coming into the Hills by wagon from Omaha via Cheyenne and Fort Laramie in the spring of 1876 and witnessing the departure of troops to the Battle of the Little Big Horn.[15] In Deadwood he first sold supplies out of a tent but soon built the "Bighorn Store," named in honor of his arrival. Within the year he had sold out to Jake Goldberg and moved to Lead, where he started a grocery store serving the miners on the more promising Homestake Mine, and within two years he had married the niece of the Manuel brothers who had founded it. The Gushursts' was the first marriage in Lead, consecrated with a ring made from the first gold taken from the Homestake Mine.[16] The Gushurst family ran the Wholesale and Retail Grocery (also advertising mining supplies as well in the early years) for nearly a century. Goldbergs continued to sell groceries on the Main Street of Deadwood until the building was converted to a casino with the opening of low stakes gambling at the end of 1989.

William E. Adams and his brother James H. Adams opened another mercantile firm that sold both wholesale and retail groceries on Main Street in 1877. When James left for California in 1889 and disposed of his share of the business in 1893, William built the Adams Building in 1901 and eventually created one of the largest wholesale houses in South Dakota. The building featured a water-powered electric generator that not only ran the elevator but also ground coffee beans.[17] His first wife and two daughters died within two days of each other in 1925; two years later he married Mary Mastrovich, a successful California businesswoman who was in Lead to visit relatives. Adams was mayor of Deadwood for six years, president of the First National Bank of Deadwood, and director of several civic organizations. Four years before his death in 1934, Adams spent $75,000 to construct the Adams Memorial Museum, his gift to the townspeople, only recently refurbished with just over $300,000 of historic preservation funds coming from low stakes gambling in Deadwood.

James M. Fish and John Hunter also came to the Black Hills in 1877 and formed a partnership and business that lasted 101 years. First opening a lumber mill, they later added a mercantile and grocery. Fish and Hunter Company, with various other partners from time to time, acquired other businesses, but when a fire in 1961 completely destroyed the main Deadwood building, the company discontinued the retail grocery and hardware business to concentrate on wholesale distribution of building materials and hardware.[18] The Fish and Hunter Warehouse presently houses the city of Deadwood offices, including the Historic Preservation Commission responsible for conserving the legacy of these early entrepreneurs. Other early wholesalers included Adams-Webster Wholesale Grocers and Paxton and Gallagher. Pioneer Fruit and Black Hills Mercantile operated into the latter half of the twentieth century. In addition to the Stebbins Post and Company Bank and the First National Bank of Deadwood, Daniels Greenhouse and the Deadwood Granite and Marble Works became early and longstanding retail businesses. Sam Schwarzwald opened a furniture store in 1877 that became one of the largest furniture stores in the state and operated for 102 years within 200 feet of its original location. Between Deadwood and Lead, the Light and Fuel Company would by 1904 build a new coal gas plant, producing methane gas with coke as a by-product to replace the old oil-fueled plant. Not only was this a more efficient source of gas, for the first time providing enough pressure to reach the houses up the gulch in Lead, but by 1909 doctors were prescribing the breathing of gas fumes for their patients suffering from congestion.[19]

Perhaps Ayres Hardware best exemplifies the mercantile spirit of the community of Deadwood. George V. Ayres first came to Deadwood in May 1876, but he went to Custer for a short time. He returned to Deadwood in the fall of 1877 and took employment in the R. C. Lake Hardware Store, which he would later purchase. For most of its history, Ayres Hardware shared the building with hardware on the street level and the Star and Bullock sixty-room hotel on the second and third floors. (Seth Bullock had initially sold hardware and supplies and started the hotel but soon became occupied with his position as sheriff.) Originally selling heavy hardware and mining supplies, including explosives, as prospecting diminished the retail hardware was supplemented with a sheet metal and pipe shop. George Ayres died in 1939, but his son Albro ran the store except when he served in the South Dakota state legislative sessions for three months biennially.[20]

The building was sold in 1975, but the business did not disappear by any means. Ayres Hardware moved across and down the street, and

Albro's wife, Agnes Vancas Perkovich Ayres, continued to operate the hardware store after Albro's death in 1981. The building has one of the most frequently photographed front doors in town. When the property speculation associated with the legalization of gambling began heating up in Deadwood, Agnes posted a handwritten sign on her front door that said, "Do not ask! This building is not for sale. Don't even think about it!" The sign remained until November 1996, when poor health forced her to sell the store, albeit with a covenant that the building not be used for gambling until after her death. Meanwhile the original Ayres Building now houses the Bullock Hotel once again. Its first floor no longer features fifteen-foot ladders on rails to reach the floor-to-ceiling bins of bolts and nuts. Instead it houses, on a plush figured carpet, colorful, noisy slot machines and blackjack tables.

Other early hotels did not all survive into the twentieth century. An African American woman, Lucretia ("Aunt Lou") Marchbanks, ran the Grand Central, locally famous for the quality of its food, but she left in favor of a roadhouse north of the Hills. Jacob Wertheimer's Merchant's Hotel not only served French cuisine but provided "sample rooms" where commercial travelers could display their wares. The Overland Hotel was notable for advertising that its kitchen was presided over by a white cook and for having no bar and allowing no intoxicated guests.[21] The Mansion House, however, survived as the Fairmont Hotel, which currently operates a casino and boarding house. The grandest hotel, the four-story, eighty-room Franklin Hotel, opened in 1903, featuring electric lights, steam heat, and baths in half the rooms. Maintaining a conspicuous presence at the primary intersection of Deadwood's Main Street, its current owner would be one of the early backers of legalized gambling in contemporary Deadwood.

None of Deadwood's eleven early theaters, of varying reputations, persisted even as a movie house past midcentury, even though one of them premiered *The Mikado*, which ran 130 days in 1886, and another offered both *Cavaleria Rusticana* and *Il Trovatore* on the same day in 1916. But the Deadwood Library Association had been formed in 1882, and, with the help of the Andrew Carnegie Endowment and a major contribution by Phoebe Hearst of the Homestake Mining Company, the Deadwood Carnegie Library opened in 1905. It was approved for a major historic preservation grant for renovation in 1994. Deadwood also spawned the usual array of lodges—Masonic, Odd Fellows, Knights of Pythias—and a Ladies Relief Society. There was a Business Men's Club, an Olympic (health) Club, and not one but two competing pioneer societies even before the turn of the century. Five churches had established themselves, but not all had their own buildings, and the Methodists lost their first church to a devastating flood that washed away 150 buildings in 1883, bracketed by major fires in 1879 and 1894.

Several public buildings, still in use, appeared in the first decade of the century, including the Federal Building and the U.S. Post Office in 1905–6 and the Lawrence County Courthouse in 1908. Deadwood High School, now the Lead-Deadwood Middle School, was built in 1925. The Deadwood Auditorium, built in 1912, later became a recreation center and has also been recently refurbished with historic preservation funds.

In the first thirty years of the century, before Rapid City became the wholesaling center of the Hills and until the Homestake Mining Company took over virtually all milling operations, Deadwood saw itself not only as a complete community but as a "metropolitan" one. It was a relatively prosperous one, with bank deposits of $200 per capita, 2.5 times the state average. Obviously this wealth was not evenly distributed, but historian Watson Parker, at least, argued that there was "enough to go around."[22]

Part of Deadwood's metropolitan image clearly included tolerance of gambling and prostitution. Both had a nearly continuous presence in the culture and economy of the town but were marked by occasional raids to remind the citizens that they were illegal activities. In a prime example of celebrating its "bad press," the *Deadwood Daily Pioneer-Times* published on January 29, 1909, a "sample of the bunk which the four-dollar-a-column dopesters are in the habit of sending out from this section of the country." The story in the *Chicago Tribune* described the successful effort of the local ministerial association to force the sheriff to close bars at 11:00 P.M. and on Sundays. It claimed, "Deadwood, the Toughest Town on Earth, has at last been shorn of the name which it boasted for about a quarter of a century. The one time terror of the mining country now approaches the prosaic quiet of New England village." The article also described how side doors were boarded up, roulette wheels were shut down, slot machines were carried out, faro boxes were seized, and faro dealers were ordered out of business. The piece also noted the presence of a mere twenty-four saloons in a town of nearly four thousand inhabitants.

When this story was reprinted in the "Special Gaming Edition" of the *Lawrence County Centennial* on November 1, 1989, writer Scott Randolph noted that, rather than a crucial point in changing the course of Deadwood, it would be more accurate to say that the belief in a changed Deadwood existed primarily in the mind of the journalist who wrote the piece.[23] Indeed, the next major gambling raid that would finally drive gambling underground in Deadwood did not occur until 1947. Prostitution, also experiencing raids in 1952 and 1959, would not be formally closed down until 1980. In both cases the townspeople responded to the closures in terms of the negative economic impacts on the city. But for most of Deadwood's early history, its saloons and brothels operated as a normal and central part of the community's commerce. George Moses, who grew up in Deadwood in the early part of the twentieth century, remembered the brothels as being places where he and other youngsters could perform odd jobs such as sweeping the stairs or washing the entry and count on being paid "more than the job was worth." As residences were arrayed on the steep slopes of Deadwood Gulch, a good proportion of the population had clear views of the back doors of the brothels, which, ironically, local citizens preferred to use. Referring to the Bodega Rooms, Moses said, "It was not uncommon to see those who were on their way to the second story enter by this back door. . . . Those who lived there at the time thought this was a regular practice and no thought of ever mentioning the incident was discussed, either in private or in public."[24]

Lead: The Company Town

For a century, the economic fortunes of Lead and Deadwood, only three miles apart, would be linked inextricably as the "Twin Cities," yet their image of culture and community would be as different as the rough camps of Placerville and the gentility of San Francisco. Indeed, Homestake headquarters, as a Hearst enterprise, were always in San Francisco, and that is where Lead citizens always looked for signals about their fortune.

The original Homestake strike was made by two seasoned prospectors, the French Canadian brothers Fred and Moses Manuel. They had previously prospected in Montana, Utah, Idaho, Arizona, and Nevada. Moses had been in Alaska and was about to leave for Africa when he heard of Custer's discovery of gold in the Black Hills. They made their big strike in the spring of 1876, but, being short of money, they sold North America's principal gold vein almost immediately for $70,000 to an agent of George Hearst, who wasted no time consolidating it with other mines and properties in the gold-bearing draw. The Hearst syndicate incorporated Homestake Mining Company on November 5, 1877.[25] Lead (pronounced "leed" from a mining term for a vein of ore) would become the principal mining town in the Black Hills, sitting atop the richest gold veins in the Western Hemisphere. With a population of 3,777, Deadwood was the largest city in Lawrence County in 1880, while its sister city, Lead, had a population of 1,437. However, only ten years later, Lead's population

(2,581) had surpassed Deadwood's (2,366) on its way to becoming the dominant city in the county, and by 1910 Lead's population had peaked at 8,392, compared to 3,653 for Deadwood.[26]

If Calamity Jane and Poker Alice characterize the way Deadwood saw its women, Phoebe Apperson Hearst personified the mining community Lead endeavored to be. Lead's residents have insistently characterized Hearst's Homestake ("The Company") with an interest many scholars call a benevolent paternalism, and it appeared in the person of Phoebe Apperson Hearst, who became majority owner of the company upon her husband's death in 1891. Mrs. Hearst gave Lead a library with four thousand volumes and eighty-one periodicals as a Christmas present in 1894.[27] Books and periodicals in Italian, Slavonian, Finnish, German, Swedish, Spanish, Lithuanian, Norwegian, and French reflected both the ethnic diversity of the community and Hearst's interests in the miners' access to information. The library also hosted monthly chamber music concerts.

In 1900 Mrs. Hearst took over support of the kindergarten started by the Woman's Club to provide English language and socialization experiences for children ages three to six with teachers who had graduated from her Kindergarten Training School in Washington, D.C. Education in Lead represented the company's relation to public services as well as any social institution. Since Homestake was for most of the city's history by far the greatest taxpayer in the district (homeowners did not even own the lots their houses sat on until 1988), the company essentially had the choice of paying for schools outright or simply supporting them through taxes. In many ways the company did both and exhibited interest in both the Americanization and stability of its mining families. The first public school in Lead opened in 1877 with a Mrs. Snyder teaching fourteen students, but by 1895, when the Independent District No. 6 was organized, two buildings were already required, soon to be joined by the Hearst Free Kindergarten.[28] Phoebe Hearst subsidized the construction of public buildings by buying bonds at low interest rates. For most of the twentieth century Lead's schools were to have the best athletic, library, and laboratory facilities, the highest paid teachers, and some of the most rigorous academic programs in the state.

The diverse population of miners and their families in the employment of Homestake would be found residing in stable, albeit fairly segregated, residential neighborhoods. The Italians lived on the hill called "Sunnyside," while the Serbs and Croats lived together on "Slavonian Alley" but attended different churches. Lead's few Chinese families ran laundries on Mill and Bleeker Streets, and its African American population lived in an area local newspapers referred to in the vernacular of the period as

"Coonville."[29] Even the Scandinavians sorted themselves out into sizable Finnish, Swedish, and Norwegian neighborhoods, each with their own Lutheran church. Only the English-speaking Cornish and some Welsh seemed to lack a specified neighborhood, probably because they were thought to be the mainstream, while two thirds of their mining coworkers spoke other languages. In addition to a number of fraternal organizations, several ethnic groups organized marriage brokerages to bring women "of their own kind" to the Hills.

Medical care, first contracted by the company in 1878 for miners and their families for a monthly fee of $1.10, eventually became a free benefit with a hospital and staff of doctors. Likewise, persistent shortages of supplies prompted Senator George Hearst to open a company store in 1879. The Hearst Mercantile carried mining supplies and retail goods and became a wholesale distributor as well. While employees could get interest-free credit with the deposit of their paychecks, and the Homestake offices were in the same building, there was apparently, unlike many nineteenth-century company mining towns, no attempt to pay wages in company scrip redeemable there. The Homestake Opera House and Recreation Building, available to the entire citizenry, opened in August 1914 with a one-thousand-seat auditorium, a bowling alley and swimming pool, social rooms, and billiards, pool, chess, and card rooms. The library was now on the top floor of the building designed by the Chicago architectural firm of Shattuck and Hussey.

Even though Lead was the largest city in the Black Hills by several thousands, all other merchandising in Lead paled in comparison to the Hearst Mercantile Company. Built on Mill Street, the long, straight, if steeply sloped street perpendicular to Main and connecting it to the mining operations, the first Hearst Mercantile suffered the fate of the rest of Lead's commercial district when subsidence from the lack of backfill in the underground mining forced the entire town to move up the hill in the 1920s. Perhaps nothing less than company sponsorship could have made the mercantile as resilient as it was. Even the first "Brick Store," opened in 1879, was a sizable sixty by two hundred feet. The New Hearst Mercantile Store, which opened on Main Street in 1922, occupied a building 160 by 130 feet, with two stories fronting Main Street and two more floors below that opened onto Julius Street. The store sold blasting powder and mining machinery and was a wholesale distributor of mining equipment. But it also sold dry goods, carpets and draperies, millinery, ready-to-wear clothing, furnishings, shoes, trunks and valises, groceries and baked goods, buggies, automobiles, furs, plumbing supplies, and lumber. In addition to a full range of merchandise and seventy sales employees, the Hearst housed the Homestake Mining Company main offices.[30] It burned in 1931 and was rebuilt, only to be completely destroyed by fire in 1942, after which Deadwood increasingly became the retail center of the Twin Cities.

Not only was the commercial market dominated by Homestake, but banking and politics were as well. The original Thum, Lake and Company gold rush bank had become the First National Bank of Lead with assets of over half a million dollars by 1891. T. J. Grier, the mine superintendent, was president; R. H. Driscoll, his confidential agent, was cashier; and Dr. J. W. Freeman, the chief Homestake surgeon, was a member of the board of directors. Grier also ran the company railroad and supervised the Hearst Mercantile.[31] Ironically, although the Hearsts were Democrats (George was a U.S. senator from California), Homestake Republicans dominated politics in Lawrence County and the second congressional district and wielded power in the state legislature for at least sixty years. It was understood that whoever represented Lawrence County and the second congressional district was to defend the interests of Homestake against the largely Democratic agricultural voice in the state.

Altogether, Mrs. Hearst, and eventually the townspeople, would see Lead as a cosmopolitan community and an oddly urbane one honoring "high" culture as well as ethnic diversity. It is telling that while the Smead Hotel, with more than a hundred rooms, was built in 1901, no mention is made of a saloon in Lead until 1911, although the Welcome Saloon may have been built in 1903.[32] Most Lead residents felt not only geographically but socially above their downgulch neighbors in Deadwood. It would take a century for their fortunes to be reversed, when a unionized Homestake Mining Company would turn a large part of Lead into an open pit gold mine that will provide no more ore by the year 2000, leaving only underground operations.

The First of the Colorado Gold Rushes

Numerous reports of gold discoveries surfaced in Colorado during the 1840s and 1850s, but the first significant find was in Gregory Gulch on May 6, 1859, soon to be followed by a major find on June 1, 1859, in an area known as Russell Gulch. John Gregory, on his way from the played-out gold mining in Georgia to the Frazer River of British Columbia, got stuck for the winter in Fort Laramie in 1858–59, when rumors of Colorado gold ran rampant. The Russell brothers, also from Georgia, had found placer gold along the South Platte Valley, and they and Gregory encountered each other at the source of Clear Creek the next spring. Within weeks there were settlements up and down the mountainsides— Black Hawk, at the mouth of Gregory Gulch, and above it Mountain

City, Springfield, Missouri City, Bortonsburg, Eureka, Nevada City, and scattered tents at other creek junctions, all within two miles.[33] The dream of prospectors, lode gold, was unearthed. The rush was on, and by year's end over two hundred miners were encamped in the Central City/Black Hawk district. During the winter of 1859 word of the gold strike spread primarily through the reporting of New York newspaper editor Horace Greeley, who visited the gold camp. Commenting on what would be Central City, he wrote, "As yet, the entire population of the valley—which cannot number less than four thousand, including five white women and seven squaws living with white men—sleeping in tents, or under booths of pine boughs, cooking and eating in open air. I doubt that there is as yet a table or chair in these diggings, eating being done around a cloth spread on the ground, while each one sits or reclines on mother earth."[34]

Spring brought wave after wave of miners, merchants, and hangers-on, all seeking quick fortunes and many risking their meager resources. Prospectors poured into the gulches, cities were platted, and the area took on the appearance of an urban area with a population of around six thousand. Growth continued at a dizzy pace, with an infrastructure of mercantiles, schools, churches, and, of course, saloons and dance halls taking shape by 1862. Central City may have been named by W. N. Byers, who convened a citizens' meeting to propose what they hoped would be new laws and a constitution for the "future State of Jefferson," as he felt they were too far from the Kansas legislature for appropriate territorial jurisdiction.

Considering that Central City/Black Hawk developed a decade earlier and the Cripple Creek District fifteen years later and in greater proximity to burgeoning urban areas than Deadwood or Lead, we might expect quite different histories, and indeed they each produced a unique cast of characters and idiosyncratic events. And yet, the twentieth century brought similar fates to these towns.

Given Gilpin County's forty years of gold mining before 1900, most of the community building was a nineteenth-century phenomenon. It came from white men of means, to be sure, but not necessarily those who had already amassed vast experience or fortunes in mining. So Central City and Black Hawk had been from the beginning much more tenuous experiments in mining business and mining communities.

Much as the Manuel brothers would disappear from the Black Hills after a few years, John Gregory and William Green Russell, who made the first gold discoveries in Colorado, experienced a relatively brief presence in the communities they spawned. Russell and Gregory not only had quite different personal styles, but they ended up being mining rivals and had brought countersuits against each other by 1863. Gregory may have returned to Georgia or died in Montana, poor from gambling losses by 1865. Russell died in Oklahoma (Indian Territory) in 1877.[35] Other bonanza barons had chosen to live in more comfortable environs: D. Joseph Casto moved to Golden, Colorado, and Harry Gunnell to Denver; W. H. Doe had returned to Oshkosh, Wisconsin.

Concerns about nonwhites and women surfaced in Central City as they would in Deadwood. Fragments of a diary entry from Central City in 1865 worried especially about women who were able to turn profits from vice into property ownership.

> Dec. 10 . . . There are many here who seem to have come from fine homes and have good manners and are well educated; others who appear to be just human drift-wood, wanderers from many lands, dissolute and tough beyond description. My face burns with shame for the very shameless-ness of some of the women around here on pay nights tempting the young men into bawdy houses, screaming from their doors and windows, using the most obscene language.
>
> I have observed some of these women in the saloons and they appear to be as bad after the drink as the men, they contribute largely to the crimes that are being committed around here, keeping the mining camps aflame with sin. . . . Some of the madames or proprietress [*sic*] of the disrep-utable houses have purchased mining properties and are having them worked by men they have "set up." It is all a very deploring state of affairs and I think the religious character of this place presents a dark picture as far as any hopes of clearing out the undesirables is considered.[36]

The *Daily Central City Register* reported the opening of a "brothel dance house" at the head of Dry Gulch on November 24, 1868, with the warning that "unless they are properly and severely dealt with, we shall be overrun with ruffians from the railroad," only to receive a response from a Black Hawk citizen that there could be no such institution, as "Black Hawk would not allow it."

Distress over the demeanor of local citizens is reflected in vigilant reports in the *Register* of the city attorney playing billiards during the hours of Sunday service, "another hell-hole" opening somewhere in the rear of Washington Hall (with other parties looking for new locations), and two "nymphs du pave" becoming intoxicated and taking refuge, unsuccessfully, in John Chinaman's house as they fled from police. However, the image the paper wanted to reflect is clear in its announcement that "strangers fed on Bret Harte stories of mining camps would be surprised at the high moral and religious tone of Central City."[37]

News accounts in both 1864 and 1867 report "Indian uprisings" and some reports of deaths, but with the army occupied elsewhere there was no great call for military assistance, and perhaps that contributed to the avoidance of major conflicts. A small band of Utes that camped nearby from time to time on their way from the western slope of the Rockies to Denver to get provisions were regarded with ample suspicion.[38] There is no sign that Native American people were engaged in the commerce of the various mining towns, certainly not as citizens.

Census data, however, do show a significant number of black and Chinese settlers in various occupations in Central City and Black Hawk. In 1873, unsuccessful politician Frank Young worried openly about the 187 Chinese laborers who, having completed work on the transcontinental railway, were taking over placer mining from white miners.[39] But in addition to placer mining, at least nine Chinese ran laundries, and ten or twelve were prostitutes. One African American woman, "Aunt Clara" Brown, was a pillar of the community. Having bought her freedom from slavery, she came to Black Hawk in 1859 and worked as a laundress, caterer, and midwife. Methodist church services were held in her home through most of the 1860s, and one of the hickory chairs in the Opera House would eventually memorialize her. On the other hand, in 1869 Negro parents retained a lawyer to force the opening of the public school to their children.[40] Other black settlers had occupations and businesses ranging from forges to service in the posh Teller House.

Nevertheless, when Harriet and George Randolph appeared in November 1864, after they and their government escort along the Platte had been held up for eight weeks by Indians and snowstorms, a very real vacuum in benevolent community building awaited the new general manager of the Boston Milling Company and his wife. Randolph came from the Randolph family of Virginia and was a Civil War hero at Gettysburg. In 1868 he was chosen as Gilpin County representative to the Territorial Republican Convention in Denver and within eight years had applied considerable ingenuity to making the mining industry, specifically his Ophir and Narragansett mines, profitable even as the surface ores played out.[41] Harriet's chief contribution seemed to have been as a model of gracious living, especially after the Randolphs were able to move from a remodeled log cabin in Nevadaville to a fashionable house on Casey Street in Central City, although she spent most of her time in San Francisco and Europe.

The gold field quickly became a continuous settlement comprised of Black Hawk, Mountain City, Central City, and Nevadaville. Population peaked in the 1870s, when Central City prided itself on being an economic and cultural oasis. The Colorado Central Railroad arrived in 1872, the same year the five-story, 150-room Teller Hotel was completed, with the fifth floor devoted to high stakes gambling.

> Completed June of 1872, and the total cost was said to have been $104,000 . . . The dining room would seat one hundred and the range in the kitchen, in the words of the *Register* correspondent, "Looked like a narrow gauge locomotive." The parlors were "elaborately furnished with the latest approved styles in walnut and damask and carpets of the finest Brussels. . . . The piano—a Knabe square grand . . . had great volume and richness of tone. [A majority of the sleeping rooms were] ordered in suites for the better accommodation of families, but without transoms, ventilation being obtained by adjustable windows.[42]

Even the sporting life in Central City seems always to have played second fiddle to its high culture. "The Row" of parlor houses and cribs was segregated high on the hillside at the end of Pine Street in Central City, and the nightlife was never as wild as in most western mining camps or even early-day Denver, according to local historian Caroline Bancroft. In her monograph on "Six Racy Madames of Colorado," the only mention of Central City is in an anecdote that reflects both the theatrical and moral tone of the town. One of the six biographical sketches is of Laura Evans of Salida, who while visiting Della Warwick, a madam friend of hers in Central City, attended a charity masquerade at the Teller House dressed as a nun. She was so successful in her portrayal that she had herself photographed in the nun's habit to prove that the "soulful eyes" were indeed hers.[43]

Although adjacent, the contrast between Central City and Black Hawk was noted early on by Sara J. Lippincott: "narrow and dingy as is this mining town [Black Hawk], its people are making a brave effort to give it a look of comfort . . . scarcely a tree or shrub is to be seen, or even a flower, except it be in some parlor window; but as we drove up into Central [City], we came upon a very pretty conservatory, attached to a neat cottage. It was something strangely cheering, yet touching, in the universal dreariness."[44]

Central City's commitment to cultural niceties was more substantially revealed through the construction in 1878 of the Opera House, which could seat 750. This same year spelled the end of the gold field's growth, with lode strikes of silver and gold discovered across the divide at Leadville and Central City's placer mines petering out.

If Harriet Randolph had neither the inclination nor the resources to be a Phoebe Hearst, there were locals who would be much more involved in community building. Peter McFarlane had the glamour neither of name nor of gold discovery. He came to Gilpin County from Prince Edward Island in 1869 to join his brother William in operating foundries and machine shops in Black Hawk and Central City. Eventually William and his family and Peter's own family moved to Denver to open shops there. But Peter, a self-taught lover of Shakespeare and Robert Burns, remained in Central City for sixty years, being elected mayor in 1878, resisting the rush to Leadville in the 1880s, and serving on the city council before and after. By the 1890s McFarlane had a thriving construction and real estate business. Eventually he would help to refurbish the Opera House, which he had helped to build fifty years earlier.

McFarlane was mayor at the peak of Central City's economic success. In the decade of the 1870s there were thirty-five hundred residents in Central City, plus another fifteen hundred in Black Hawk and a thousand in Nevadaville. In 1873 there were forty businesses, some in the wholesale trade, the Rocky Mountain National and the First National banks, plus six churches in Central City, two more in Black Hawk, and two in Nevadaville. The Masons, Odd Fellows, and Turnverein lodges competed with traveling lecturers, including Horace Greeley, Henry Ward Beecher, and P. T. Barnum, for community attention. A glee club and orchestra supported amateur acting productions.

Then, as was seemingly inevitable in these early wood-frame towns, a six-hour fire consumed 150 buildings, including the Montana Theatre, in 1874. Only three brick buildings, including the Teller House, remained in the center of town. The *Daily Register* reflected the spirit of the town two days after the fire: "we are going to have a new, and, if properly directed, much more substantial and better city than that which disappeared on Thursday. At no previous period has there been manifested such enthusiasm on the present and future prospects."[45] Over the next year and a half, 188 new commercial buildings of brick and stone filled the downtown of Central City. A new theater, the Belvidere, was among the early erections, but by 1877 it already seemed inadequate after the Amateur Dramatic Company's performance of *The Bohemian Girl*, which played to overflow audiences in the spring of 1877.[46]

The McFarlane brothers emerged as substantial citizens with a prosperous construction business. The year that Peter McFarlane was mayor, 1878, was a turning point. The Central City Opera House opened, and rich deposits of silver were discovered in Leadville. The Opera House would become an icon of Central City culture and its sustenance as the population and resources rushed to Leadville and Denver. McFarlane not only was the contractor for the construction of the Opera House but managed the installation of electric lights in 1896 and became program manager in 1900. Shortly after the turn of the century McFarlane acquired majority stock in the Gilpin County Opera House Association; he oversaw the renovation of the theater in 1903 and installed motion picture equipment in 1910. McFarlane and the Opera House had withstood several threats. In 1882 the owners of the Opera House had sold the property to the county for $8,000 so that it could be converted into a courthouse. The new wealth from Leadville had already built in Denver the Tabor Grand Opera House, which would become the leading theater of the state and would, happily, provide continued venues for theatrical troupes who were willing to play in Central City at the end of their Denver engagements.[47] It is not clear that McFarlane ever made a profit on the Opera House or that it was important to him that he did. McFarlane operated it not only as a theater but as a community center where civic, religious, and political meetings could be held, often without a rental fee, including the two years after McFarlane quit booking outside shows in 1908 and the beginning of film showings in 1910. Films were shown at least one night a week until 1927, except for the five months the theater was shut down during the flu epidemic of 1919.

The Central City Opera House had become not only a symbol of the town's endurance but indeed its lifeblood in subsequent years as the summer theater festival attracted both Denver opera lovers and a national audience to the historic mining town for at least a few weeks each summer. McFarlane would not live to see the grand reopening of the Opera House, which featured Lillian Gish in *Camille* in 1932. The review in the *Rocky Mountain News* recalled the "good old days" and unknowingly foreshadowed a distant future with a banner headline reading "CENTRAL CITY ROARS WIDE OPEN IN REVIVAL OF OLD MINING DAYS." The story described an "uproarious throng estimated at more than 5,000" streaming up to Gregory Gulch for opening night of the Central City Play Festival. But only a few hundred of the thousands actually viewed the play. The rest took advantage of free-flowing bootleg liquor, roulette, craps, and faro games in the gambling establishments hastily set up in the long vacant buildings on "the richest square mile on earth."[48]

Gilpin County's population had decreased by a third, to 4,131 in 1910, and even more dramatically to 1,364 by 1920. The urbane town of Central City, which had produced Henry Teller and Nathaniel P. Hill, early Colorado senators, Frank Hall, the secretary of the territory, and James B. Belford, Colorado's first congressman, had long ago been eclipsed by Denver. Central City was, at the opening of the summer play festival in 1932, a town of only 572 souls, and Black Hawk, the only other remaining community, had a population of only 253.

The Greatest Colorado Gold Rush

Much more immense in economic significance was the last great gold strike in what became known as the Cripple Creek District. Although numerous rumors and some limited documented gold finds occurred in what today is Teller County, the area depended primarily on marginal cattle ranching until October 20, 1890, when Robert Womack filed a claim with verifiable gold content. Due to previous fraud (salting of mines to encourage commerce) the gold rush was slow to develop, yet by the middle of 1891 twenty-two claims had been filed in the Cripple Creek District. By December 1891 a real estate boom was under way, and stock in gold mines sold in Denver and Colorado Springs amounted to an investment in excess of four million dollars and more than sixty million shares—an indication of the diversification of mine ownership and the requirement of extensive capital investment.

The emergence of the Cripple Creek District was truly a "rush." Almost overnight an urban infrastructure emerged along with the thousands of adventurers who produced it. Mining was the game; more than 450 mines were developed from 1891 to 1896, peaking at 700 mines, and the game was played in numerous robust and exciting communities such as Cripple Creek, Victor, Independence, Gillett, Ajax, Elkton, Goldfield, Cameron, Altman, and Anaconda. Although dominated by Cripple Creek, which emerged with something over 20,000 residents by 1896 (according to city directories), other communities had substantial populations. Victor possibly included 18,000 residents. By 1896, the peak of gold fever, the Cripple Creek District achieved sufficient growth so that it contained the fourth and fifth largest cities in Colorado. Some writers estimated that the district contained more than 50,000 residents. The significance of the gold field is revealed in the establishment of three separate rail lines to transport people, commerce, and, of course, gold ore to Colorado City and Pueblo for processing. Furthermore, the district, towns, and major mines were serviced by two electric trolley lines.

At its peak, the district supported fifteen newspapers (eight published in Cripple Creek alone), an extensive business section, and several notorious red light districts, the most famous being found in Cripple Creek on Myers Street. Although few in number (32), churches were present in most of communities, with the greatest concentration, 16, in Cripple Creek. But churches were vastly outnumbered by saloons (149, with 73 in Cripple Creek and 37 in Victor), dance halls, sporting establishments, and cribs. Prostitution, gambling, and opium use were relatively open and tolerated, even encouraged, in Cripple Creek.

The year 1896 also marked the decline of limited placer mining and the winnowing out of the less productive deep mines. The closure of marginal mines resulted in a rapid decline in population so that by 1900 only about 30,000 people remained in Teller County, most of them in the Cripple Creek District. Here too the familiar characteristics of mining boom towns would shape the image of the amenities and law enforcement concerns of the dominant communities of Cripple Creek and Victor.

After half a century of gold-mining flourishes and failures in the American West, the *Denver Times* began a series of articles on the necessity of "reform" in Cripple Creek, with the hopeful headline "CRIPPLE CREEK IS HERE TO STAY: Enough Gold in Sight Now to Keep It up for a Quarter of a Century."[49] The article emphasized the replacement of shacks and frame tenements with solid brick houses. Betsy Jameson, who spent two decades exploring the highly unionized working-class life and politics of Cripple Creek and Victor, reported the somewhat unusual demographics in these "family" mining towns, where 40 percent of the population was female and three of five adults were married. Jameson confirmed that, unlike the company towns in the East, 48 percent of the district household heads owned their homes, and those who rented did so in private agreements; they paid in cash rather than company scrip, traded with private merchants, and elected school officials. Colorado women had the vote and were active in district politics, including two women on the police court jury in Cripple Creek in 1893.[50]

But if there were indications of community stability, some of the social deviance endemic to mining booms appeared in the district as well. The same article that began by celebrating the "solidity of the city" and went on to comment on "cosmopolitan transient visitors" also discussed "prospectors seen in large numbers on Bennett Avenue every day, talking long and learnedly of 'good propositions' to any one who will listen," and included concerns about "clairvoyants" and robbers, most especially the female variety, because their victims were so often unwilling to press charges.[51]

By the first half of 1900, the issue of controlling gambling, prostitution, and related robberies dominated the news of the newly formed Teller County. The district was on the precipice between the nineteenth-century view of vice as inevitable, perhaps beneficial, and at most subject to government control and profit and the progressive reform impetus to abolish gambling, prostitution, and related sins. On February 9, 1900, the *Times*, under headlines reading "Revenue from Crime and Vice" and "Gamblers and Fallen Women Required to Pay a Tax in Cripple Creek," the paper's lead paragraph acknowledged:

This wide-open camp is now having the usual troubles over the collection of so-called fines from the gaming houses and the depraved women. The neighboring camp of Victor has been wrestling with the problem for the last few weeks and after having removed a police justice and the night watchmen, who collected the fines, has not yet solved the question—at least satisfactorily to the city treasury. . . . [T]he judge claimed that the fines were not fines, and that as the money was illegally collected, the city was not entitled to it. . . . In this city, also the gaming houses and houses of ill-fame are likewise subjected to a tax or fine—a regular sum per month for each offender. The fines are regularly collected by a "collector." Several days ago the collector was removed.

The issue was resolved in favor of taking a census of "all the immoral characters and gaming house keepers, requiring them to come into court every month and pay their fines." At the same meeting the city council considered the petition to open a dance hall "with the necessary equipment of handling painted high kickers in abbreviated skirts." The matter was referred to a select committee.[52]

The second reform effort in the same month attempted to require the removal of the gambling operations in the twenty-four saloons on Bennett Avenue (the main street) to second floors. Once again, the moral case is ambiguous. The problem seems to have been in part one of congestion, with the closing of gambling houses in Leadville and an incipient reform movement in Denver, and partly one of weather, given the descriptions of the "shivering crowds" (at an altitude of 10,000 feet, with nowhere else to go) being attracted to the saloons, "brightly lighted with a large stove fire." Presumably by confining gambling operations to the second floor, temptation would be removed from the drinking saloon patrons. Featured prominently is the following prototypical and speculative story: "one of the saddest incidents that I [reporter unnamed] have seen lately was that of a woman with her little boy shivering in the cold at the door of a saloon last Saturday evening. The woman was crying bitterly. She had sent in for her drunken husband, who was gambling off his wages at the roulette wheel. The woman was thinly clad, and perhaps she and this child had not had their supper."[53]

While some efforts to enforce an ordinance against all gambling ensued, a countereffort was launched by small gambling concerns that prevailed in their argument that the required move to second-floor space constituted a trust that would freeze out all gambling operations of only one or two tables. Demonstrating the speed with which gambling interests could move, even in 1900, within the first year of the Cripple Creek gold strike, the *Denver Post* reported the presence of a hundred slot

machines, each of which paid in "fines" $5 per month; twenty-two rou-
lette wheels, each paying $10 per month; and a number of craps and brace
faro games, which made a total revenue in fines of between $900 and
$1,000 a month.[54] Some of the leading citizens tried to compel the sheriff
to close all the gambling houses in the city or remove him from office. But
it was argued that as long as gambling was not shut down at Victor,
Cripple Creek could not afford to allow the profits to go there, and Victor
made the same argument about Cripple Creek.[55]

The campaign against prostitutes as well contained less moral rationale
than economic concern. In May 1900 a petition from a number of property owners on Myers Avenue requested the removal of all the disrepu-
table women from that avenue (about fifty) due to the decreased rents and
prices of property on the street.[56] Cripple Creek's legal policy (state law
was essentially circumvented) depended on weighing the income from
prostitutes against property values and petty crimes and danger from fire.
Revenue derived from "immoral women" and dance houses was about
$500 per month, at the rate of $4 per month for each of the "degraded
characters," plus $10 per month for establishment owners and an addi-
tional saloon license. But there were also "gangs" of female crooks rob-
bing victims who were usually too embarrassed to appear against them.
Some even engaged in fairly large scale fraudulent land deals.[57] But at the
same time, new dives were being opened with the misleading name of
"theater," staffed with female toughs imported from Denver.[58]

But the concern in Cripple Creek was not simply over women's relation
to gambling and prostitution. This was a "family town" in which the
unions worked hard to win a "family wage," and if class issues were
paramount, gender issues were not. Nearly 19 percent of women listed an
occupation, including twenty-five nurses, in the 1900 census, but married
women rarely worked outside the home, even though they might take in
laundry, cook, clean, or run a boarding house.[59] There was plenty of
suspicion of the "ADVENTURESS IN CRIPPLE CREEK: They Work for a Song,
Hoping to Capture a Rich Miner Some Day." This *Denver Sunday Times*
article actually did not get beyond issues of squatters and mine salting for
a full column, but eventually the story addressed its headline by worrying
that women were willing to work

> for half rates, throwing men out of employment. Women will accept
> almost any wages in order to escape what they term the drudgery of
> household work. . . . But the young thing who has taken work at half rate
> spends her money upon herself and is boarded by her own family. Her
> wages are her "pin money" by which she is enabled to dress finer. It is this
> which is mainly demoralizing the labor market of this camp—excepting of

course the organized unions. If it were possible to unionize all classes or employment it would be much better for the camp and also for employees generally.[60]

In fact, several hundred women belonged to the unions in 1900, even though the lowest wages were still paid for "women's work." But both the Dressmakers Union and the Female Clerks #28 had all-female unions.[61]

If women were segregated into the spheres of private homes, prostitute cribs, and female unions in Cripple Creek, so were racial groups. Here ethnicity took on more of the historical character of turn-of-the-century America than had its mining camp predecessors. African Americans were segregated from the rest of the population, Asian workers were banned, and southern and eastern Europeans were kept out of Cripple Creek as well. While ethnicity and ethnic fraternal organizations were dominant in the social life of the district, it mattered a lot whether you were Irish, Cornish, or Welsh.

Teller County had 310 African Americans in 1900, 188 of them in Cripple Creek, most living in or near the entertainment district. Black men were saloon porters, janitors, cooks, and laborers, while the women listed washerwomen, cooks, and servants as their occupations. Slurs appeared in the press, but black townsfolk had public gathering places (Mahogany Hall and the Just a Few club), and a black delegate was sent to the state and congressional Republican Party conventions. There was not only a Colored Republican Club but an organization of black Democrats.[62]

National anti-immigrant sentiment would be strong enough to help shape the formation of Cripple Creek. Unlike the Black Hills mining towns, especially Lead, in which southern Europeans would form an enduring and celebrated segment of the community to the present, Cripple Creek residents made it clear that Slavs, Italians, Greeks, and Hispanics were not welcome, presumably because they were willing to work for less than union wages. "The town guns would stone 'em out." The press also reported worry about the Italians, Austrians, and Slavs in Leadville who did not buy enough from the local merchants and sent their earnings to families abroad. In any case, in 1900 only eighteen Italians, no Greeks, and five Asians lived in Teller County.

Anti-Asian prejudice was vitriolic, if misplaced. In 1902 the Cripple Creek Union #19 asked the police chief to run the "Japanese harlots and their lovers out of town," and the Trades Assembly then thanked him for expelling from the city "the Japanese women and their consorts." While the unions argued about whether the Chinese or Japanese were more dangerous, the press argued that exclusivity was essential because of the "higher standards of living of the Caucasian race" and because the "presence of Mongolians was inimical to overall scholastic success."[63] The Chinese were run out of Silverton, to the south, the same year.

Even the vice district of Myers Avenue was laid out according to racial and class distinctions. The Old Homestead, fanciest of the parlor houses and the playground of mining kings, kept a separate building at the back of the lot where a few black women worked. The Royal Inn, ironically, staged *The Mikado*. The smaller houses farther down Myers Avenue toward Poverty Gulch housed (in order) French, Japanese, Chinese, Mexican, Indian, and black prostitutes. But if melting pot sentiment was absent in a Cripple Creek highly politicized by class at the turn of the century, so were inclinations for progressive proscriptions against prostitution. An article titled "Regulate It" in a local paper advised: "under the present social and industrial system, the breeding and propagation of a female prostitute class is as inevitable and unavoidable as the appearance of maggots in the putrid carcass that lays [*sic*] in the July sun."[64]

But the prostitutes were not only participating in the economic boom, which could allow them to charge a dollar a "date" and a dollar for a bottle of beer, they participated in labor politics as well. In 1902 the dance hall girls called a strike to oppose the 10 percent reduction in their share of liquor sales and formed the Dance Hall Girls Protective Association. When in response the Trades Assembly mounted a campaign to close the dance halls, the Musicians Union protested. The strike succeeded, although the union was apparently short-lived.[65]

While women had a place in the entertainment business and even the labor organizations of Cripple Creek, the fundamental business of the town was mining, in which both laborers and owners were mainly men of western European extraction. The Cripple Creek District condensed the history of discovery, bonanza, and community into a remarkably brief period. While the rush to "the world's greatest gold camp" had taken place in the decade before the turn of the century and spawned no fewer than twenty-five mining villages, by 1910 Cripple Creek and Victor were the principal towns, and only Goldfield and Independence had populations of more than a hundred. Cripple Creek still had over 6,204 of its 10,147 inhabitants from the original census, and Victor held relatively steady at 4,986.[66] After a devastating fire in 1901, Victor rebuilt in brick and stone. Cripple Creek as well not only had survived the 1896 fire, which burned the business district and left five thousand homeless, and the bloody labor strike of 1903–4, in which 33 men died and 3,550 laborers were idled, but had recovered to stake out its identity as the home of mine owners, managers, and foremen.[67]

In the familiar pattern, Bob Womack, the discoverer of Cripple Creek gold, lacked the capital to develop the necessary deep mining, sold the claim for $500, and died poor. But a range of other folks made fortunes. In 1900, of the twenty-five superintendents of the largest mines, 35 percent were foreign born and had worked at an average of four mining camps previously. The thirty-five predominant mine owners were all native born. Forty percent owned mines elsewhere, and only 14 percent had ever worked as a miner or prospector. This summary, however, disguises the differences among them. Betsy Jameson categorized them in four groups.[68] Four of the thirty-five had working-class roots, the most famous of whom was Winfield Scott Stratton, founder of the Portland Gold Mining Company and Cripple Creek's first millionaire, who became a major benefactor to Colorado Springs and, reflecting his sympathies, joined the Carpenters Union after he became a multimillionaire. Very wealthy and influential older mining magnates who expanded their already major holdings in the new gold camp included David H. Moffat and Eben Smith. Turning from Leadville interests after the silver crash, their Cripple Creek District holdings eventually included the Bi-Metallic Bank of Cripple Creek, the Metallic Extraction Company, the Florence and Cripple Creek Railroad, and fourteen mines. Moffat and Smith lived in Denver and seldom visited the Cripple Creek District.[69] Warren, Frank, and Harry Woods of Woods Investment Company held a kind of middle ground in relation to the community and their workers. Starting out by selling town lots in Victor, they hit pay dirt while digging the basement for a hotel that would be called the Gold Coin. While this family enterprise ended up owning several power companies, a mining supply company, the Short Line railroad, and twenty-four mining companies and built mansions for themselves in Colorado Springs, they also built an elaborate clubhouse and the Pinnacle Peak amusement facilities in the district for their workers. The "socialites" from wealthy eastern families, including Albert E. Carlton, Charles MacNeill, Charles Tutt, and Spencer Penrose, were neither friendly to labor nor patronizing of its welfare, according to Jameson. Although younger than the mining magnates, they ultimately were able to destroy organized labor and develop the "mill trust" in the district. All but Carlton lived in Colorado Springs.

The crushing of the Western Federation of Miners over mill workers' wages did not by any means solve Cripple Creek's problems. A long period of consolidation of the nearly five hundred mines and mills eliminated jobs. Water filled the mine shafts, some as deep as 3,000 feet. In 1911, the three-mile-long Roosevelt Tunnel was bored into the gold field to lower the water level, enabling about 150 mines to continue to operate until World War I closed them. In 1920 only forty mines were operating, but when the price of gold was increased to $35 per ounce in 1934, 135 mines again operated.[70] The population of Teller County, having dropped to 4,141 in 1930, increased to 6,463 in 1940 but would plummet to 2,754 in 1950. Indeed, Cripple Creek and Victor could not sustain their former populations, even as the shift of families from the lesser villages to the two centers continued.[71]

At the same time, the town's long-term fame would come not from its mines or wealth but from its entertainment history. The Cripple Creek District purportedly had the only bullfight staged in the United States (in Gillett in 1895). Jack Johnson staged a twenty-round bout with Mexican Pete in Cripple Creek in 1902; Jack Dempsey fought seven rounds with a local fighter named George Coplen in 1913. But whole books were written about the painted ladies of Cripple Creek's red light district. Their names were known and their funerals were attended by local bands, mounted policemen, and buggies of women from "the row."[72]

While Cripple Creek residents were almost proud of the tenderloin, even well into the twentieth century, they wanted it to be their story on their own terms. When Julian Street, a travel writer for *Collier's Weekly*, did a story in 1914, principally on Colorado Springs but with a few paragraphs on Cripple Creek, all focusing on the sordid lives of the prostitutes, in particular one Madame Leo on Myers Avenue, the citizens were very upset. A letter-writing campaign garnered neither a retraction nor an apology from the magazine, and a contest for an essay in response did not produce rhetoric meeting the magazine's standards. In frustration, a meeting at the Elks Club to discuss possible retaliation produced a suggestion on which the city council members acted immediately. That night an ordinance was passed that changed the name of Myers Avenue to Julian Street, after the offending author.[73]

The characterization of Cripple Creek/Victor comes more accurately from Lowell Thomas, who grew up and began his career in journalism there. In the foreword to Mabel Barbee Lee's *Cripple Creek Days*, which is dedicated to Thomas, he describes getting to school: "on our way to school in the morning we all had to pass Dingman's gambling emporium, and the swinging doors of Diamond, the Monarch, and other saloons that never closed. Then there was the lurid red-light district almost next door to the schoolhouse. And just outside our windows was a mine boiler repair shop. The man who ran it had the most colorful variety of purple profanity I have ever heard."[74] The "greatest gold camp on earth" would create a reputation for itself that would be hard to live up to over the long haul.

Deadwood/Lead's and Central City/Black Hawk's earlier frontiers had permitted a wider variety of female and ethnic participation for a time than in the Cripple Creek District. However, Cripple Creek/Victor foreshadowed public policy that would provide revenues through the taxation of social vices. The institutionalization of community forms in these settlements in the early twentieth century would give a clearer view of how they differed from and how they resembled small towns across America. The comparison provides some clues as to why the three mining sites would hitch their fortunes to the allure of localized gambling in the 1990s, their residents once again proving themselves to be adventurous prospectors in the latest rush for the extraction of gamblers' cash.

CHAPTER 3

Stagnation and Decay in Retrospect

Placer and hard rock gold mining, which provided the lifeblood for the creation and development of the three pairs of communities, also placed constraints on the growth of the communities and eventually contributed to their decline. Gold ore, located in relatively inaccessible mountain ravines, dictated that the communities supporting the influx of miners would be isolated and burdened with expensive transportation in terms of both time and money. Gold provided the substance for the population boom of mining and support occupations, along with the infrastructure to service the mining industry and to provide a stabilizing influence for the communities during the early part of the twentieth century. But consolidation and mechanization of mining operations also contributed to the communities' eventual deterioration.

The decline these towns faced, however, was not unlike the fate of small towns all over the country at midcentury. Although the United States has a long history of rural to urban migration (the only exceptions being the Depression and the rural revival of the late 1970s and early 1980s), after World War II many rural areas and especially small towns were decimated by widespread out-migration. Throughout the United States smaller communities lost population through this migration; in most cases it was their brightest and most capable young adults who left to seek economic opportunities in large urban areas. As a result of selective migration, small town populations began to age, and many lost their vitality; businesses closed, and the cultural foundations of the communities, including churches, theaters, opera houses, and even schools, lost their clientele. A general decline of human capital sent many once vibrant communities toward an accelerating tailspin into decay and, in some cases, extinction.

Cripple Creek, Victor, Black Hawk, Central City, Lead, and Deadwood were all adversely affected by this diaspora, in spite of local efforts to diversify and revitalize their economies through the 1950s, 1960s, 1970s, and 1980s. Although Gilpin, Teller, and Lawrence Counties had seen some increase in population from their lows in 1920 (Lawrence County) and 1930 (Gilpin and Teller Counties), the six communities had experienced substantial decline, with slight fluctuations since World War II. For example, Deadwood steadily decreased from a high of 4,100 in 1940 to only 1,830 by 1990. Lead had peaked at 8,392 in 1910 and with the stability of Homestake still had 6,211 in 1960, but it lost a thousand residents each decade to 3,632 in 1990. Cripple Creek too had dropped from 10,147 in 1900 to 425 in 1970, with a minimal increase to 655 in 1980 from the mining resurgence of the 1970s,[1] but it declined to 584 in 1990. Victor's nearly 5,000 souls in 1900 had dwindled to 700 in 1950, 450 in 1960, and 258 by 1990. Central City and Black Hawk achieved their peak populations of 3,114 in 1900 and 1,540 in 1880, respectively. But since 1920 they together had not more than about 1,000 people and for the past thirty years maintained populations of around 300 for Central City and 225 for Black Hawk.[2] As this shift from stable to declining communities reflected national trends, particular efforts to reverse the decline in South Dakota and Colorado must be placed within a national context to understand the difficulties faced at the local level.

National Patterns and Government Policy

The historical movement away from agricultural and extractive industries to other types of employment in the United States was particularly abrupt during the second half of the twentieth century. Researchers have devoted substantial energy to understanding the dramatic restructuring from primary industries (mining, forestry, fishing, and agriculture) to secondary (manufacturing) and tertiary (service) industries. Explanations began with increased mechanization of both agriculture and extractive industries coupled with the attractive pull of industrial jobs while, more recently, analyses have focused on the global marketplace and its relationship to financial stress on American agriculture and extractive industries. By the mid-1980s social scientists documented the most recent downturn in agriculture, noting that depressed farm prices, excess supply, declining land values, declining exports, and high interest rates together had created a farm economic crisis that resulted in high rates of farm foreclosures and a restructuring of agriculture. Similarly, competition in extractive industries, primarily from abroad, led to increased mechanization and consolidation of mining companies.[3]

Warren Trock, Thomas Miller, and S. Lee Gray and Russell Youmans have all documented that in times of financial crisis many farmers and miners turned to temporary alternative employment as a way to maintain their economic viability.[4] Of course, another outcome was a net transfer of labor out of primary industries. From 1940 to 1980 the number of people working solely or primarily in agriculture dropped from 8.4 million to fewer than 2.5 million nationally, accounting for only 2.7 percent of the labor force. There were fewer people working in agriculture in the United States in 1980 than in 1820. A similar but less dramatic decline occurred in mining industries, with employment dwindling from 901,000 in 1950 to a low of 514,000 in 1970 with a slight rebound to 723,000 in 1980. This transfer of labor out of agriculture and mining generally meant a movement of population into the manufacturing and service industry opportunities in metropolitan areas.

Even though the United States experienced substantial redistribution of population from rural to urban areas, and a boom-bust pattern characterized many U.S. mining and railhead towns, the majority of small towns until the 1960s had been able to sustain their populations through high fertility. This trend began to change rather suddenly after World War II, when the exodus from rural areas and small towns increased, particularly from those areas dependent on agriculture and extractive industries. For example, sociologists Lichter, Fuguitt, and Heaton noted that just during the decade of the 1950s towns of less than 2,500 in nonmetropolitan counties declined 1.7 percent (an absolute decline of 588,000) in spite of high fertility.[5] It was during this decade that numerous government policies unintentionally accelerated the depopulation of rural areas and small towns in the United States. Foremost among the programs were the interstate highway system, federal housing policies that tended to favor metropolitan areas of 50,000 or more, and government (state and federal) agendas that provided subsidies for attracting basic industries, with many of these programs also restricted to communities of fifty thousand or more until 1981.[6]

These development strategies in concert with regional and national economic trends resulted in rural areas and small towns experiencing substantial out-migration, while middle-size towns and especially metropolitan areas gained population from substantial in-migration, particularly those located on or close to the interstate highway system. Lichter and Fuguitt demonstrated that town growth was strongly correlated with the timing of the completion of the interstate highway system and that even communities that had experienced out-migration previous to interstate highway construction were likely to have net in-migration and net creation of employment, particularly in service-related activity, both non-local and tourist-related.[7] They concluded "that interstate highways have the effect of redrawing trade or service areas," implying a net loss of population from noninterstate counties. Thus, the loss of jobs from agriculture and ancillary industries juxtaposed with the expansion of manufacturing and service jobs in metropolitan areas, along with the ease of commuting, allowed for an increase in the growth of metropolitan population during the 1950–1970 decades both in terms of population size and number of metropolitan areas.[8]

Indeed, if the rural Rocky Mountain mining towns were too small to avail themselves of the federal housing and industrial programs, they were all affected by the interstate highway system. I-90 generally replaced U.S. Highway 16 across South Dakota, but as it headed north across Wyoming and Montana, it bypassed U.S. 85 through Deadwood and Lead, making Rapid City and Spearfish the new commercial centers. Similarly, Central City/Black Hawk and Cripple Creek/Victor, on less major thoroughfares near metropolitan areas, would be threatened as destinations by their relative proximity to I-70, which crosses the Rockies via the Eisenhower Tunnel west of Denver, and I-25, which enables traffic to speed through southern Colorado at Colorado Springs.

Confronted with massive migration into urban areas, the federal government responded in the late 1960s to counterbalance the magnetic pull of metropolitan areas. The Economic Opportunity Act of 1964, the Public Works and Economic Development Act of 1965, the Appalachian Regional Act of 1965, and the Rural Development Act of 1972 explicitly mandated industrial relocation as a primary instrument for improving conditions in nonmetropolitan areas. Rural industrialization is one example of governmental policy designed to stimulate job creation in rural areas and to energize rural revitalization.[9] Once enacted, this legislation provided incentives for industries to move into rural areas, which, coupled with cheap land, low taxes, and a low-cost available labor force, led to the development of some manufacturing jobs, particularly in the rural South during the late 1960s and 1970s.

In addition, a number of programs, both federal and state, were enacted to encourage a good business climate. Joseph Schumpeter summarized in "An Introduction to State and Local Economic Development Policy" the rationale for these programs when he noted that economic vitality "comes from the new consumers' goods, the new methods of production or transportation, the new markets, the new forms of industrial organization that capitalist enterprise creates, the impulse that sets and keeps the capitalist engine in motion."[10] His focus was on the private risk taker; the function of the entrepreneur was to be an actor with vision who would stimulate the economic engine. He was not looking for stimulus by governmental agencies or programs; for him risk taking would come in response to market demands. Writers including Peter Eisinger took issue with Schumpeter by arguing that there were circumstances when private activity would not suffice, particularly given regional and international competition for jobs and capital.

Several federal programs reflected Eisinger's point of view. The Community Development Block Grants (CDBGs), Economic Development Administration (EDA), Urban Development Action Grants (UDAGs), and Small Business Administration (SBA) were designed to affect the supply side by providing inducements, including low taxes, tax exemptions, cheap land, and capital subsidies (usually unconditional but changing criteria), to attract new enterprises in communities undergoing "stress." Most of these programs were designed to improve local infrastructures such as water, sewage, streets, and similar amenities, so that smaller communities could compete for new enterprises and eventually new jobs and perhaps population. It was generally assumed that more jobs would lead to fewer unemployed people, more income, greater tax revenues, fewer social expenditures, lower-cost government, a more robust employment multiplier, and, of course, a more dynamic community.

Of particular relevance to the Rocky Mountain mining communities was the EDA, created in 1965 and designed to promote economic development in distressed areas of the country with a focus on structural unemployment. Within the act establishing the agency were a public works bill (Title I), which provided matching grants and long-term loans to communities and counties for fixed-capital projects; a business loan and loan guarantees bill (Title II); a technical assistance and planning grants bill (Title III); and an economic adjustment bill (Title IX).

CDBGs, which consolidated seven different programs, including Urban Renewal and Model Cities, were originally limited to metropolitan areas of 50,000 or more but were modified in 1981 to include smaller towns. This legislation was designed primarily to assist in developing new housing stock or rehabilitating the existing housing inventory. Passed in 1977, the UDAG program, authorized by the Housing and Community Development Act, was designed to permit a wide range of public investments in major development projects. According to Eisinger, this act is the "single most important federal contribution to subnational economic development policy in the modern period." These programs provided grants to severely distressed cities and urban counties to help alleviate physical and economic deterioration (PL95-128, sec. 119[a][1977]). "Approximately 70 percent of commercial projects and 43 percent of industrial projects involve brand new construction."[11] CDBGs and UDAGs were used extensively by Lead and Deadwood and explored in Black Hawk and Central City, at least to provide sewer and water improvements, in an effort to jump-start local economies and reverse community decline.

Like numerous small towns throughout the United States, the Rocky Mountain mining towns launched diverse economic development schemes to counteract their steady decline, both in terms of economy and demographics. These included Main Street projects, rural manufacturing, low-skill service enterprises, and development of potential tourist attractions. Many of these development schemes focused on unique local assets such as lakes, mountains, or rivers or a reconstruction of their history through the creation of local interest museums, living history exhibits, or historic preservation projects. Initially these efforts were funded primarily through private entrepreneurs or by philanthropic organizations. But, beginning in the 1970s and expanding in the 1980s, communities were assisted by federal money and expertise, primarily through the UDAG and CDBG programs. Money from these programs encouraged communities to preserve their heritage through Main Street programs and other historic preservation efforts. These efforts to make communities more attractive spotlighted some inherent trait, such as a western motif, with the objective of encouraging tourism and diversifying local economies. The three pairs of communities investigated here were active participants in these "redevelopment efforts," focusing on the scenic terrain and nineteenth-century western history, albeit with limited success.

At the national level these programs provided for a brief but significant rural turnaround or, more properly, a nonmetropolitan turnaround for some thirteen hundred counties during the 1970s. In addition to the draw of rural industrialization, nonmetropolitan areas grew in the 1970s at a faster pace than metropolitan areas, ironically, because of the availability of more and better highways, mass telecommunications, and a higher disposable income that allowed residents to pay a premium for their dream of the bucolic residential life.[12] However, with a declining economy in the 1980s, many small towns and rural areas lost their ability to attract migrants. In addition, metropolitan job creation accelerated during the 1980s, providing a pull toward larger cities, with the most favored located in the Sunbelt.[13]

The national rural turnaround proved short-lived in general and had no appreciable effect on the six mining towns, four of which would eventually turn to gambling. Thus, all six communities were likely candidates for development schemes that might lead to expanded opportunities and the hope of a revival of population and economic growth.

The Rocky Mountain Mining Towns' Experiences

Mining towns all over the West had for half a century been turning to tourism to supplement dwindling income from mineral sources. Those that have survived at all have known that tapping renewable resources is a necessity to bring stability to their communities and new riches where old precious metals are playing out. Leadville and Georgetown, Colorado, and Butte, Montana, all continued mining at some level, with various interruptive labor strikes, buyouts, and shutdowns, while turning more and more to the attraction of tourists as a more "stable" source of community revenues. The tales of the gold rushes, the nineteenth-century architecture, and especially the seedier complements to society—saloons, gambling halls, dance halls, and even opium dens—fashioned the lore of the communities. With the downturn in mining, these mountain towns attempted to exploit their past to ensure their future by attracting tourists to relive the towns' notorious history in visits to the sites of these adventures. Yet, as the towns continued to lose population, even buildings with historical significance, the main draw, began to deteriorate.

Uniqueness was an important lure, so appeals to tourists adopted different themes. Of the communities central to this analysis, Deadwood, South Dakota, focused most on the gold rush into the Black Hills with its Days of '76 and re-creation of a wild, rough, frontier atmosphere. Stopping to see where Wild Bill Hickok was shot and buried alongside of Calamity Jane became a tourist staple. Its neighbor Lead, just up the gulch, concentrated instead on the continued mining of Homestake, once the largest and now the oldest operating gold mine in North America. In Colorado, Central City staked its fortunes on the more highbrow Central City Opera, restoring a nineteenth-century opera house to a grandeur suitable for staging complete classical productions. In Cripple Creek, continued mining along with narrow gauge mine train tours drew tourists to a longstanding melodrama and the most famous red light district in the Rocky Mountains, as if the past were unbroken. Only Black Hawk and Victor settled for a time as residential adjuncts to their more famous neighbors. Reliance on tourism for at least four of the communities required the reconstruction of their past and a minimal restoration of historic buildings and relics (i.e., cemeteries and museums).

Although providing some diversification in economic structure, tourism as a solution to community stagnation proved to be problematic as a source of stable revenues. The towns' unique locations in scenic, though isolated, mountain canyons (gulches) and their distance from the interstate highways meant that, in the long run, tourism would provide seasonal employment that peaked during the summer months but left the long winters with many businesses closed.

The Black Hills first became a tourism destination with the advent of the motor car. The mountains, Mount Rushmore National Memorial, and scenic highways and lodges built during the 1930s by the Civil Conservation Corps gave the Black Hills an early advantage as a summer destination for midwestern family vacationers and an occasional president, from Calvin Coolidge to Dwight Eisenhower. If Lead had become the purest form of a mining town and Deadwood the commercial center, both began to recognize the possibilities of tourism as early as the 1920s. The northern Black Hills towns, including the agricultural community of Spearfish twenty miles down the canyon, began to attract short-term visitors interested in participating vicariously in the gold rush of 1876. For all its celebration of a poker-playing sheriff, a gun-toting smallpox nurse, and a cigar-smoking madam, not to mention the largest expropriator of a precious mineral in the Western Hemisphere, the Northern Hills' image of itself was as a "less commercialized" scenic area than the Southern Hills. Lead-Deadwood with Spearfish set the area up as the gateway to Yellowstone (the first national park), with Devil's Tower (the first national monument) on the Wyoming edge of the Hills. This was a direct challenge to the "tourist traps," including commercial "crystal" caves, "gravity spots," and reptile houses on U.S. Highway 16 between Rapid City and Mount Rushmore, which was also adjacent to Wind Cave National Park, Custer State Park, and the range of rustic lodges and highways built by the Civil Conservation Corps in the 1930s and led to Custer, the site of the original gold find. The Northern Hills offered, within half a dozen miles, not only the Wild West atmosphere of Deadwood, with nightly performances of *The Trial of Jack McCall,* the killer of Wild Bill Hickok, but continuing surface tours of the Homestake Mine in Lead. Just down Deadwood Hill on U.S. Highway 85, or through the spectacular limestone formations of Spearfish Canyon, is Spearfish. Having claimed moral superiority over the mining camps up the hill virtually since its founding in 1882, Spearfish offered on three nights a week during the summer the Black Hills Passion Play, an outdoor amphitheater reenactment of the last seven days in the life of Christ. Patterned on a medieval German play, it used the same family of professional actors for over forty years, plus several dozen "extras" provided by local churches for each performance.

In 1920, with a growing demand to see the Homestake operations, surface tours for a fee were conducted by the "Homestake Guides." The tours became a project of the Lead Civic Association in 1947 and, in addition to providing funds for city projects, became one of the prime sources of seasonal employment for "employees' daughters who were college students."[14] Besides allowing the young women to wear a pseudo miner's uniform of bluejeans, white shirt, and hard hat, the job was preferable to waiting tables or making beds, the other main summer employment possibilities for young women. The Homestake surface tours during the summer months increased from 7,500 visitors in 1986 to 36,000 in 1989 and planned for additional growth with the recent addition of a mining museum.

Deadwood began its summer celebration, the Days of '76, in 1924, featuring Wild Bill Hickok, Calamity Jane, Poker Alice, and assorted other gold rush characters. In addition, the city opened Pine Crest Park, with a community house and campsites, at the top of Deadwood Hill north of town. "Deadwood Dick" was installed in a cabin there in 1927 to entertain visitors. Although a number of people have claimed to be the authentic Deadwood Dick, including black cowboy Nat Love, Richard Clark was the local resident who regaled tourists with historical lore as various women's groups conducted songfests.[15] Cabins were later constructed, but the entire site burned to the ground in the forest fire of 1959, which started at the other end of town in Gayville. It completely surrounded the city of Deadwood but miraculously burned only a few houses on the highest slopes of the gulch and left the downtown intact.

By that time a number of motor lodges and motels provided less expensive overnight accommodations than the various hotels in the two towns, and a joint Lead-Deadwood Motel Association was formed, perhaps the first truly cooperative effort between the two functionally different and socially antagonistic towns. Tourism would provide a significant, if seasonal, secondary economy for Deadwood and Lead during the middle part of the century.

Consequently, Deadwood and Lawrence County both had longstanding experience with and fairly ample facilities for visitors' eating and sleeping requirements, even apart from the resources of the rest of the Black Hills and Rapid City to the southeast. In 1993 Deadwood and Lead offered 600 rooms in 34 motels, while Spearfish had 650 rooms in 26 motels, some of them larger franchises.[16] Yet the seasonal cycle of tourism meant that many motels had not stayed open in the winter, at least past hunting season, while during the summer they offered a range of possibilities for staying over, from rustic cabins to newer motel chains at either end of the price spectrum.

The Colorado mining/gambling towns also had previous experience with tourism, but they differed from Deadwood and each other in ways that had much to do with proximity to metropolitan areas. As early as 1932, Central City had its opera festival in the reopened Opera House, which was clearly intended to draw outsiders to a mining town that had largely played out its mineral resources.[17] But the opera season was a relatively short summer run, it drew a particular clientele, and numbers were limited. Certainty of its even remaining in Central City was debated in 1948 when efforts were made to move the opera to Red Rocks only a few miles from downtown Denver. That year, a group of residents petitioned to have Mayor John C. Jenkins Jr. recalled, supposedly because of his close connections with the Central City Opera House Association. Then on August 11, 1948, Jack Foster of the *Rocky Mountain News* editorialized that the opera festival should be relocated to Georgetown or Red Rocks, thereby providing two benefits: proximity to Denver, where most patrons resided, and resolution of the divisions in Central City over the place of the Opera House in city politics.[18] Frances Wayne, editor of the *Central City's Register-Call*, quickly responded to Foster as follows:

> NO CHANCE, JACK.
>
> Jack Foster, editor of The Rocky Mountain News, goes haywire when he learns of political differences in Central City, and suggests that the cause of these, the Central City Festival, be removed from Central City to, of all places, the Red Rocks Park.
>
> If his idea were accepted it could be written down that nothing more disastrous could happen to Central City since the great fire which consumed half of the town in 1874. . . .
>
> But the Central City Festival belongs to Central City and the people here. They are intelligent, thoughtful, grateful for the benefits which have come to the community through the establishment of the festival as an honor to its pioneers, and are not afraid that it will be removed, any more than the eternal hills which cup this old camp be removed by a suggestion of Jack Foster.[19]

Wayne was proven correct. A poll commissioned by the *Denver Post* found that 89 percent of Central City residents favored the retention of operas and plays in Central City (3 percent elected to stop the opera, while 8 percent didn't care); 84 percent were opposed to moving the operas and plays to Idaho Springs or Georgetown (16 percent didn't care or didn't know); and six out of ten supported their four-term mayor.[20]

Generally, the split occurred between "old-time" and "newcomer" residents, with concerns being voiced over the tax-free status of the Opera House (and its adjoining properties) and the illegal gambling associated with the opera festival.

Putting aside local animosities, Central City retained the opera and gradually increased its tourism to 262,000 visitors in 1950.[21] By 1960 the Highway Patrol estimated that 578,421 persons visited Central City, of whom 54,722 attended the operas and plays. During the summer months of 1960 Central City operated seventy restaurants and bars, of which only three remained open during the winter months.[22] Tourism steadily increased until 1971, when Central City police estimated 1.5 million visitors to Central City, most attracted during the summer months, a figure that seems to have been stable until 1990.[23] The exact number of tourists is debatable, but given the consistent methodology of using car counts multiplied by a passenger factor, it is obvious that tourism increased substantially from the late 1940s to the early 1970s and that the tourist trade remained cyclical. Yet, even with the cyclical nature of tourism, Central City in 1990 had at least three local hotels, plus a large motel in Black Hawk, and it was possible to drive to Idaho Springs, a resort some fourteen miles away, or even to Denver or Golden, thirty-eight miles down Clear Creek Canyon.

Cripple Creek, the youngest of the mining communities, founded in the 1890s, continued to support a large assortment of fairly small operating mines to the present. Its location some fifty miles up the mountains from the prosperous metropolitan area of Colorado Springs on rugged, high altitude terrain meant historically that most tourists would choose to ride the Short Line Railroad, assessed by Vice-President Theodore Roosevelt in 1901 with the oft-quoted words, "Bully! This is the ride that bankrupts the English language!"[24] Before the advent of gambling, Cripple Creek still had several hotels to accommodate those automobile drivers who could make their way up the winding road, which featured a single-lane tunnel with a stoplight, but did not want to make the return in the same day. The attraction to Cripple Creek may have been a more general interest in a twentieth-century mining area, a place where gold strikes, gambling, prostitution, labor strikes, and adventurous characters came late, and one could see an authentic rather than a reconstructed Rocky Mountain gold town.

After World War II Cripple Creek underwent a slow general decline, with a decrease in year-round mining and limited, cyclical summer tourism. With no new businesses entering and disinvestment occurring, the community experienced increased deterioration of structures and was on the verge of losing important historic buildings. But in 1946 the Imperial Hotel was bought and refurbished by Dorothy and Wayne Mackin, who hosted a teachers conference in the fall of 1948, the highlight of which was an acting troupe from Georgetown who had been "ousted" from Central City and provided "historic" melodramatic entertainment. The melodrama proved a great success, leading to ever larger audiences and a longer season. Although additional tourist attractions were soon to follow, the historic melodrama became the "Central City opera" of Cripple Creek.[25]

A 1951 headline, "New Gold Rush of Tourists Goal in Cripple Creek," announced the arrival of a Colorado Springs business group headed by Blevins Davis, president of the American Ballet Theatre, which was interested in making Cripple Creek "more attractive to the tourist trade" while maintaining "the original architecture" of the town.[26] Blevins Davis, along with Margaret Giddings, member of a prominent Colorado Springs family, bought the old Midland Terminal Station with the intention of creating a district museum. The consortium also planned to restore five brick houses on First Street. By 1952 the group hoped, with government assistance, to develop a general program of infrastructural improvement consisting of new streets, sidewalks, lighting, and utilities.[27] June 14, 1953, marked the opening day of the Cripple Creek District Museum donated by Davis and Giddings.

In 1954, the *Rocky Mountain News* headlined an article on how the "deluge of tourist hints new boom." The optimistic forecast was based on the 1953 visitations of 45,000 people to the newly opened Cripple Creek District Museum and the Molley Kathleen, an 1882 authentic gold mine on the hill above Cripple Creek that provided an underground, informative, historic tour of a thousand-foot-deep "operating" mine, which had 22,000 visitors and was featured in *National Geographic*.[28] In 1953 the *Rocky Mountain News* reported that "more than 200,000 tourists in all came up over Tenderfoot Hill from Divide, or over the beautiful old Gold Camp Road from Colorado Springs," and referred to the Cripple Creek/ Victor areas as a "Mecca" for visitors.[29] They were heady times, no doubt. These attractions were soon joined by the Cripple Creek and Victor Narrow Gauge Train, which provided tourists a two-hour scenic trip to the top of Mount Pigasus and a panoramic view of the Cripple Creek valley. By the 1960s Cripple Creek attracted half a million tourists annually. Although the Imperial Hotel remained open year-round, the melodrama, mine tour, narrow gauge train, and museum were closed from October through May. Seasonal tourism proved the dominant force in setting the pace of economic and social life in Cripple Creek.

Albeit cyclical in nature, tourism had for over forty years become a central industry and internally diversified from curio shops to performances and food and lodging in Cripple Creek, Central City, and Black Hawk, as well as in Deadwood. Nevertheless, the fortunes of the towns had diminished as interstate highways and high speed attractions encouraged tourists more and more to keep moving, only fifteen to forty miles from these old destinations.

Historic Preservation

Cripple Creek, Central City, Black Hawk, Deadwood, and, to a lessor extent, Victor and Lead have relied on tourism to supplement or drive local economies. While these towns had long been in the business of attracting outsiders to help support their economies, all had been in a state of gradual decline, with population loss, deteriorating housing, and limited investment in infrastructure to support Main Street businesses. That historic restoration should become part of a revitalization effort is not surprising.

In Central City the Opera House was restored as early as 1932. Once restored, the Opera House summer season became the major draw to Central City. Beginning in the 1940s, private donations permitted the Central City Opera House Association (CCOHA) to purchase and restore numerous historic properties. For example, in the 1940s Mrs. Spencer Penrose, a major benefactor of the CCOHA, purchased and redecorated several Victorian Era houses for use by the opera cast. In 1950 the CCOHA, through the efforts of Mrs. Penrose, Davis Moore, and Frank H. Ricketson Jr., invested $30,000 to remodel the Chain of Mines Hotel (donated to the CCOHA in 1942 by Ricketson) with its twenty rooms and eight baths for year-round use.[30] Consolidation of CCOHA property holdings on Eureka Street was further enhanced through the purchase of the First National Bank, with its turn-of-the-century brass vault and hand-carved walnut fixtures. The purchase, made possible by a gift of $25,000 from Helen Bonfils, enabled the association to remove the last neon signs from Eureka Street.[31] Then in 1954 a Penrose donation of $35,000 allowed the purchase and reconstruction of the historic Williams Stables. Penrose's donation stipulated that the facility, once restored, would be available to the Central City community during the winter months.[32] That same year the CCOHA committed $20,000 to the restoration of the Teller House. By the 1950s Central City was able to offer a tour of the historic district.

Yet in the 1970s the purchasing and restoration work of CCOHA, which provided measurable improvements to the physical appearance of the community, also generated conflicts with some local business owners and residents. The CCOHA was viewed as a closed circle of Denver residents that controlled almost thirty of Central City's choicest properties, which were exempt from property taxes. At the same time association members complained about the quality of the shops in town as well as the "honky-tonk atmosphere."[33] By 1973, in an effort to reconcile differences between the CCOHA and townspersons, association members began to work within the Little Kingdom Historical Foundation to preserve not only CCOHA properties but other significant historic properties in the district.

Down the hill in Black Hawk, restoration efforts were less successful until Mrs. Evelyn Hume deeded the Lace House, a turn-of-the-century mansion noted for its unique architecture, called Carpenter Gothic, to the city of Black Hawk. Lace House, a distinctive landmark built in 1863 and noted for its gingerbread detailing but in badly deteriorated condition, was selected by the Little Kingdom Historical Foundation as its preservation effort of 1976. A ten-thousand-dollar restoration grant awarded by the National Park Service along with $5,000 from the Colorado Centennial-Bicentennial Commission attested to the significance of the Lace House. Additional donations of $52,000 for restoration efforts enabled the Lace House to open as the Black Hawk City Museum.[34] The significance of this

Lace House, a Carpenter Gothic residence built in 1863 in Black Hawk. Its designation as a historic site in 1976 prevents its removal for a casino parking lot.

effort would not be realized until 1997, when it became clear that the conditions of the 1976 restoration would be the only obstacle to moving the Lace House to make room for a casino parking lot.[35]

Both Central City and Black Hawk were designated as National Historic Landmarks in 1961 by the National Park Service. In 1970 the Little Kingdom Council was established with the purpose of developing "an operational plan in several steps for complete and logical restoration and preservation of the two cities as a historic district."[36] Efforts to implement the restoration and preservation of the communities resulted in the Little Kingdom Council meeting with officials from the National Register and National Park Service, Farmers Home Administration, Bureau of Outdoor Recreation, Urban Renewal, and Small Business Administration. Government officials stressed the need for a master plan if federal funds were to be used for implementation of the restoration and preservation plan, but all were encouraging in regard to grants and/or loans being available. Projects in development stage included a seven-hundred-thousand-dollar water and sewage project for the "district" to be funded by the Farmers Home Administration and a proposal by the Bureau of Outdoor Recreation to fund the beautification of the Opera House gardens and flume area. An Urban Renewal official noted that his agency's mandate was to provide funds for planning, rehabilitation, and preservation.[37] Little came from the meeting except for the creation of a historic district, yet citizens continued to grapple with preservation issues in a series of town meetings, funded by the federal government and held in Black Hawk, that were designed to specify problem areas and solutions. Perhaps the most significant product of these town meetings was a solidifying of community spirit and the creation of "The Black Hawk Song."[38]

Likewise, in 1961 the National Park Service designated the Cripple Creek District as a National Historic Landmark. But in general, federal programs had little or no impact on the revitalization of the Teller County historic and tourist facilities beyond the private efforts of the 1940s and 1950s.

Lead-Deadwood: A Case Study of Community Development

Ironically, the town that worked hardest on community redevelopment had the worst prospects in 1997. Lead looked well on its way to becoming a ghost town in 1986, when a local group calling itself the Community Action Nucleus (CAN) began working on a redevelopment program that would be multifaceted, innovative in its entrepreneurial arrangements, and cognizant of the longstanding and continuing relationship of Lead to the Homestake Mine that still sustained it. Led by former high school coach and administrator Wendell Handley, Homestake attorney spouse Jacque Fuller, and local businessman Bev Hink, CAN organized a campaign for the citizens of Lead to stop depending on Homestake and to begin taking responsibility for their own fate. The development efforts they spawned are characterized by a peculiar combination of an uneasy alliance with Deadwood, continued dependence on Homestake's fortune and good will, and a desire to carve out Lead's distinct identity in the commercial tourist trade, which taken together produced some unusual entrepreneurial arrangements.

Out of their mutual hard times, Lead and Deadwood worked to forge joint redevelopment projects in the mideighties. A major project reaching fruition was the 7.8-million-dollar Twin City Shopping Mall, funded in part by a 1.3-million-dollar UDAG, for which Deadwood could qualify but Lead could not because of the relatively high average salaries of Homestake workers.[39] The multistory shopping mall, designed to look like a mine hoist building, was located on the hill above Main Street in Lead but very much in its new "center." Built in 1986 without much opposition, the mall housed a large grocery store, a discount store, and a total capacity of sixteen smaller retail stores. In 1988, when $700,000 of the grant was to be used for a 7.5-million-dollar hotel and convention center, Deadwood's mayor Tom Blair expressed concern about the inclusion of a city recreation center in the hotel plans. This truly unusual arrangement effectively voided any real possibility of a tri-city recreation center serving Deadwood, Lead, and Central City (which lay in the three-mile span between them). Lead's new YMCA building, constructed adjacent to the Golden Hills Resort and built in part with a 3.7-million-dollar bond underwritten by Homestake and $700,000 in interest from a fire insurance claim and connected by a "mine" tunnel, was to be made available to hotel patrons at a one-dollar-per-day room rental charge. The mall, hotel, and YMCA were all completed and remained by far Lead's greatest redevelopment success, although a major landslide in the winter of 1994 had the effect of closing the mall stores, and two years later, only the grocery and discount stores had reopened.

Lead's independent commercial efforts were slower in coming. CAN continued to meet and sponsored an award-winning beautification program and an annual Fourth of July festival and oversaw a parking authority, park board, tree board, Twin City Development corporation, and the YMCA. The town, which had been in commercial decline for thirty years, began to look immeasurably better. A mining museum, first housed in a vacant variety store on upper Main Street, moved to a vacated supermarket on lower Main, where it continued to develop. The museum prided itself not only on its archival collection of mining artifacts but also on its educational tour, which focused on changes in mining technology at Homestake. The museum linked itself to the longstanding surface tours of Homestake in order to lure those 40,000 summer mine visitors to the old Main Street of the town.

But in fact the old lower Main Street business venues were increasingly vacant or disappearing into the Open Cut, the open pit portion of the mine that was expanded enormously in the mid-1980s and required the demolition of ninety-two houses. The half-million-dollar City Center Redevelopment Project, funded with a CDBG and matched with local funds, included $138,000 from the sale of house lots in the rest of the town that had previously been owned by the Homestake Mining Company. The project aimed to develop the "Triad": the old Homestake Recreation Building to be reminiscent of the Hearst Mercantile, which burned in 1942; the Mining Museum, which is a conversion of an old grocery store; and the Mining Hall of Fame, to be created in the lobby of the Homestake Opera House, a National Historic Landmark of American Music gutted by fire in 1984. The proposal included brick sidewalks and Victorian lighting intended to keep tourists in the lower end of Main Street, where one restaurant and the Hearst Library (restored after not one but two fires in the 1980s) currently operated. But the other side of the street, which once housed a regionally known men's clothing store, a fine jewelry shop, a photo studio, a bakery, and a couple of bars, continued to be marginally occupied, and while the buildings had been purchased by various new mining companies, no clear plans for their use were evident.

There had been other efforts. One group, calling itself GOLD, for Greater Old Lead Development, had talked in 1986 about creating an artists colony in those buildings. But the notion was based on the assessment of a local artist who hoped that anywhere from twenty to thirty faculty and graduate students from the University of Wyoming and some local artists, attracted by the low rent, would be ready to set up studios in those buildings. In fact, there were never that many members of the University of Wyoming Art Department, nor was there ever serious consideration of the arrangement. A woodcarver occupied one corner of the Mercantile across the street until it became a pizza parlor, but the artists colony failed to materialize, as did the brick sidewalks and Victorian lighting. However, other efforts at renovations were successful. The city council got permission to tear down a number of abandoned and dilapidated buildings. They also bought the Burlington Depot and tore it down to make way for a new apartment building. Homestake was generous with rebates from the house lot sales for people who wanted to improve the sidewalks, retaining walls, and exteriors of their homes.[40]

Both improved housing and protection of historic sites were required before the second expansion of the Open Cut in the 1990s. This time, rather than simply buying out and burning houses, the company, according to its application for an expanded mining permit, had to relocate 170 households, including 107 single-family residences and 6 businesses displaced either by the mine expansion or the highway realignment necessitated by the expansion. It was the goal of Homestake's mitigation program to retain 60 percent of the 170 displaced households in Lead by constructing a new mobile home park, multifamily developments, and single-family residences. In addition to buying the houses at their appraised value, residents were to be given relocation assistance in several forms corresponding to individual needs.

According to Lead's financial officer, Harley Lux, "Homestake needed to find about thirty-five new residential home lots as part of the Open Cut project. We went together with them [and] now have up to a possible ninety lots." These lots, developed west of town on the hill opposite the high school, are a third to half an acre and on grades of about 8 percent, almost flat by Lead standards. A bond issue for $1.2 million plus another $1.3 million from Homestake provided funds for lot preparation, sewer and water lines (and a tank to provide adequate pressure), curbs, and gutters. It remains unclear what the city has done and what Homestake has provided, partly because the water system belonged to Homestake, although the company negotiated in 1994 to allow a joint Lead-Deadwood water commission to take over operation of the water system in spite of opposition by both city governments because of the system's poor condition. On a more optimistic note, the city hoped that with the addition of high quality houses the city tax base would improve and that the population decline would be halted.

In addition, Homestake assisted in developing an Ethnic History Park in the downtown area. The Mining Area Clearance and Buffer Zone Development Plan of February 1989 included a cultural resource analysis that surveyed 217 structures in the proposed expansion area and surrounding zone within the area nominated for the National Register of Historic Places in 1974. Only two (the Homestake Opera House and Recreation Building and the Homestake General Office Building, originally the Lead City Hall and now a hotel) were listed on the nomination petition. Ninety buildings "contributed" to the historic area, while 110 were found to be nonconforming structures and 15 had unknown eligibility. Plans were simply to record and then destroy these latter structures, with the exception of a hundred-year-old Finnish Lutheran church and two large houses. These houses were to join three presently located behind Main Street to create a historical park focusing on the various ethnic groups contributing to Lead's longstanding history of ethnic diversity.[41] This effort complemented Lead's installation of signs that designate the ethnic composition of neighborhoods based on a major study of Lead's ethnic history compiled by Don Toms. Plans included a park containing the old Finnish church that would be built in connection with the widening of U.S. Highway 85, but most of the rest of plans had not been implemented by 1997.

While the Homestake underground mine will likely produce for some time longer, this third major move of the city's downtown, because of either subsidence of underground mining or the consumption from the top of the mountain on which it resides, must provide the town something more than a decade's reprieve if it is to be worth the effort and expense. It is this focus on Lead's unique history as a prosperous and civilized mining town, as an appreciative magnet for cultural diversity, as a tourist town in its appealing Black Hills setting, and as a refuge adjacent to but separate from the gambling mecca of Deadwood that gave its hard-working and enthusiastic citizens hope for a new lease on life, at least for a time. However, the additional physical devastation of the still unexplained landslide of 1994 behind the new shopping center continues to threaten new commercial additions to the town.

The New Gamble

All six towns have spectacular mountain scenery, an assortment of Victorian architecture, the titillation of a rough and dangerous history, and the romance of a time when people dreamed of amassing a fortune after taking a tremendous risk. Through a combination of private venture capital, with substantial risks involved, and state and federal grants, the six mountain communities entertained efforts to preserve their past in order to attract tourists. As John Findlay described the midcentury effort in Las Vegas to encourage tourism, "the bold new West first dressed up as a remnant of the old West in the nineteenth century."[42] Successful to some extent, at least in regard to an increase in summer tourism, the communities continue to decline or stagnate and suffer from the problems of a cyclical economy or a population dependent on consumptive mining operations. No wonder these adventurers in search of a year-round, stable, vibrant economy turned to another form of risk taking: local option, limited stakes gaming. Lead was never included in the "Deadwood You Bet" initiative, and Victor chose not to contribute the $10,000 necessary to join the proposal by the "Preservation Initiation Committee" in Colorado. But four of these communities would have in common the hope that legalized low stakes gambling would promise that not only an occasional lucky tourist but the communities themselves might become rich from having staked a new claim.

C H A P T E R 4

Gold Rush Returns

The second boom in the Rocky Mountain mining towns took place with clearer legal sanctions than the first, but it would include much of the same perceived individual risk taking matched by considerable government sponsorship. The most aggressive local entrepreneurs in Deadwood hopped on the gambling bandwagon wearing historic preservation as a culturally legitimating uniform with elaborate economic incentives sewn in the linings. Fourteen of the bravest of the local entrepreneurs in Deadwood converted their buildings to "gaming halls" immediately, while others hoped to add a few slots as a sideline to their ongoing retail businesses. Few were prepared for the scale or the rate at which Deadwood would become a new single-industry town.

Property Speculation:
The First Phase of the Boom

November 1, 1989, was Deadwood's opening day, but the months preceding gaming proved indicative of future changes. During the summer of 1989, a land speculation boom began, buildings were traded or bought, leases were canceled, and risk taking was at high pitch. Land values skyrocketed. One building appraised at $75,000 before the April 1989 election sold for $300,000.[1] Some locals became millionaires. With escalating property values and tremendous potential gaming revenues, many business people either sold their enterprises or became gaming proprietors by converting their retail stores to gaming parlors. Those who initially resisted the gaming fervor were compelled to reconsider once property valuations reflecting "fair market value" were announced. For example, a "steeply sloped lot skyrocketed from a $4,000 appraisal in 1990 to $756,250 in 1991."[2] The high valuations had the unintended consequence of accelerating the conversion of retail and wholesale properties to a more profitable enterprise, gambling.

Much of downtown Deadwood is part of a historic preservation district as well as a designated National Historic Landmark. Therefore, the Deadwood Historic Preservation Commission had control over the external appearance of buildings; however, few constraints were placed on the interiors of buildings, which were generally gutted to make room for new, glitzy, noisy slot machines. Buildings were viewed as commodities to be used to maximize profits. During the first nine months of legalized, local option gaming, more than seventy buildings were converted from retail/wholesale enterprises to gaming parlors. For example, the A&W Drive Inn was transformed into the Deadwood Gulch Resort and Convention Center, Anthony's clothing store became the Gold Dust Gaming Hall, and the Coast to Coast Hardware was turned into Rotten Luck Willie's.

Michael Madden's 1988 study had predicted that gamblers would wager $2 million in the first year of so-called limited gaming, but by July 1990 gamblers were betting $1.2 million a day. In the first twelve months gamblers had bet a total of $281.5 million in Deadwood's gaming halls, most of which included bars or restaurants. The initial four hundred gaming devices more than doubled twice, to nine hundred in June and more than eighteen hundred by July.[3]

The Seasons Come and the Seasons Go

Nevertheless, old business patterns persisted. By November some operations were closing on weekdays and curtailing hours. Autumns had always been lean in Deadwood, with hunters helping to keep some motels open until ski and snowmobile season, but most closed over the winter. A business or two with entertainment was able to book holiday parties. But October's 29.4-million-dollar gambling action was a 15.3 percent drop from September. In fact, November and December would be worse, with a slow turnaround in January. The recovery would not reach the first October figure until the next July.

In mid-December the Deadwood Historic Preservation Commission and the Business Improvement District retained the Colorado marketing firm of Broyles, Allebaugh and Davis to develop an advertising plan for the town. They first met in the Deadwood Middle School, and more than a hundred people turned out to hear ideas for improving profits for the businesses of Deadwood. The first priority was to create a "brand awareness" that would separate Deadwood from its competitors, presumably Colorado, which by then had authorized but not yet opened casino gambling. The second and third points were to interest and attract travel agents and tour operators in a Deadwood destination, and the fourth and fifth were to create a "perceived quality" that with a fair price would generate a "highest perceived value" to induce return visits. In addition to stressing that businesses had to be willing to increase their advertising activity, claiming a direct correlation between number of ads run and return for profit, the marketing team launched the historic preservation theme, recognizing that historic preservation funds had to be used to advertise heritage tourism, not gambling per se. "Deadwood! The way it was is the way it is!" or "Where the West was won!" figured prominently in the display.[4]

A Model of Community Development and the Reality of Gambling

Our understanding of the transformation on which the town was embarking can be strengthened by referring to Eisinger's community development analysis of the relations between entrepreneurial activity and the state. Eisinger's view of state entrepreneurialism focused on supply-side initiatives.[5] His model posits that through government efforts such as tax breaks, infrastructure enhancement, low interest loans, industrial bonds, and other subsidies, new industry can be attracted, thereby creating jobs and increasing property values, which in turn enhance the well-being of community residents. The ensuing increase in consumer spending creates more jobs. He saw governmental initiatives as essential to jump-start local economies. But the problem with supply-side incentives, according to Eisinger, rests with the inevitable intergovernmental competition for the "same" jobs.

While many communities are in bidding competitions to attract or retain industries, other communities attempt to create new jobs by filling an existing demand or creating a new one. The development of tourist attractions is a typical example of using unique local assets (here both scenic and historical) to create a demand. Here too, according to Eisinger, communities rely on governmental entrepreneurialism to provide incentives "to underwrite the process of business planning, product development, initial production and marketing."[6] Government, then, provides the initial stimulus for economic revitalization.

In the early stages of Deadwood's new gaming industry we see involvement by governments and public agencies, but not in the way Eisinger describes them. First, in terms of political initiatives and controls, local option gaming was launched by local residents (primarily a coalition of local business persons) via ballot petitions to amend state constitutions, eventually winning statewide approval.[7] Once approved, the state legislatures were charged with enacting regulatory legislation that not only provided restrictions on gaming but also specified how gaming would be taxed for the benefit of the state and local governments. Rather than jump-starting these local economies with diverse economic incentives, the states ensured that they would gain financially from gaming. This legislation, however, was vastly different in South Dakota and Colorado, and these differences in turn determined how communities in each state would be transformed by gaming.

Once the regulatory mechanism was in place, private risk takers in both states were instrumental in providing the capital that transformed the respective communities. The infusion of capital into high risk ventures provided dramatic economic changes in the form of accelerated property values, expanded employment, and large increases in revenues for governmental entities. But it must be emphasized that once private capital began the transformation of community economies, local and state governmental agencies became active participants in encouraging additional gaming investments by means of touting tourism, investing historical preservation funds into building restoration, and developing and improving infrastructures such as water and sewage systems.

Ultimately these towns would all discover that this particular form of economic development, like most development endeavors, was not without costs, such as increased demand for municipal and social services and amenities. Finally, although having created a new legitimate and astoundingly large demand for gaming, entrepreneurs and government officials in both states worried at least privately about the saturation of that demand, the relationship of the gambling venues to each other, and the myriad gaming opportunities with their varying legal restrictions sprouting up all over the country.

The Colorado Variation and the Competitive Threat

But for the first year or two the focus of gaming in Deadwood was on improving the wretched winter months and hanging onto the town's amazing summer boom. A *Denver Post* feature on Deadwood in October 1990, after ten months of gambling, pointedly queried where the gambling clientele came from, reporting that a brochure by gambling proponents of Colorado's not-yet-passed Amendment 4 claimed that $100 million of the $145 million wagered during most of the year in Deadwood came from Colorado gamblers. Lead-Deadwood Chamber of Commerce director and local newspaper publisher Vince Coyle called the statement "absolute fabrication." Former mayor and founder of the You Bet Committee Tom Blair said the figure was closer to one million than a hundred million. "To say that two-thirds of the gross revenue comes from Colorado is so far off base. There's no way they could substantiate that figure. We have good support from Colorado, but we have far more from South Dakota," Blair argued as diplomatically as possible.[8] Once gambling had been approved in Colorado, its five gaming commissioners flew to Deadwood in the staunchly opposed Governor Roy Romer's state plane "to get an idea of what Black Hawk, Central City and Cripple Creek might look like some day."[9] The visit preceded by a week the meeting that would first set the Colorado gaming tax rate structure. Don Gromer, director of the South Dakota Commission on Gaming, told the Coloradans that even after two years of gaming there still needed to be changes in state laws to make gaming more fair and uniform.

Foretelling the direction Black Hawk, Central City, and Cripple Creek would take, the commissioners paid a conspicuous visit to Dan and Kevin Costner's Midnight Star: "decorated in mahogany and rosewood, [it] appeared to be one of the most elegant of the sixty gaming halls in Deadwood."[10] Dan Costner admitted spending "a couple of million dollars" on the town's last department store, adding a third-floor sports bar to expand the available space nearly fourfold to 18,500 square feet.

Although a mere twenty-one casinos divided among the three towns were ready for opening day of gambling in Colorado on October 1, 1991, by early December locals in Deadwood were already being assured that Colorado gaming showed no impact on Deadwood. Jeff Zeiger of the Center for the Advancement and Study of Tourism at Black Hills State University had his students do a visitor intercept study during six survey days between September 21 and November 11, 1991. Zeiger's survey showed the same proportion (under 5 percent) of visitors from Colorado gambling in Deadwood as a spring intercept survey had shown, with increasing numbers from Nebraska and Wyoming.[11] Jody Severson, a consultant for Deadwood's Historic Preservation Commission and the Joint Marketing Committee, agreed. "Colorado is still there," he said, adding that there had been more concern voiced about traffic from Wyoming and Nebraska being lost to the Colorado market. "Those are our 'bread and butter markets.' I thought we were going to get cut into when Colorado opened. I think we will be able to hold them but not without a fight." Severson's marketing survey showed that Deadwood's most promising market outside the Black Hills was Milwaukee, followed by Chicago, Minneapolis/St. Paul, then Denver, followed by Des Moines, Iowa, Omaha and Lincoln, Nebraska, Sioux City, Iowa, Sioux Falls, South Dakota, Regina, Saskatchewan, and North Dakota.[12]

In December two casinos took advantage of the slow season to close for remodeling, one deciding to dump the colorful local figure (Calamity Jane's) as its name and reopen as the French Quarter. But there was little doubt that gambling was the biggest news in South Dakota in 1991. Revenue from wagering in Deadwood was $8 million higher during the first nine months of 1991 than the previous year. Wagering totaled $47,243,426 in July alone. But gambling did not all take place in Deadwood. The video lottery that had ridden in on the coattails of limited gaming in Deadwood had become the third highest revenue producer for the state's general budget, at $29 million, and Governor George Mickelson had already proposed a property tax rollback to be financed with video lottery funds for the following year. Two reservation casinos were opening at Pickstown and Lower Brule in eastern South Dakota.[13]

Speculation in the Colorado Sites

As in Deadwood, land speculation in Teller and Gilpin Counties in Colorado preceded the onset of gaming, with property values doubling and redoubling as downtown businesses converted to casinos. A full year before gaming started and even before gambling was approved by the voters, Teller County Assessor Reta Bowman recorded seventy-eight property transactions between January and September 1990 totaling $3.2 million, almost as many as in the previous five years.[14] Similar real estate transactions occurred in Gilpin County. In November a ditch eight hundred feet long and thirty feet deep— the old mine flume long since filled with worn-out tires and a collapsed bridge—sold for $124,000 the week after gambling was approved. A four-story building with a large hole in the wall that had sold the spring before for $36,000 drew an offer of $250,000, and the charred remains of the Gilpin Hotel were valued at 50 percent more than its price before it burned the previous December.[15] Although many property owners planned to hold out until they could see how profitable gambling would be, Gilpin County saw $6 million in property sales in the single month of February 1991 and $8 million in March.[16] The Central City town council imposed a seven-month building moratorium over the winter, but by the time it expired in mid-April, $8 million had been invested in Central City and Black Hawk.[17] Central City then kept the building ban on until June 1 to give the town time to revise zoning laws and building, fire, electric, plumbing, and mechanical codes, as well as historic preservation guidelines, an admirable planning decision that may have been costly in the long run since Black Hawk continued to build at a rapid pace.

Not all the transactions were happily regarded. Ten families residing in the Black Hawk Trailer Court, including five senior citizens, lost their homes in March when the 1.75-acre property, across the street from the Gilpin Hotel, was sold for $1.3 million to accommodate the casino serving the hotel. The purchasers, Mountain Casino Properties, who bought the lot from Black Hawk alderman Herb Bowles and Denver lawyer Albert Dawkins, then made a public offering of $7.5 million in limited partnership shares within a week.[18] In June trailer park residents, faced with inevitable evictions, were offered $1,200 each to move before July 31. Eighty-year-old Bertha Toney, who decided to move into a suburban Denver trailer park twenty miles away with her eighty-five-year-old husband, E. J., said, "I wouldn't be able to move it they didn't offer it. What else can we do? It sure the heck helps us better than not getting anything." Gilpin County nurse Jeanne Nickolson, who was to help relocate the elderly, was less sanguine. "I wouldn't call it a purely philanthropic gesture. I would call it a good business decision. I mean, how would you put a value on something like moving out of a place where you lived for twenty years? There's no value in that."[19] One alternative for these displaced residents was the only other trailer park in Gilpin County, located several miles from town. It would cost new residents at least $20,000 to drill wells for their water and install septic tanks for sewage. The rent at another park, in Golden, Colorado, was about $100 higher than the $145 they had been paying in Black Hawk.

Obviously, development at the multi-million-dollar level required both investors and financing from far beyond the borders of Gilpin and Teller Counties. Deadwood had tried to keep investments local by requiring at least 50 percent ownership from inside Lawrence County. Kevin Costner's brother Dan had therefore bought a house in Lead and claimed residency. But that restriction on interstate commerce was thrown out by the South Dakota Supreme Court. In Colorado there were no such pretenses of local ownership. Denver real estate developer Rick Mellicker, heading a group of ten investors in a limited liability company, bought the Gilpin Jail Exhibit, which became Annie Oakley's Casino, and the Chandelier House Gift Shop, which was transformed into the Silver Slipper, totaling nearly $4.5 million. Mellicker said, "We're going to have a lot of fun. We're going to have seventy slot machines and three blackjack tables. We'll have video poker built into the bar. We're going to have a chef with a white hat to serve roast beef sandwiches for $1."[20]

Bradford Whatley, from the Denver suburb of Lakewood and owner of Black Hawk Gaming Inc., bought the Prospector even though it was in the North Clear Creek floodplain. A group of investors called Limited Gaming of America Inc. spent $4 million on a hundred acres of Central City property, promising to build a twenty-five-million-dollar complex of casinos, a hotel, and housing. The proposal comprised two acres of land along Gregory Street, six acres of hotel and restaurants, nine acres for gift shops and parking, fifteen acres for single and multifamily homes, and sixty-eight acres of open space for hiking and biking in what was called Mountain City, once inhabited by twelve hundred people in the late 1800s. City Manager Jack Hidahl was skeptical that the plan would meet historic preservation guidelines.[21]

But investment dollars were scarce in the first year. Banks steered clear of gambling-related loans, and venture capital groups in Denver and Colorado Springs were prepared to pour in millions, but not until the legislature clarified the provisions under which gambling would take place. Ted Meuller, president of the Bank of Cripple Creek, the town's sole lending institution, said the bank had made several loans "in the lower five-figure range" for minor renovations but would not lend the millions gaming operators were seeking. David Wahl, co-owner of the proposed Grubstake Inn and Molly's Casinos, concurred in less restrained language: "basically the banks in Colorado are so conservative anyway; they'll laugh you right out the door if you went in to get a loan for this."[22]

That did not prevent speculators from making huge profits in turning over property ownership. Jay Williams, another Denver businessman, scored a profit of $9.9 million in July by selling the Belvidere Theater in Central City. He had bought it in 1990 for $117,500 and sold it on July 15, 1991, for $10 million. If Rick Mellicker intended to have fun, Williams planned a lot more fun. Robert Leisen Jr., one of the Belvidere's new operators, said (and gambling license applications confirmed) that plans called for a casino and restaurant with 340 slot machines, 2 poker tables, 4 blackjack tables, and 60 video betting machines. Leisen said he and three other partners "all had backgrounds in gambling," but despite the high price for the building they intended to keep the "dust-covered" theater, with "rat-chewed stage props" littering the attic, as described by the *Gilpin County Advocate*, intact.[23]

Even some people who objected strongly to gambling reaped enormous profits. Dan and Donna Melson and their two school-age children had moved to Central City in 1989 and bought an eighty-five-thousand-dollar home in which to "spend the rest of their lives." By September 1991 they had sold their house for $182,000 profit. Dan Melson said, "I've had to deal with this as a death. This town is not the same. This is an end to a part of my life."[24]

Other community business people were not so fortunate. Some operators of the town's little shops were among the biggest backers of gambling but ended up dealing with broken leases and no shops at all when building owners opted instead for casinos. In the view of the proprietors of Floyd's Gifts and Jewelry, "they found a little glitch and managed to get us out early. We definitely were sold a bill of goods in a good con game."[25] Some who owned their buildings were better able to hold on. In a reflection of Deadwood's by now nationally televised "Don't Even Ask" sign on Agnes Ayres's hardware store, Rosemary Hennings's Rock and Lite Antique shop window said, "We approve of gambling. However, this shop will stay as is—we are not going out of business. Merchandise is not fifty percent off."[26]

Like Deadwood, Central City, Black Hawk, and Cripple Creek had long faced bleak winter months. Although closer to major metropolitan areas, the Colorado towns were also three to five thousand feet higher than Deadwood's nearly mile-high elevation. Tourists had traditionally come through the Colorado mountain towns until the aspen leaves had fallen about the first week in October and didn't return until the first week in April. About 60 percent of the businesses in Central City were usually closed nearly half the year, and Rosemary Hennings and her daughter Mary Green wondered not only about staying open but hiring extra help. Her location, next to the Golden Rose Hotel (whose owners had been offered up to $5 million and were about to sell), encouraged her to hold out for at least $2 million.[27]

Foreshadowing the collusion of public agencies on gambling development out of their growing dependence on it, within two weeks after legalized gambling commenced in Colorado, the Gilpin County school district began negotiations with the Lady Luck Casino of Las Vegas to build a casino and concert hall on school property in Central City. The Gilpin school district, one of the smallest and poorest in Colorado, was the first public or private entity in the state to negotiate a gambling deal with a Nevada casino operation.[28] The lease agreement, which included approval to demolish the Quonset gym, built in the 1930s (a deviation from Central City's historical guidelines), would give Gilpin County schools the first income from any gambling operation since the 1950s, when Denver mobsters reportedly brought school kids hot lunches so they could keep illegal gambling halls open.[29] The school district did not wait for gambling to come to it. School Board President John Rittenhouse, Superintendent Paul Coleman, board member Forrest Anderson, and the school's accountant went to Las Vegas to talk to gaming board officials and Lady Luck Casino owner Andrew Tompkins.

Ironically, that trip may have marked the beginning of the shift in focus from Denver investors to those from a much larger region, but in fact the county of Gilpin had also been negotiating the relocation of the county courthouse since the previous May. A Walden, Colorado, ranch wanted to trade 383 acres of Gilpin County land two miles outside Black Hawk for the Clark Annex, a former elementary school, vintage 1900, which had been housing the county's Department of Social Services and Friends of the Library. The transaction, a 1.7-million-dollar deal, would provide parking access for county business, which the courthouse on Eureka Street across from the opera house did not, once gambling traffic appeared.

Meanwhile Central City officials wanted to get out of their one-room, wood-floored city hall—the oldest public building in the state—and into the Gilpin County Courthouse. While the preservation and restoration of the Lawrence County Courthouse in Deadwood had been one of the first projects (and controversial at $4.8 million), Gilpin County preservationists had no argument with the proposed move. Bonnie Merchant, president of the Gilpin County Historical Society, favored the sale of both buildings as long as they were preserved and restored by new owners. "If they build a new courthouse in mid-county, then all the offices could be in one place. With property values as they are today, it would be an ideal time to sell them."[30] Central City and Gilpin County were not yet in the position of depending on gambling for operating funds, but they were already in the land speculation game.

Opening day in Colorado had much less of a hometown celebration feeling about it than it had had in Deadwood. For one thing, there was little pretense of the small-scale "limited gambling" that governed Deadwood. None of the first casinos to open limited themselves to the thirty devices per building that Deadwood mandated. No one pretended that local entrepreneurs were responsible for upgrading their city. A lot of the new owners were real estate developers rather than gambling professionals, so they relied on Nevada experts. IGT, the world's largest slot machine manufacturer, held seminars. Paulson Card & Dice of Las Vegas, supplier for the Taj Mahal in Atlantic City and Excalibur in Las Vegas, expected to do about $425,000 worth of business in Colorado the first year, selling cards, chips, tables, and chairs.[31]

The historic Teller House, adjacent to and owned by the Central City Opera House Association, had done considerable facelifting of chandeliers, bars, and murals in order to accommodate 168 slot machines (including Jackpot Jungle, Earth Quake, and Home Run) plus 82 video poker games. It was, however, described as "the class act of both towns," thanks to a 6.5-million-dollar investment by the Swiss-based Tivolino Corporation.[32] Although the Teller House operation totaled 250 devices, the twenty-one Colorado casinos that opened October 1, 1991, averaged about a hundred devices apiece, mostly slot machines plus smaller numbers of video poker and blackjack tables. The Gilded Garter stood alone, with only forty-nine slot machines and no remodeling.[33] By October 1, Central City was in the lead in property turnover, with $27 million in sales, more than Black Hawk and Cripple Creek combined. Moreover, the metropolitan connections of the Colorado towns were recognized by four shuttle companies that operated on opening day from Denver to Central City and Black Hawk and six to Cripple Creek from Colorado Springs and Pueblo.[34]

Perhaps with some sophisticated vision of the long haul and also a dread of bad publicity about traffic jams and auto accidents, the Colorado towns actually discouraged visitors from coming to gamble on opening day, even as the media hyped it heavily. In fact, even with eleven months' lead time since the election, most casinos were scrambling to be ready for opening day. Owners and managers of Annie Oakley's in Central City were still helping work crews clean up the place as the board of directors arrived for a black-tie gala the night before. The Gold Mine Casino started from the ground up on August 15 and still had fifty workers painting, installing telephone lines, and unpacking china the day before.[35] By 6:30 A.M. several dozen people were lined up outside the Teller House, waiting for the 8:00 A.M. opening, and an estimated 5,000 waited for a chance at 1,175 slot machines in Central City and Black Hawk. A gift store had been completely gutted and refurbished to open as the Long Branch and was waiting for an early morning city inspection on October 1 for its certificate of occupancy, but the doorman was ready in his Buffalo Bill suit promptly at 8:00 A.M.[36] So the opening ceremony with speeches from city and state officials was brief, and Ava Brackett, cochairwoman of the Colorado Limited Gaming Control Commission, and former Black Hawk mayor Bill Lorenz pulled the first slot machine handle together with a shout of "Let the games begin!" Prospective gamblers scrambled around on their hands and knees to gather up what they could of $500 in quarters dropped from a rooftop.[37]

Cripple Creek was as much under construction as Central City, with scaffolding and paint buckets all over the sidewalks.[38] But that town attempted to duplicate some of the Deadwood spirit in its opening by importing buckskin-clad, seven-foot one-inch Big Dave Mura from Deadwood to fire replicas of Wild Bill Hickok's pistols down the length of Bennett Avenue. Early morning in October at 10,000 feet is inevitably chilly, but at least four hundred people were there waiting for the last-minute slot machine glitches to be fixed before the casinos could open their doors. As in Deadwood, the event was seen not as a beginning but a revival, thirty-seven years after FBI agents had shut down the town's last illegal slot machines.[39]

Shades of what was to come were apparent by day three. One Wisconsin grandmother on her way to Las Vegas had seen the television coverage on Colorado gambling in a Laramie, Wyoming, motel room. Detouring to Central City, she won $10,000 within twenty minutes and then proceeded to Las Vegas to use her winnings there. Meanwhile, in Cripple Creek, the owner of the Goldminer's Daughter Boutique, which had moved once during the year to make way for a casino and was about to be displaced again, made only one sale, to a local citizen, on opening day and complained, "The purpose of the gambling was to help the gift shops. This isn't the way any of us planned it. . . . [W]e did as much work as the gambling houses to get the law passed."[40] And in recognition of decades of sponsorship, the Teller House closed to the public at 4:00 P.M. on Friday, October 4, to accommodate the Central City Opera House Association members and patrons who paid $300 per couple to attend a charity event.[41]

By the weekend, casino operators were complaining that television coverage was "killing [them] with stories about traffic problems and parking." While 11,217 vehicles traveled Colorado Highway 119 to Central City, a 155 percent increase (7,000 more cars) on October 1, 1991, over the year before, the 4,000 new parking spaces on top of the mountain seemed to have handled them.[42] And after deciding that more weekend business should be encouraged, the towns experienced their first freezing cold snap, which would ultimately have some of the same effect in Colorado as it had in Deadwood. New Year's Eve and New Year's Day provided the first big disappointment in Colorado casinos, when even fireworks, church bells, a ragtime band, and the promise of ten dollars in quarters failed to avert newspaper notice of the quiet atmosphere of the gambling towns.[43]

If Black Hawk, the downgulch "mill town," seemed somewhat left out of the excitement about legalized gambling in Colorado, a particular conjunction of geography, history, and Colorado gaming legislation would soon change the fortunes of Central City's poor sister. Some feared that Black Hawk would become a parking lot for Central City (which instead routed visitors' autos above the town and shuttled them back down in buses), but city officials began to realize that Black Hawk had nearly three times the space for gaming that Central City had. While several historic buildings in the "core gaming" district had opened immediately as casinos, or planned to, the vacant lots along North Clear Creek, which stretched about a mile along Colorado 119, would allow developers to build on the "millsite gaming district" creek banks, as long as the buildings resembled the warehouses and mill sites of the late 1890s.[44] Given the Colorado gambling law, which stated that buildings need not *be* historic but only built in the historic architectural style and that establishments were not limited in the *number* of gaming devices but only in the percentage of space devoted to them, space became everything in terms of attractiveness of operations. Nothing could be better than a building that resembled a nineteenth-century warehouse or mill, and a vacant lot made it that much easier to erect.

Black Hawk councilwoman Kelle Sunter, who also served on the planning commission and historic preservation committee, made reference to the tortoise and the hare,[45] but within a month after gaming began, Central City and Black Hawk were playing even when Los Angeles developers Hemmeter Partners, which had built six huge hotel resorts in Hawaii, closed deals for a twelve-million-dollar Bullwhackers Casino in Central City and another twelve-million-dollar Bullwhackers Casino in Black Hawk on November 4.[46] The next day, plans for a thirty-million-dollar casino were announced for Black Hawk. Tommyknockers, which anticipated opening by spring, was to have 1,200 slot machines, 40 blackjack tables, and 18 poker tables in 100,000 square feet. To comply with the space proportions, it would include a 1,500-seat coffee shop, a 350-seat lounge, and a 90-seat gourmet restaurant. Black Hawk city officials announced that an even larger casino with a 300-room hotel plus recreational vehicle parking and a permanent housing complex, plus an airport valued at $100 million, was in the works.[47]

Central City responded with plans by Terry Christensen, former president of the company that owned the Desert Inn in Las Vegas and current director of the MGM Grand, to open "what will be Colorado's largest gambling hall here in May, choosing Central City over Deadwood, South Dakota."[48] The Gold Coin Saloon and Casino would have 559 gaming devices, with $4 million invested in the property and another $6 million in renovation, providing 7,783 square feet for gaming. Three days later, a California group announced plans for a thirty-five-million-dollar casino that would have 50,000 square feet of casino space (enough room for 2,000 gaming devices) on a piece of property near the entrance to Central City purchased for $9.6 million. Six days after that, the Glory Hole, holding the current record with 326 gambling devices actually operating, announced plans to expand, having bought the Gilded Garter (which had opened with only 49 slots and no remodeling), to give the Glory Hole 43,000 square feet and allow 700 slot machines and card tables.[49]

Expansion would not be completely simple or linear. Tommyknockers, named for the ghost that haunted western miners, proved to have chosen an appropriate appellation. The original owner of the millsite property said the stocks it had received in a 1987 trade with Brush Prairie Minerals Inc. of Spokane, Washington, were worthless. The property was subsequently deeded to New Allied Development Corporation and another intermediate owner, all of whom shared the same address in Arcadia, California. Meanwhile the U.S. Securities and Exchange Commission had investigated New Allied and suspended it from stock trading. In addition, the property was adjacent to the Golden Gilpin Mill, a Superfund site, which would involve a cleanup of the Millsites 12 and 13 on which Tommyknockers was to be built.[50] By April 18, Casinos Austria International withdrew its planned 3.5-million-dollar investment, saying, "The climate wasn't right."[51]

A Pause, and a Shift in Dominance

Even confident, urbane Central City seemed dizzied by the developments and called a nine-month moratorium on casino development on April 18, 1992, to allow time to deal with issues of water, parking, and other services. Put in a holding pattern were not only deals by local businessman Lary Brown, who spearheaded the move to legalize gambling, and the Gold Point investors, who planned the twenty-five-million-dollar Grand Central Casino project, but also the new county courthouse deal with a Black Hills developer and the Gilpin County school district sale to the Las Vegas casino. Immediately noticed was the fact that eighteen of the twenty-one projects that had been allowed building permits were linked with current or former city officials, existing casino owners, or long-time residents.[52] Although challenged in court by Brown and Gold Pointe Inc., Judge Kenneth Barnhill upheld the moratorium, saying that even if he granted an injunction overturning the council resolution, it could simply adopt a city ordinance nullifying his order.[53]

However apparent Central City's need to catch up with its infrastructure may have been, why it attempted to take care of those problems independently of Black Hawk, only a mile away, can only be explained by history. Water and sewage had long been a problem in Central City. A joint proposal to the FHA for a water and sewer project had been prepared in 1972, but nothing had come of it. The urgent need for a new water system and the absence of local or state monies to fund the improvements figured prominently in the discussions of the gambling initiative in 1989.[54] In the spring of 1992, Central City's water still came from a "hole-in-the-ground" reservoir that could meet the town's needs in the spring, summer, and fall. But two new ten-million-gallon reservoirs would be needed to store spring and summer runoff for the expected boom in the winter season. The city had begun selling bonds to build a new water treatment plant and to replace its hundred-year-old water lines. Central City and Black Hawk had shared governance of the sewage treatment plant, which could treat 500,000 gallons of raw sewage per day, but the plant was already nearing half its capacity, which would trigger state department of health requirements for expansion plans. Black Hawk had just signed a contract with Coors Brewing Company of Golden for ten million gallons of water a year and was selling $5.1 million in bonds to build its own new water treatment plant and replace its one-inch water lines with twelve-inch mains. But neither town wanted to share water rights or water treatment plants and refused to create a joint water district.[55]

So while Central City replaced its water system and worked on parking lots, the Hemmeter family, which had opened one Bullwhackers casino in Central City along the historic district, proceeded to build its other big new casino at the entrance to Black Hawk and to move its Los Angeles corporate headquarters to Golden, Colorado. The two casinos, costing more than $12 million each and housing a total of twelve hundred slot machines, promised to employ eight hundred people in Gilpin County. The Hemmeters also announced plans for their Outlaws Casino with an adjoining "inlaws" day-care center between Crook's Palace and the Black Forest Inn and Otto's Casino, but the property apparently became too valuable for day-care, for Black Hawk was still without any three years later.[56] Merv Griffin made a bid to manage Lilly Belles in Black Hawk, and Las Vegas slot machine leaser Stan Fulton invested in casinos in both Cripple Creek and Black Hawk.

By November 1992, a shift in dominance among the Colorado gambling towns was emerging. In midsummer Black Hawk's revenues from gambling were steadily growing while Central City's had shown a decline. Seventeen casinos in Black Hawk had grossed $4.8 million in July and, with two additional enterprises, increased to $6.7 million in October. Meanwhile, Central City peaked in July with $8.5 million from twenty-two casinos, dropping to just over Black Hawk's revenues with $6.8 million from twenty-three casinos in October. Two casinos in Black Hawk had closed, and six in Central City had shut down; two more filed for Chapter 11 bankruptcy protection. Meanwhile Cripple Creek revenues had also dropped from the peak summer months. Thirty-one casinos had grossed $6.4 million in August, while thirty-three casinos took in only $5.5 million in October.

Within the first year of Colorado "limited gaming," the differences legislation would make were already apparent. The twenty-one casinos ready for opening day had grown to seventy. The 1,949 slot machines licensed during October 1991 had risen to 11,723, 4,000 more than the industry experts had projected the state would ever support. Already, smaller casinos were losing out to big operations, despite the three-tiered tax structure to protect the "mom-and-pops." Average daily yields per slot machine had dropped from $154 to $58 per machine, making loan repayments difficult for some investors. And even before winter, workers were being laid off.

With patterns becoming apparent to the state gaming commission, Colorado changed its tax system in October 1992 from a three-tiered rate structure of 4 percent, 8 percent, and 15 percent, depending on revenues, to a two-tiered system of 2 percent and 20 percent in an attempt to protect the smaller operations. Some people thought that would not be sufficient to save the little casinos. "The big mistake they made was, they didn't limit the number of gaming devices," observed the owner of a medium-sized casino in Central City. "Now they have Las Vegas–type casinos when they wanted Deadwood-type casinos."[57] Even Lary Brown, author of the gambling amendment that became part of the Colorado Constitution, was upset about the direction of gambling in Colorado. He said, "In our campaign, we tried to create an attraction to our tourist industry. But what we've created is an industry."[58] Whatever one's economic philosophy, the industry was behaving as expected. Colorado Gaming Commission Chairwoman Ave Brackett said, "We can't regulate competition, nor would I want to. It's still a free enterprise society. While gaming is highly regulated, it's still subject to market forces."[59]

A Central City real estate developer predicted that Central City and Black Hawk would end up with four or five big casino owners and no others, with big operations spreading domino-style until they engulf entire streets. Indeed, a total of twenty-two small casinos had closed by the end of 1992. In Cripple Creek, small properties at either end of Bennett Avenue that had been sold after gambling commenced and opened late were already closing by the next fall. Jerry Johnson, the South Dakota owner of the eleventh biggest casino in Colorado, said, "Supply and demand will take care of itself."[60]

But Colorado found itself where Deadwood had been when the weather started to turn cold.[61] John Sharpe, president of the Cripple Creek Chamber of Commerce, noted that there weren't enough people to occupy all the stools at the gaming devices. "We did reach the numbers of people who were predicted to come. At the same time, we thought we would have

2,000 to 2,500 gaming devices, and we got nearly double that. . . . Our challenge is to get aggressive in our marketing programs, and fill those seats. And it will be a challenge."[62]

Revenues and Returns

With regard to gambling revenues from limited gaming developments, several observations could be drawn from the first year of gambling in both South Dakota and Colorado. First, gaming action was far greater than anyone had predicted. Second, profits, employment, and tourism would remain highly seasonal. Third, large enterprises would squeeze out smaller ones, and the effect would be much greater in Colorado than in South Dakota, given the relative rather than absolute limit on gaming devices. Fourth, state bureaucracies would be mandated to control gaming. Fifth, local governments would have to contend with the impact of the influx of visitors. Finally, both state and local governments would become contentious about and dependent on the taxes from gaming profits.

In a variation on Eisinger's model of community development, about the only government assistance needed to increase private investment was the legal permission to proceed. Having seen the speculation and expansion of revenues in Deadwood, Colorado began with Denver money and expanded quickly to investors from Los Angeles, Las Vegas, and abroad. Given the size of the investments and operations, there can be no argument that what followed would be increased taxable capital stock and a larger volume of jobs and payrolls leading to a larger tax base and expanded tax revenues. Some kinds of improved public services would be not only an outcome but an almost immediate requirement in order to handle the growth in tourist visitations. But all of this produced wholesale business transformations that would ultimately transform the communities themselves, and it is the impact these revenues had on communities and governments that suggests a model of community development based on gaming that is quite different from Eisinger's.

Dramatic as the shift was, gaming in Deadwood would never show revenues comparable to the Colorado towns. Although astounding nearly everyone with more than a million dollars in revenues in the first month and rising to an average of $3.5 million for each of the summer months the next year, even Deadwood's five-million-dollar peak in July 1991 would be dwarfed by $8.4 million in revenues the first month of Colorado gambling in October of that year. The low points would show even more dramatic differences. When in December 1991 Deadwood had dropped to $2.1 million in gross revenues, Colorado was holding at $8.1 million. The next December, when Deadwood again showed $2.1 million, Colorado gambling had climbed to $14.2 million. In July 1993, Deadwood gambling had turned $5.5 million in gross profits, but Colorado gambling had climbed to $26.5 million, up from $19.3 million in July the year before. By December 1996, the differences were even more dramatic, with Deadwood's gross revenue climbing to only $1.9 million compared to Colorado's adjusted gross profit of $30.9 million.[63]

Apart from this overall trend, community comparisons show growth patterns even more clearly. In October 1991, the first month of Colorado limited stakes gambling, Central City had adjusted gross profits of $4.1 million, Black Hawk showed $1.7 million, and Cripple Creek brought in $2.5 million, while Deadwood, after nearly two years of gambling, had $3.3 million. The next July, Deadwood's $5.2 million compares to $8.5 million in Central City, $4.8 million in Black Hawk, and $6 million in Cripple Creek. The December trough of $2.1 million in Deadwood compares to $4.5 million in Central City, $6.1 million in Black Hawk, and $3.7 million on the mountaintop at Cripple Creek. By July 1993, Deadwood's $5.5 million was overshadowed by Central City's $8.3 million in profits, not much more than half Black Hawk's $10.4 million, and more than two million short of Cripple Creek's $7.8 million. In December 1993, Deadwood's repeat of $2.1 million was less than half of any Colorado gambling town's gross revenues. Cripple Creek had $4.4 million; Central City had returns of $5.6 million; Black Hawk took in about twice that of the other Colorado towns, with $10.5 million in adjusted gross profits. By August 1996 Black Hawk had peaked at $20.5 million, more than doubling Central City's $8.4 million and Cripple Creek's $10.6 million, compared to $5.2 million in Deadwood.

Initial employment changes were dramatic, with local option, limited stakes gaming in South Dakota generating approximately eighteen hundred new gaming jobs, albeit many of them part-time and without benefits, in a town with a population of 1,830.[64] Generally, wages for these jobs were toward the low end of the pay scale with most paying between $5.00 and $6.00 an hour. Furthermore, given the cyclical nature of gaming in Deadwood, employment demands are greatest in the summer months and decrease substantially during November, December, and January. Unfortunately, limited employment opportunities outside of gaming in Deadwood have resulted in labor turnover during the slack gaming months, although the summer recruitment of teachers, college students, and Homestake miners who had been put in early retirement plans mitigated that issue somewhat.[65]

The Colorado communities as well began to experience some cyclical shifts in gaming-related employment. Although there was some decline in employment in the winter of 1992–93, employment in the gaming industry in July 1992 had created 1,576 jobs in Cripple Creek (a town of only 600 population), 1,056 jobs in Black Hawk (with a population of about 250), and 2,128 jobs in Central City (population 300). By July 1996 Cripple Creek had 1,819 casino jobs, Black Hawk had 2,751, and Central City was down to 1,413. The unemployment rate was half the rest of Colorado (about 2.7 percent as of September 1991), and hourly wages at the low end were around $7.00 and about $9.50 at the high end. Although about three hundred jobs had been created for local residents, most employees commute from surrounding Denver and Jefferson Counties or from Colorado Springs.

In addition to expanded employment and a larger tax base, direct gaming tax revenues would provide significant return to the communities and to the states. Tax payments are reported on a monthly basis but are difficult to analyze at that level, as a grace period in payment makes the statistics fluctuate in ways unrelated to profits. Also, while South Dakota's flat 8 percent rate on profits (as enacted in the enabling legislation) has made gaming taxes stable, the Colorado Gaming Commission used its prerogative to adjust rates five times in six years, leading to some uncertainty in a volatile industry. The initial assumption that casinos would fall into categories of small, medium, and large, with a 4 percent tax on those with less than $440,000 profit, 8 percent tax on gross revenues between $440,000 and $1.2 million, and 15 percent tax rate on those profits in excess of $1.2 million, had been demonstrated as faulty in the first year. In October 1992, a two-layered tax structure recognized that casinos were either big or small. Those making less than a million dollars would pay a 2 percent tax, and those with revenues in excess of one million would pay 20 percent on those revenues to the state. Mark Grueskin, counsel to the Casino Owners Association of Colorado, attributed the failure of twenty-four casinos to that excessive taxation.[66]

By 1993 the tax rate had gone from two tiers to four, with taxes levied at 2 percent on the first $1 million, 8 percent on revenues of $1 to $2 million, 15 percent on revenues of $2 to $3 million, and 18 percent on revenues exceeding $3 million. Furthermore, the state annual device fee reverted back to $100.

September 29, 1994, witnessed the fourth change in state gaming taxation policy. The change, designed to aid small and midsize casinos, set taxes on revenues under $2 million at 2 percent, on revenues between $2 and $4 million at 8 percent, on revenues of $4 to $5 million at 15 percent, and 18 percent on revenues exceeding $5 million. Colorado was still in the process of balancing state and industry interests. In October 1996 it moved to a five-tier tax with 2 percent on the first $2 million adjusted gross proceeds, 4 percent from $2 to $4 million, 14 percent from $4 to $5 million, 18 percent from $5 to $10 million, and 20 percent above $10 million. In addition, state slot device fees were raised from $100 to $150 and then lowered to $75.

Certainly as important to the communities as who made profits was how the tax revenues would be distributed. This would affect not only the relationship of the gambling communities to the state and the outcome of the stated goals of historic preservation but also the relationship of gambling communities to their nongambling neighbors.

In South Dakota, the 8 percent tax revenues were divided so that 40 percent went to the South Dakota general fund and 10 percent to Lawrence County. The remaining 50 percent went to the state gaming commission, from which its operating expenses were drawn. Any remaining monies, plus a two-thousand-dollar annual fee levied on each gaming device, were returned to the Deadwood Historic Preservation Commission. Perhaps reflecting either the state's naiveté about how profitable gaming would be or possibly its firm commitment to historic preservation, the city of Deadwood, or more precisely its Historic Preservation Commission, has reclaimed nearly 70 percent of all gaming tax revenues from limited gaming in Deadwood. Those amounted to $2.3 million in fiscal year 1990 and over $5 million annually from 1991 to 1996, counting the local fees on devices. Although the state gaming commission was entitled to half the tax revenues, it had used less than a million dollars for operating expenses annually. The struggling town of fewer than two thousand residents meanwhile suddenly found itself with enormous public resources, all of which were to be spent in the name of historic preservation. The creative uses of these funds are the subject of chapter 5.

Colorado made different choices in its distribution of tax revenues. There would be differences in scale from the start. While Deadwood's first eight months (FY 1990) resulted in just over $1.1 million in tax revenue, the nine months of Colorado's first year (FY 1991) produced $10.8 million in state gaming revenue. Of that the Colorado general funds received 50 percent (with 0.2 percent earmarked for advertising state tourism). In the first budget year the state dedicated a portion of its gaming tax revenue (4.7 percent of the total state gaming taxes) to the counties for impact mitigation, half of which went to eight neighboring counties, based on how many gambling-related workers lived there, and the other half in the form of grants.[67] Twelve percent would be returned outright to Gilpin and Teller Counties annually, proportionate to the volume of gaming revenue produced, and 10 percent would go back to the three communities themselves, also based on the volume of gaming revenue. The biggest difference is that 28 percent would be designated for historic preservation *throughout* Colorado. Each of the respective communities also had an annual licensing fee per gaming device. In Central City the fee was $1,000, in Black Hawk it was $800, and Cripple Creek charged $1,200. Like the state tax rates, annual device fees have shifted over time, but in 1991 the annual licensing fees produced more revenue for the communities than their proportion of state gaming taxes. Moreover, these fees and the tax revenues returned directly to city government, allowing local communities to address impacts generated by gaming without having to make a justification to a historic preservation committee.

The first tax returns from gambling in Colorado were distributed in September 1992. Of the 9.1-million-dollar disbursement, the state general fund received $4.1 million, and the state historical fund got $2.5 million. Gilpin County, which had generated 72 percent of the gaming revenue, collected $790,000, while its two gambling towns collected almost the equivalent, with Central City getting about $395,000 and Black Hawk nearly $264,000. Teller County was eligible for not quite $304,000, and Cripple Creek got $253,000. In addition, the gaming commission awarded $425,000 to the Contiguous County Impact Fund. It took $3.4 million off the top for expenses and salaries and kept another $875,000 in escrow for estimated expenses.

Tax revenue disbursement for 1996 totaled $48,007,951, after expenses, with each entity receiving approximately four times as much revenue as in 1992 (except Central City, whose share tripled, and Black Hawk, which garnered almost a 1,000 percent increase). The Colorado general fund received $17,506,173, while the State Historical Society obtained $13,442,226.

Gaming devices (slot machines and poker and blackjack tables) are taxed on a per item basis, so owners and managers have had to make decisions about the optimal number of devices, the proportion of tables to slot machines, and the amount of "hold" on the slot machines that will maximize profits while still attracting customers. As the number of gaming devices increased, their profitability or "daily hold" decreased. Deadwood started out with a hold of $102 per unit (representing 10 percent of the total wagered) and averaged $90 over the first eight months. Colorado began with an average daily adjusted gross profit per device of $160 and averaged $110 per device in the nine months that covered its first fiscal year. But gaming profits per device would plummet in the summer of 1992 in Colorado. As the number of devices increased from 7,202 in June to 10,525 in July, average daily profits dropped from $80 per machine to

$63, and they would bottom out in December, when 11,030 devices produced only $43 per machine. Slot machines, always dominant, increasingly returned the biggest revenues, and quarter slots returned the biggest part of the slot machine revenues.

Deadwood had initially included nickel slot machines, controlled by the city and exempt from taxes as a low revenue come-on. But soon places like Costner's Midnight Star had the "loosest" dollar slots with enormous machinery and oversized handles placed strategically in the big windows at the front of the building. In Deadwood the average daily hold per unit increased slightly in fiscal year 1992 after dropping in 1991. While nickel slots increased from $26 to $33 per machine, quarter slots (with three to six times the gross revenue of other slots) increased from $40 to $51, and dollar slots increased from $51 to $67, despite their having the smallest hold percentage rate at 8.7 percent. In Colorado, the hold was similar in 1992, except that dollar slots held $103 each daily, and five-dollar slots (not then available in Deadwood) held an average of $306. But by 1996, the difference in average daily hold between Deadwood and Colorado was significant. While in Colorado nickel slots held $38, quarter slots $62, dollar slots $116, and five-dollar slots $170 each, in Deadwood they were holding $19, $24, $49, and $75 each, respectively.

Table games occupy peculiar positions in the gaming halls. They count as "devices" and are taxed as such. Their average daily hold is almost always greater than for a slot machine, averaging 18 to 20 percent. But they take up more space, and they entail higher labor costs. Most casinos include them so that their tuxedo-clad dealers will lend an atmosphere of the big time to the enterprise, but they occupy a small and decreasing proportion of the devices and revenues. In 81 locations in Deadwood at the end of FY 1992, there were just 73 blackjack tables and 27 poker tables but 1,875 slot machines. At the same time, Colorado had a total of 265 table games and 10,805 slot machines in 65 businesses. By December 1996, having "found" more buildings, Deadwood had gambling in 97 locations, but there were 48 blackjack tables, only 13 poker tables, and an increase to 2,367 slot machines. In Colorado table games had decreased to 258, while there were 13,176 slot machines in 56 businesses.[68]

When Transformation Is Not Enough: The Drives for Further Expansion

The "shakedown" in the new gambling boom would not discourage everyone. Indeed, further expansion was proposed on several fronts almost as soon as gambling was in place. Within a month of the passage of Colorado's Amendment 4 and long before any casinos were open, eleven more small towns in southern and southwestern Colorado vowed to get the 52,000 signatures needed to qualify for an initiative on the 1992 ballot when, as expected, the legislature refused to authorize gambling in their towns. Senator Sally Hopper, the author of the original legislative bill supporting Colorado gambling, said she would oppose it, and so did the mayor of Manitou Springs (one of the towns proposed), down the hill from Cripple Creek.[69] However, Historic Rural Communities for Limited Gambling (eleven southern Colorado towns), Colorado WIN Committee (which focused on sixteen municipal airports), the Dollars for Education Gateway Group (seventeen towns and counties in eastern Colorado), the town of Parachute (which wanted gambling and a moratorium on all other gambling expansion until January 2000), and Old Town Arvada (in metro Denver) would produce much community and legislative debate, and a two-year moratorium on expanded legal gambling would die on the Colorado House floor in February 1992.

Several towns took advisory votes that opposed gambling, and the House then passed a bill requiring a local vote as well as statewide approval for expansion "for the protection of local governments."[70] Proponents of expanding gambling invoked technical challenges to try to stop other communities from getting their petitions on the November ballot; a whole new town, to be called $ilver $take $trip, filed a proposal, and an initiative for gambling in lower downtown Denver (LoDo) was added to seven other potential ballot measures by March.[71] *Denver Post* columnist Dick Kreck observed that in the business of limited stakes gambling, " 'limited' . . . means limited only by the length of time it takes quick-buck artists, poachers and developers to elbow their way to the trough."[72]

In June a Colorado Supreme Court ruling opened the door to a November vote on legalized gambling in seventeen Colorado towns, sweeping aside a petition from two rival progaming groups. Ultimately five different gambling initiatives were approved for the November ballot. Four gaming expansion initiatives, representing thirty-three Colorado communities, survived the signature drive by eleven groups aimed at getting gambling in their communities and began campaigning against each other. One of the initiatives would have added roulette, craps, baccarat, and big wheel as legal games and would cap the state tax at 15 percent instead of the 40 percent that the original law allowed. The fifth would provide that, after a statewide vote approving casino gambling in a city or county, local residents would have the final say in a separate election.[73]

Casino owners in the three gambling towns quickly organized a campaign against competition from more casinos. The director of marketing for the Swiss-based company operating the Teller House casino in Central

City predicted that the industry shakeout would continue for at least three years. "People who put this on the ballot overestimated the possibilities," Massimo Schawalder warned.[74] Mayor Wellington Webb of Denver was vocal in his opposition to the LoDo proposal. Two University of Nevada professors added their warnings. "The whole thing is predicated on the idea that gambling money is on a tree and you just pick it off. It's not," William Thompson, professor of public administration, said. "It is money that is taken away from other things." Bill Eadington, director of the Institute for the Study of Gambling and Commercial Gaming at the University of Nevada–Reno, argued that the proposed expansion of gambling in Colorado is part of a "create and destroy" syndrome in which, by creating more gambling, existing gambling would be destroyed. But some local proponents thought the assessment of Nevada academics lacked credibility, since Nevada might lose much of its Colorado customer base.[75]

In the end, after much editorializing, a barrage of letters to local and regional newspapers, local straw polls, and expensive television advertising, all the gambling expansion amendments were voted down in Colorado by large margins. The lower downtown Denver amendment and the one from Parachute lost by the widest margins. Even though Parachute, thanks to the oil-shale bust of the early 1980s, was uniquely overbuilt with water and sewage systems, fire stations, paved roads, and other facilities, its "dog in the manger" position, which would have called a moratorium on any other gambling expansion, seemed not to have served it well. Only Referendum C, which would allow local votes on gambling even if approved statewide, passed, and that by a wide margin.[76] New initiatives to put slot machines at Colorado airports and limited gambling in Manitou Springs were reintroduced in September 1993. One, to try again for gambling in Trinidad, failed to garner enough legal signatures for the 1994 state ballot.

Colorado was not alone in the pursuit of gambling expansion. Even though Deadwood had much more uniform limitations on the size of operations, given its thirty-device limit per building, several different efforts, some legislative and some administrative, would push at that restriction. In addition, a judicial decision in December 1991 declared unconstitutional under the equal protection guarantees the South Dakota law that specified that majority ownership of Deadwood gaming halls must be held by South Dakota residents, clearing the way for more outside investors.[77]

Late in 1991, as Colorado was debating the expansion of gambling, a proposal was first announced in Deadwood that never mentioned gambling at all. Actor Kevin Costner and his brother Dan, who managed the

Midnight Star Casino in downtown Deadwood, had purchased an eighty-five-acre tract atop Deadwood Hill on Highway 85 and were proposing to build a new hotel and business conference center. With five to nine hundred rooms, it would match the six hundred hotel and motel rooms that Lead and Deadwood presently had. The need for services like water and sewage treatment were obvious to Mayor Bruce Oberlander, but as the Department of Transportation had planned to close Highway 85 for a full year to expand the curvy, slow, two-lane road to a four-lane highway from Interstate 90 twelve miles down the hill near Spearfish, there seemed plenty of time to solve those problems.[78] The Costners were not available for comment, and no mention of gambling was made in the articles.

However, by February, the *Denver Post* reported that gaming officials in Deadwood said they couldn't compete with other cities that offer gambling unless bet limits were increased. A bill squeaked through the 1991 legislature allowing twenty-five-dollar bet limits on blackjack, but the governor vetoed it. In 1992 hundred-dollar bet limits, increased numbers of slot machines and card tables per casino (with up to 400 machines in hotels), and 490 machines allowed each individual investor found their way into a legislative bill.[79] By this time Kevin and Dan Costner had called the governor to lobby in support of the increase in limits on Deadwood gambling, but Bill Walsh, one of the earliest supporters of limited gambling in Deadwood, went to the capitol to say that the expansion of gambling would go well beyond what was sold to the people of South Dakota by the Deadwood You Bet Committee. "I think we're breaking our treaty with the people of Deadwood and the people across the state." For that he was branded a "Maverick."[80] The Senate passed the 1992 bill, but the House was ordered by the governor to wait out a two-week spring break in order to get public input and added a provision that the changes would not take effect until July 1993. But faced with a likely veto and fading support in the legislature, the bill was withdrawn in March.[81]

The following November the Deadwood Gaming Association hosted a political action retreat in Rapid City for members of the gaming industry to discuss their concerns. Sixty-six of eighty-one gaming license holders attended the retreat, and a majority voted for higher bet limits, expressed support for the Costners' project, rejected drug testing for employees, and left unresolved the method of determining the number of gaming devices they wanted per establishment. Several people expressed the hope of a change to a square footage formula (the Colorado model). Dan Costner's presentation (always referring to the development as "a dream") to the group reflected the "need for a maximum of 180 devices per retail license with one device allowed per fifty square feet, a room incentive, a $100 bet limit, and a liquor license."[82]

This would be the public debut of the link between bet and gaming device limits and the "Costner Project," as it came to be called, and the first round in a statewide debate about the limits of gambling in Deadwood and across South Dakota. The legislation proposed by Deadwood Economic Development Corporation attorney Jon Mattson for the next legislature was a compromise on the Colorado model, with ample room for the Costner development. In the revision, each building would be allowed thirty devices or one per fifty square feet of building blueprint (whichever was greater) for buildings in the historic district, with a maximum of ninety devices in one building. An individual would be limited to a financial interest in 180 devices. Buildings outside the historic district that existed as of January 1993 would be allowed ninety devices, but facilities built after that date could have only thirty per building, to prevent the proliferation of "slot houses" on the edges of town. Hotels, however, would be allowed one additional gaming device for every two rooms up to a maximum of four hundred devices.[83]

Not everyone fell in line with this effort either. Mike Gustafson, owner of the First Gold Hotel at the lower end of Deadwood Hill, said a "Save Deadwood Committee" had been formed to study the legislation. Asserting that his committee represented 57 percent of the gaming devices in Deadwood, he claimed that they did not want the ninety-device maximum raised and wanted a smaller increase in the betting limit.[84] (The reference to ninety devices reflected the degree to which not only new structures, such as First Gold, but old buildings, such as the Midnight Star, had been successful in arguing that they occupied not one but two or three buildings "historically" and were thus eligible for multiples of thirty gaming devices; each owner was limited to ninety slot machines regardless of the number of "buildings.") Gustafson was reflecting not only on his location in Deadwood, which would be the closest to the Costner Project of any gaming/ hotel establishment, but also on his ownership interest and "recent significant financial loss in Central City, Colorado, because of the different gaming rules of that state." He argued that the large gaming halls with four to six hundred devices took the lion's share of the business and were ruinous to smaller operations.[85] Motel owner Lee Colbert also pointed to Bullwhackers in Colorado and its effect on smaller gaming operators. Additionally worrisome was the threat that Governor George Mickelson would claim 80 percent of the increased gaming tax revenues for the state. John Mattson argued for continuation of a fifty-fifty split, but in fact Deadwood had been getting much more than that via the Historic Preservation Commission, through the gaming commission operating surpluses and the device fees.

But soon after the Save Deadwood Committee appeared, another called "United for Deadwood's Future" organized to support the creation of the Tax Increment Financing District (TIFD), which would provide the bonds for extending water and sewer up the hill to the Costner Project. This referendum would allow property taxes on improvements to the undeveloped land to be used to pay off the TIFD bonds, after which the taxes would go to the city, school district, and county. Some, including city commissioner and gaming device distributor Mike Trucano, who opposed the TIFD, argued that gambling expansion and taxes were unrelated. The issue was one of tax fairness, not "Anti-Costner/Pro-Costner, or Anti-development/Pro-development."[86] Three hundred people attended an information session on the Costner Project three days before the January 19, 1993, ballot, and although Deadwood citizens had defeated a bond proposal the previous spring to use sales tax revenue to fund the installation for water and sewer lines to the site, the measure passed overwhelmingly, and the Costner Project had cleared its first hurdle.

Immediately, the dual effort to sell the development project and to expand gambling opportunities was launched. The largest architectural firm in South Dakota was announced as the winning entry for the Costner resort. The Spitznagel Partnership of Rapid City and Sioux Falls displayed the designs for "Dakota Springs," a seventy-five- to ninety-five-million-dollar development modeled consciously on the "grand lodges in the National Parks."[87] Meanwhile, in the capital, Pierre, lobbyists got a boost when Governor Mickelson came out in support of the Costner Project. Back in Deadwood, Jon Mattson, representing the Historic Preservation Commission and the Economic Development Corporation, reported that most gaming investors, about half the casinos, and virtually all the nongaming retail businesses in Deadwood supported the idea of the resort. But whether small casinos or large ones felt more threatened remained a matter of contention.[88]

At this point in the campaign, Mattson took the ironic position in front of a legislative committee that expansion of gambling was needed not to support the Costner Project but because "fifty-three percent of the businesses in Deadwood [were] losing money. The bill was drafted to meet the competition and the need for more rooms." Dan Costner followed and described the conception of his dream and the first steps of making the dream a reality.[89] The South Dakota Senate defeated the bill twice on February 23. But with heavy lobbying and a late afternoon deal, after which only three speakers, all in favor, introduced a new bill (nearly identical to the original), the Senate voted 23–13 to concur with House amendments to pass the gambling expansion bill. By this time the measure was identified in the press as "allowing Deadwood an estimated $95 million development."[90]

But gambling expansion in Deadwood was not to have clear sailing at this point either. Within a week, JoDean Joy of Miller, South Dakota, who had organized a petition drive to make video lottery face the electorate in 1992, started working on the referendum to kill the Deadwood legislation and to collect 12,836 signatures to put it on the ballot. A rally in Deadwood on March 19 was intended to ask Mrs. Joy "how one person could completely disrupt the work of the 1993 South Dakota legislature on this issue."[91] Several hundred people turned out to do so, with Dan Costner front and center as the cause célèbre of the day. From then on, bet limits and the threat that the Costners would *not* build their resort became one cause.

One brave citizen in Spearfish wrote a seven-point letter to the editor on democratic rights and responsibilities, the fifth of which stated:

> The issue before the voters is not and never has been the Costner project. No one is telling Dan Costner he can't build his resort. He's telling us he won't build it unless we give him higher bet limits. But that decision is entirely up to him, and any conscious attempt by anyone to make voters believe it's up to them amounts to blackmail at the worst or petulance at the least. The issue before us is whether or not we want higher stakes gambling, and that issue concerns the entire state in various ways. What Costner does with the decision for the citizens is a private enterprise decision, not a public policy one. Supporters of higher bet limits and the Costner project are attempting to get us to confuse the smaller issue—the resort—with the larger one—higher stakes gambling—because such confusion works to their advantage. We have to resist that confusion.[92]

JoDean Joy had collected nearly twenty thousand signatures by mid-June and filed them with the South Dakota secretary of state, qualifying for a September 14 vote on the expanded Deadwood gambling law. In response to Joy's "It's NOT what we voted for" campaign, Deadwood opened its "Vote YES for South Dakota" committee headquarters. Joy felt confident that the sound defeat of her referendum on the video lottery the year before had come from having to vote yes to end video gambling. On this referendum a no vote meant no to expanded gambling.[93]

Joy won the day. After massive letter writing, fund-raising campaigns, hired experts, and public debates, 55 percent of the voters said no to expanded gambling on September 14. The Missouri River divides the state's sixty-four counties economically as well as culturally, and while twelve West River counties favored the bill (by the largest margins in Lawrence and Pennington Counties), it lost in ten of the western counties and barely won in four. But expanded gambling lost by more than twenty-six thousand votes east of the Missouri, failing in forty-two of forty-four counties.[94]

Extensive blame laying and some soul searching followed, including the questions of whether South Dakotans voted against expanded gaming because it would be a boon to tribal casinos in the state, which would be subject to the same expansion. Voters in every county with a tribal casino rejected expanded gambling, reflecting either a distaste for Indian casinos or opposition from tribes to a measure that might bring further competition from Deadwood.[95] But state senator Paul Valandra from the Rosebud Sioux Reservation said that the bill's drafters tied possible boosts in Indians' table numbers to their ability to put up a large, Costner-scale operation (with fifty connected acres, at least fifty hotel rooms, and a convention space for four hundred). Such provisions could keep big profits from small Indian operators who did not have major backers. Moreover, when the Cheyenne River Sioux chairman asked for Costner's help and a cut of the profits in its fight with the state over two new casinos outside Pierre and Deadwood, Costner responded with a terse "not interested."[96]

However, by February 1994, the Costner Project, now downscaled to a fifty-million-dollar resort to be called "Dunbar" after the *Dances with Wolves* character that first brought the actor to the Black Hills, was back on the agenda of the Deadwood Planning and Zoning Commission. Dan Costner asked for another seven-million-dollar tax increment finance district to avoid higher property taxes in March. By October an on-site open house to look at plans was held for Deadwood citizens, and a new legal battle was in the works, establishing a railroad authority to provide train connections to Deadwood from the population center and airport at Rapid City. In addition, multiple action blackjack was introduced in Deadwood in April 1993 to allow players to make three bets at once, even though each player gets only one hand. Some people thought that was a way to triple the bet limit, but it was currently being played in nine states.[97]

The most ingenious and efficient form of gambling expansion, however, has been the South Dakota Gaming Commission's ability to discover and declare that buildings that were formerly thought to be one unit are in fact "multiple" buildings and thus eligible for a larger number of gaming devices under the original legislation. In June 1994 four Main Street casino operators asked for multiple building designations. Building owners and their attorneys argued, with the aid of old maps and photographs, that what appeared to be one old structure was actually two or more separate buildings. For instance, the original Lucky Wrangler building was only fifty feet long when it was built in 1894. A second building was placed on the lot sometime in the 1930s, and two separate businesses operated there for many years. Although a third structure was added later, attorney Jon Mattson requested only a two-building designation. Another casino, Hickok's, was granted a three-building status on the basis of plans that never came to pass. The argument went like this: A series of cast iron interior columns were to be used as partitions between the two Main Street businesses. The partitions were never built, but a separate business operated in the rear of the structure and used an entrance on Deadwood Street. If the wall had been put up, the commission would likely have agreed that it was two buildings, but because the interior wall was *never* constructed, the three-building designation was granted and a fire wall to separate the two front businesses was not required, since it had never been built in the first place. Another building that had originally housed the post office and telephone companies, with separate entrances, had been consolidated as the Montgomery Ward store, and since the original interior wall was removed more than forty years ago, no separation was required for the two-building designation. Finally, a 1930s building was granted a two-building, but not the three-building, classification it asked for on the basis of three separate postal addresses and its use by three separate businesses. Mark Aspaas, the gaming commission's consultant architect, said the third portion was really an addition, not a separate structure.[98]

Again in October, the commission added four more "buildings" and the possibility of another 120 slot machines in existing casinos. These cases were even more imaginative in their arguments. One, the newly built Four Aces Casino, had been approved as three buildings upon its completion in 1993, but the commission, having been convinced that an older auto shop was incorporated in the building, approved it as four separate buildings. In a remarkable argument, given gambling rules based on historical preservation, commission architect Aspaas was reported as saying, "They have done a wonderful job of creating the feel of a brand new facility. Such a good job that it is hard to realize there was [an older] building." The French Quarter across the street from Hickok's revived the argument of intent by saying that builder Bert Jacobs may have started out with a "two-store concept in mind."

The most novel contention held that the basement of the Fairmont

Hotel was constructed with completely separate entrances and was at one time operated as a separate business from the hotel upstairs. As the foundation of the building was recognized as a separate structural system, the Fairmont became two buildings for the purposes of gaming. Finally, for that session at least, a discussion ensued as to whether Tin Lizzies Casino, built on the site of a major old Deadwood auto dealership, occupied three, four, or five buildings, depending on whether Eddie Rypkema had constructed the showroom, used car lot, auto shop, tire dealership, and service station at different times and as different businesses. Said Aspaas, "There is a fine, foggy line between what is an addition and what is a separate building. A situation like this becomes difficult. . . . It might be stretching it to call it five buildings, but if we called it three, we could call it four." The four-building designation passed unanimously.[99] And while the pretense continued on into 1996, it was apparently no longer even necessary to make the argument in terms of what might have been historic buildings. When the Deadwood Gulch Saloon gained a two-building designation, attorney Roger Tellinghusen said the saloon structure was actually two buildings, one built in 1885 as a glove factory and a second added in 1990 when the present owners converted the building to a gaming hall.[100]

In their own ways, Gilpin County, the "richest square mile on earth," Teller County, the "world's greatest gold camp," and Lawrence County, site of the "largest single-operating gold mine in the Western Hemisphere," endeavored to maintain their legacy of extracting wealth from available resources. While governmental agencies may not have had to jump-start the businesses, they were in the business of regulating limited gambling. But they were also increasingly themselves becoming sponsors of gambling. As clear as the actions of the South Dakota Gaming Commission's architect Mark Aspaas might have made the relationship, Kay Lorenz, president of the Casino Owners Association of Colorado, would the same week put it in plain English: "in the light of the benefits we produce for Colorado and our role in the broader tourism industry, limited gaming is a partner with state government, not an adversary."[101]

CHAPTER 5

Historic Preservation, Facadism, and the Fast Buck

Gaming in Deadwood, as well as in Central City, Black Hawk, and Cripple Creek, resulted in significant transformations of both the economic and the social fabric of community life. These transformations created winners and losers in the private sector, as well as restructured state and local government roles in community economic development as gaming taxes and fees became alternative revenue sources to property taxes. As state and local governmental agencies evolved from watchdogs or overseers of gaming to active partners in the gaming industry, the short- and long-term impacts of gaming not only on these four historic mountain towns' physical structures but also on their "sense of community" became less certain. Historic preservation, the catchword that provided the necessary electoral support in both South Dakota and Colorado, was handled differently in each state and, as a result, effected different economic, physical, and philosophical responses to the benefits and costs posed by local option gaming.

In 1961, Deadwood became one of the first cities in the United States to be designated in its entirety as a National Historic Landmark. Ironically, in 1989, the year gaming commenced in Deadwood, the National Park Service downgraded Deadwood from a priority two endangered status to a priority one, noting that Deadwood was one of the eleven most endangered historic sites in the nation.[1] Three years later, in August 1992, the National Parks Service moved Deadwood from priority one level (of serious damage or eminently threatened with damage) back to priority two (exhibiting the potential for damage or experiencing threats to the landmark's integrity). According to state and national officials, much of the turnaround was due to the good fortune and foresight by the city to hire a professionally trained historic preservation officer, Mark Wolfe, in early

1990. According to historian Lysa Wegman-French of the National Park Service's Denver office, "That is a success story. The leadership is what saved its [Deadwood's] historical integrity. Mark Wolfe is just a remarkable person with a clear view and knowledge of what needs to be done."[2] And by 1993, Robert Spude, the regional chief of National Preservation Programs for the National Park Service, presented the Deadwood Historic Preservation Commission a certificate of appreciation.[3] Anticipating the award, Paul Putz, director of the State Historical Preservation Center in Vermillion, stated, "I think in preservation terms, Deadwood is a miracle."[4] These accolades, along with the $80 million invested in public and private buildings and infrastructure, suggest that the path from "most endangered" landmark designation to "miracle" is worthy of close scrutiny.

Professional Expertise and Gaming Regulation

The National Park Service established the landmark designation program in 1960, and the 1966 National Historic Preservation Act (Public Law 89-665) established historic districts and made available limited funds for the survey of potentially significant sites along with the preservation of some buildings. Embedded in the 1966 law were criteria for evaluating sites, buildings, objects, districts, and structures that should be considered before any government project would be undertaken. Title I charged the secretary of the interior to create a list of sites and properties deemed valuable—the National Register of Historic Places, which included historic districts such as Deadwood, Central City, and Cripple Creek.[5] In 1976, Congress modified the 1966 preservation act by providing substantial tax incentives to encourage preservation of historic buildings (the 1976 Tax Reform Act), a law that was modified in 1981. The 1981 Economic Recovery Tax Act provided an allowable tax credit of 25 percent for expenses incurred in restoring or preserving certified historic structures (all the buildings in Deadwood are so classified).[6] But support for historic preservation was eroded in 1986 by the reduction of federal support of historic preservation grant funds, along with a reduction of the tax credit from 25 percent to 20 percent for private dwellings and 10 percent for commercial buildings.

South Dakota law SDCL 1-19A-20 provided, in addition to federal incentives, an eight-year moratorium on state property tax assessment for improvements on historic buildings that are recorded on the State Register of Historic Places. In return for the tax moratorium on improved value, the property owner must agree to maintain the property in good order, allow public access to the improved property twelve hours per year, and insure the property against fires and floods. Such covenants reflect the philosophy that although many historic buildings are owned privately, they are a national and state treasure worthy of preservation for future generations, and they serve as a focus of community cohesion and identity.

Given federal and state tax incentives and gaming device fees of $2.3 million the first year and the approximately $5 million in revenues made available to historic preservation annually after the first year of gambling in Deadwood, the cumulative resources were significant and allowed the Deadwood Preservation Commission ample opportunity to encourage preservation efforts along numerous and diverse routes. As J. Myrick Howard noted, communities in their attempt to preserve properties have a range of options: they may acquire properties outright and resell them under protective covenants, they may buy properties (but then the agency is responsible for taxes, insurance, and maintenance in addition to the fact that the agency's funds are tied up), they may acquire an option on a property (but this also ties up funds), or they may utilize a contract to purchase agreement that might eventually lead to an outright purchase, and so on.[7] Also available are outright grants, generally to nonprofit agencies, and short- and long-term loans from a revolving fund. These various means of financing have been used, at times creatively, by the Deadwood Historic Preservation Commission (DHPC).

The success of these creative financing schemes involving historic preservation funds, private investments, and state/federal tax credits is conspicuously evident. After having been in the gambling business for seven years, even Deadwood residents who are ambivalent about gambling will say that the town looks immeasurably better. The DHPC became much more powerful than city government in determining the direction and appearance of the town. Guiding that restoration/preservation effort, Mark Wolfe, Deadwood historic preservation officer, noted that often the commission "is accused of caring more about buildings than we do about people." Wolfe continued, "The reason to try to preserve the buildings is to preserve a sense of community. When buildings disappear, people's memory of events seem to go with them."[8] Essentially, historic preservation is for the people. Even so, the critical issues involve what, how, and when buildings would undergo restoration and who pays at what costs, particularly when restoration costs more than razing an old building and replacing it with a new "historic" or "period" building.

The visible success of the DHPC's six years of restoration efforts is readily apparent in Deadwood. Changes are evident in the facades of the downtown buildings converted from retail businesses to casinos. With the emphasis on what William Murtagh calls "facadism—the postmodern design idiom,"[9] old porches, awnings, false fronts, and plank sidewalks were the first to be torn down. The usual brick cleaning, remortaring, and trim painting returned a turn-of-the-century look to several blocks. But historicity took precedence over uniformity, so several building from the 1930s have been restored to their art deco appearance.

The first and most dramatic restoration project provided the symbol, if not the rationale, for legalized gaming in Deadwood when the Save the Lawrence County Courthouse Committee intersected with the Deadwood You Bet Committee. Built in 1908, the structure that had served as post office, courthouse, and jail was declared unsafe in 1985 and had been scheduled for demolition by the county commissioners, but it was saved in 1986 by a general election ballot. The restoration of the county courthouse included stabilization and a new foundation for the large limestone building. The interior was refurbished, and office space was expanded into an adjacent annex and plaza.[10] Funded primarily through lease-purchase certificates, the restoration was completed with few historic preservation funds. However, $55,150 of preservation funds were allocated to the restoration of the *Justice and Mechanics* mural that was discovered when a drop ceiling was removed. Wolfe noted that "the project is not restoration in the purest sense, but the public has set a good example by doing it. . . . There was a lot of talk about how that building just could not be saved, and this project proves that isn't true."[11]

Infrastructure Restoration: Bricks, Lighting, and Transportation

Because Deadwood's water and sewer lines were old and inadequate, albeit historic (original wooden mains failed to provide enough pressure to fight fires at the lower end of town), the city of Deadwood, backed by historic preservation funds, issued $10 million of revenue bonds in 1990 to rebuild this infrastructural feature. Once the street was torn up, the city and the DHPC decided that the restoration of brick paving, a return to the original Main Street surface of 1907, would enhance the attractiveness of the downtown to pedestrians, since parking had been banned on the main thoroughfare.[12] The last brick on Main Street, one of 354,870, was laid June 25, 1992, thereby capping a 4.2-million-dollar investment that symbolized a recapture of Deadwood's past and a community commitment to Deadwood's future. In addition, $300,000 were spent to add Victorian-style lampposts on Main Street. The popularity of the initial project led to a second phase, the rebricking and Victorian lighting of Sherman Street in front of the courthouse.

The old depot, which had subsequently served as a fire and police station, located between the courthouse and Main Street, was restored to become a visitors center. More recently, work to restore the old Engine House was funded. The project, estimated at $403,200, was financed jointly with $250,000 from the Intermodal Surface Transportation Efficiency Act matched by a grant of $153,200 from the DHPC. The project, once completed, would allow Deadwood's locomotive to be used again, would serve as a city trolley stop (serving 97,393 individuals per quarter), and would improve access to municipal parking lots.[13]

The early commitment of Deadwood to authenticity and restoration is noted by two very different but distinctive projects: restoration of the 1912 City Recreation Center and rebuilding of the Deadwood Stage used in the Days of '76 rodeo. In both cases restoration costs far exceeded replacement costs. The initial estimate of $632,000 to restore the seriously deteriorated recreation center (originally the city auditorium) soon escalated to more than $1 million, once asbestos was removed and interior walls weakened by moisture from the swimming pool were rebuilt. Yet Preservation Officer Wolfe noted that the construction of the building using terra cotta bricks was "unique and should be preserved" and razing the building "would violate the Secretary of the Interior's rules for historic preservation."[14] Restored, the building resumed its function as a community recreation center and became one of the few places in Deadwood that catered specifically to the youth of the community.

Also in 1991, the commission provided $100,000 to bring the grandstands for the Days of '76 rodeo up to code and $75,000 to construct *new* toilets. Real commitment to preservation was evident in the piece-by-piece rebuilding of one of the small Deadwood stages that had sustained extensive damage when the stagecoach failed to negotiate a curve during the 1990 rodeo. The restoration of its 1876 appearance took two years and cost over $17,000. Used sparingly in city parades and during rodeo entrances, the stage symbolizes the rich history of Deadwood and is a major attraction for the Days of '76 museum.

Historic Preservation Projects: Public and Private

Concurrent with infrastructural restoration were demands by public and private entities for funds that the DHPC controlled. Access to these funds required an application and stringent review that ensured commitment to historic integrity of building exteriors. Projects approved initially were limited to the downtown Deadwood historic district, a subset of the National Historic Landmark designation. Only later were preservation funds allocated to worthy projects in the remainder of the landmark area. Descriptions of several notable public and private restoration efforts provide illustrations of the tactics and difficulties involved in historic preservation.

The Gillmore. One of the few efforts to improve housing in a town increasingly filled with commuting workers was the restoration of the three-story historic Gillmore Hotel. The large wood-frame structure, designed in French Second Empire style and built in 1892, was notched and pegged rather than nailed together. In its early days, numerous news articles heralded the popularity and visual attractiveness of the hostelry. By 1914 the once fashionable Gillmore had deteriorated, and the building was closed. Gradually it was transformed into an apartment building and was quite run down when the new owners, Joe Rowland and Richard and Teri Clark, petitioned to have the Gillmore brought into the historic district on December 18, 1990, thereby qualifying the property for tax credits and historic preservation revolving fund monies. Rowland and the Clarks proposed to refurbish the Gillmore for use as a luxury hotel with eleven fully furnished suites and seven studio suites at a cost of $859,000. According to Rowland, "Guests of the hotel will experience the history and lifestyle of the well-to-do during the Victorian Era."[15] An April 1991

The Gillmore Hotel, built in French Second Empire style in 1892 and renovated as affordable housing near Main Street. This housing project is to date the only one in Deadwood connected to historic preservation.

referendum dashed plans to restore the Gillmore when voters refused to allow the residential property to revert to commercial use.

After consulting with historic preservation officers and after securing creative bank lending, the owners submitted a plan to restore the Gillmore for use as "affordable housing" by combining tax credits arranged through the South Dakota Housing Authority and a five-hundred-thousand-dollar, 7.5 percent, thirty-year low-interest loan, half payable in 1992 and the remainder in 1993, from the DHPC.[16] In time to celebrate its hundredth anniversary, the Gillmore opened August 1, 1992, as an apartment house composed of fourteen one- and two-bedroom apartments with rents varying from $320 to $400 per month, based on occupants' median income. Restoration was completed by Metro Plains Development, Inc., which was able to restore the Gillmore's exterior to its 1892 grandeur; but the contractors gutted and rebuilt its interior to meet current state and federal housing codes. According to Wolfe, "The restoration of old buildings also saves another part of the community, its people. . . . We saved a building that will be used by the people that will live in it."[17] A testament to the success of the restoration was the 1994 National Preservation Honor Award given to Metro Plains Development, Inc., by the National Trust for Historic Preservation. The award, based on fifteen years of preservation work, included twelve specific projects, one of which, the Gillmore, was cited as "an excellent example of how multiple community goals can be achieved through historic renovations."[18]

The Adams House. In October 1992 the preservation commission, in spite of reservations by some board members and citizens, purchased a large home and its contents that was being used as a bed and breakfast. The property, the Adams House, steeped in the history of several prominent Deadwood families, reflected a unique turn-of-the-century architectural design, and its contents displayed the lifestyle of late-nineteenth-century gentility. In 1892 Harris Franklin commissioned Simon Eisendrath, who later became the commissioner of buildings in Chicago and a preeminent New York architect, to build a private residence. Ornate and expensive by nineteenth-century standards, the house was completed in 1896. Harris Franklin, an early liquor, mining, and cattle baron and owner of the historic Deadwood Franklin Hotel (later designated a landmark by the National Park Service), left the house to his son. In 1920 the Franklins sold the house to W. E. Adams, the wholesale grocer, mayor, and founder of the Adams Museum. After 1936, when Adams's second wife moved to California, the home went through almost fifty years of neglect and decline. Then in 1987, when it was acquired by

Bruce and Becky Crosswait, the Adams House became, for the first time, a bed and breakfast. After three years of repairing half a century of neglect, the Crosswaits sold the property to Joe Rowland, who because of financial difficulties allowed the property to default back to the Crosswaits. Unwilling or unable to continue running the Adams House, they placed it and its contents up for auction on October 24, 1992. Faced with the real possibility of house and contents being sold separately and with mounting pressure from the state historical society, Mark Wolfe, in consultation with the historic preservation board, purchased the Adams House in its entirety for $225,000, well below the listing prices of $185,000 for the house and $135,000 for its contents. In closing the deal Wolfe noted that the house was "one in a million."[19] The action, while well within the legal fiscal options available to the DHPC, meant that the Historic Preservation Commission was now in the bed and breakfast business, that the property would be removed from the local tax rolls, and that the commission would be saddled with continuing operation and maintenance costs. Furthermore, as noted by J. Myrick Howard, these funds (purchase, operation, and maintenance costs) would not be available to support other worthy projects.[20] However, another important piece of Deadwood's history had

The Adams House, purchased by the Deadwood Historic Preservation Commission, first as a Bed and Breakfast, now to become a house museum.

been preserved. A DHPC grant of $80,000 for an inventory of the house contents with an additional $300,000 for repairs will support the project of making it a house museum.

The Adams Museum. The Adams Museum, donated to the people of Lawrence County by W. E. Adams, houses a remarkable collection of Great Plains and Black Hills artifacts. The museum, one of the first benefactors of gaming revenues, hired its first full-time curator, Anne Marie Baker, in 1990. Baker, who left to do an internship at the state historical society in Wisconsin, was replaced by Carol Smith-Rogers. Under their stewardship, the museum undertook a three-phase restoration/ reorganization project. Phase I, completed in 1992, involved a historic preservation expenditure of $301,000 to restore the exterior of the Adams Museum along with some minimal interior work.[21] Kroger Restoration and Masonry, Inc., was charged with replacing worn and deteriorated mortar joints and pressure sealing foundation cracks on the building in a project to assure future generations access to an integral part of Black Hills history.[22] Under the guidelines of the National Park Service, work on the Adams Museum was intentionally a preservation rather than a restoration project. Every effort was made to retain original materials and design. Although some alterations of the interior and exterior were needed to assure handicap accessibility, an effort was made to retain the integrity of the building.[23] Phase II involved painting the building and re-designing the building's interior, especially the displays. The final phase, kicked off on September 11, 1993, called for the conservation and restoration of the artifacts and art.[24]

Smith-Rogers, with the assistance of historic preservation funding, made the museum user-friendly, particularly for children, by introducing a hands-on experience with the arts, crafts, and everyday life of the early pioneers in the basement. Aware of the tenuousness of historic preservation funding and the legal restrictions posed by the founder, E. W. Adams, that admission not be charged, the museum sought corporate sponsors. The more than 27,000 annual visitors attest to the success of the museum restoration and innovative efforts to involve the public in their museum. However, the museum, highly successful in attracting visitors and their contributions in the summer months, like many gaming parlors confronts diminished support during the winter months. The prospect of a successful, dynamic museum with year-round accessibility rests upon supplemental support provided by the DHPC, a willing patron at $50,000 for each budget year.

Deadwood Churches. If quasi-public entities were eager recipients of "gambling funds," churches that initially were either ambivalent or downright resistant to local option gaming in Deadwood were more reticent about accepting its payoff. Although perhaps still hesitant, organized religious groups began to take advantage of the success of gaming, at least indirectly, through their access to historic preservation funds, primarily through the DHPC's annual grants program. For example, the 1991 DHPC grants included numerous nonprofit organizations besides the Adams Memorial Museum, including the Historic Deadwood Arts Council, Deadwood Public Library, Deadwood/Lead Area Chamber of Commerce, Days of '76 Amusement Company, and Masonic Temple Association. Also among the nonprofit organizations were religious organizations including the First Baptist Church, St. John's Episcopal Church, and United Methodist Church.[25] Two years later, along with eight other nonprofit organizations, two churches received grants. St. Ambrose Catholic Church obtained $33,617 for repairs to the church's leaded glass "opera" windows and adjacent school building, while St. John's Episcopal Church was granted $20,000 to complete restoration work begun in 1992 with an initial thirteen-thousand-dollar grant to modernize the heating system.[26] Finally, in June 1993 Grace Lutheran Church tapped the grant fund for a "new" front door, raising issues among board members regarding the loss of a "cultural resource." Compromise was reached by Cultural Resource Manager Dana Vailancourt, who arranged financing for a replica of the old door at a cost of $1,500.[27] Implicit in these projects is the redefinition, or laundering, of gaming revenues from "tainted money" to community development funds by way of historic preservation.

Private Businesses. No redefinition was needed to encourage the private sector to take advantage of newly available funds. By the end of 1991 the largest loan awarded by the commission, $327,000, was granted to the Bullock Hotel for restoration and compliance with "safety code items." The loan amount represented approximately 20 percent of the total 1.5-million-dollar project.[28] Owners of the Adams Block, composed of three buildings, received $315,000 to cover part of the first phase of restoration. Numerous other private businesses, including the Franklin Hotel, the Windflower Building, the Peacock Club, the Lucky Wrangler, the Old Style Saloon #10 (where Wild Bill Hickok was shot), Gold Strike Gifts, the Fairmont Hotel, the China Doll Building, Deadwood Dick's, Miss Kitty's, and Hickok's all tapped into the revolving loan program during the first three years of legalized gaming. Compliance with existing life safety codes provided the rationale and highest priority for most of these initial loans. Furthermore, in all cases, substantial private funds were used as a match for historic preservation revolving loans, thereby multiplying the impact of historic preservation revenues. Second priority were the 126 buildings designated as landmarks. The 217 buildings listed as contributing to Deadwood's National Historic Landmark District status were given third priority for loans.

In 1989 the United Methodist Church sold the Howe Building to First Western Bank, thereby setting into motion one of the few complete restoration attempts, both external and internal, of commercial property in Deadwood. The new office was restored as closely as possible to the original Black Hills Savings and Trust, which had opened its doors in the Howe Building in 1904. Although the remodeling required gutting much of the first floor, every effort was made to reconstruct the interior to its 1904 appearance with some consideration given to modern banking technology. Exterior restoration was accomplished in accord with available photographs, while interior restoration was dependent upon written accounts. Gutting the interior revealed a false ceiling that had hidden ornate cornices above existing pillars and decorative beams running across the original stenciled ceiling. The beams were retained, but the pillars, which had been damaged in the placing of the false ceiling, along with the rotten cornice work, were replaced according to the identical molds provided by the original cornice company. Even the original seven-thousand-pound vault door, located some twenty miles away, was returned to the bank.[29] The uneasy wedding of historic authenticity and modern utilitarian services is evident in the interior refurbishing, which includes old-fashioned brass and mahogany teller cages juxtaposed with automatic teller machines sitting off in one corner.

By far the single largest "restoration" project thus far has been Dan and Kevin Costner's first gaming establishment, which involved a six-million-dollar expenditure of private funds in the reconstruction of the Phoenix Building. The Phoenix Building, which rose from the ashes of the 1879 fire, was a three-story structure modified in the 1960s by the removal of the top floor. The Phoenix Building restoration (named the Midnight Star by Dan and Kevin Costner and managed by Dan Costner) involved gutting the existing building and requesting a height variance of twenty-two feet to rebuild the third floor, making it the tallest building in the downtown historic district. Approval of the variance prompted a *Lawrence County Centennial* headline: "Costner to Raise the Roof in Deadwood." The Midnight Star, containing a casino on the main floor, a sports bar on the second floor, and a posh restaurant on the third floor, was given its requested variance even though Commissioner Trucano asked, "How high will the skyscrapers get?"[30] It was hyperbole, perhaps, but an indication of the community's effort to preserve the total historical context of Deadwood.

The transformation of the New York Clothing Store, long housed in the Phoenix Building, into the Midnight Star exemplified the strain between preservation of the total building and adaptive reuse centered on maximizing profit. Historic Preservation Officer Wolfe in a poignant statement noted:

> Costner's place is a major disappointment to me because the interior of the building had integrity. It had beautiful wood trim around the doors and windows, typical bull's-eye blocks and—nothing spectacular, but just very fine, very beautiful stuff. Wainscoting. Little corner cabinets. Beautiful tin ceiling in the downstairs. They just stripped it out, threw it away. They weren't interested in it, didn't want to deal with it. Wanted a Las Vegas–style casino in Deadwood. They're very proud of it. Yeah, they put the third story back on, and the cornice up there, and it is quite accurate. It was that big, but the interior is completely lost.[31]

Facadism mixed with historically correct reconstruction drove private commercial developments with few exceptions, such as Golddiggers, whose retention of original tin ceilings became a marketing come-on for gamers.

Preservation/Restoration of Private Homes. A crisis mentality for the first few years resulted in early preservation efforts being concentrated in restoring the infrastructure (i.e., water, streets, lighting), public buildings (i.e., city hall, the visitors center, the Adams Museum), nonprofit organizations (i.e., churches, fraternal organizations), and private businesses in the downtown historic district (the Bullock Hotel, the Franklin Hotel, the First Western Bank). Lagging behind were efforts to extend restoration projects into residential areas, partially because of funds limited by the number and costs of the above-mentioned projects but also because of residents' suspicions concerning the commission's control over private property once preservation funds were obtained to refurbish their homes. These concerns, according to Wolfe, were unfounded.

> People are absolutely fearful that we then have too much authority over their home, that we [the DHPC] have more authority than we should have. I'm not sure what they think would be an appropriate level. This is the Great West. People feel very strongly about "my" property. People are fearful that if they borrow from us we will have continuing authority over them that we don't already have. That's not the case. Loans are "no

strings attached." We just make sure that the work gets done right. But it doesn't give us any additional authority over the building that we don't already have. Usually outside the historic district we don't have any authority over the interior of the building. We give them advice. We ask them to try to save those things that have historic value. But we don't, we can't, tell them, "You can't do that."[32]

The first loan to renovate a private dwelling, a "loan milestone," for $3,365 was awarded in June 1992 to Linda Kottke to repair electrical wiring. It was a milestone no doubt but relatively insignificant compared to the $1.4 million lent to public and private businesses at this point.[33] One year later, a paint program was initiated at the request of homeowners. Wolfe saw it as an indication that residents were starting to develop an attitude regarding preservation as being more than an economic development scheme to attract more tourists but also a venue for establishing a sense of community based on a recognition of the community's past. Halting in its start, the five-thousand-dollar paint program encouraged private homeowners to actively participate in the total restoration of Deadwood. Crimped by some restrictions such as homes having to be fifty years old, color schemes requiring approval, and repairs supervised for quality control, the paint program through its very constraints made citizens aware of the "value" of historic precedent. The hurdles of paint removal, paint approval and purchase, and age requirements combined to try the patience of applicants; yet once a project was completed, albeit with minimal support of $500, the applicant was cognizant of the "total historic preservation effort." Wolfe concluded, "[The paint program] was probably one of the best things we've done" because, once implemented, success of the program spread by word of mouth and involved neighborhood participation.[34] More recently, private homeowner projects acquired a public relations atmosphere, as exemplified by the 1994 restoration of the eighty-six- and eighty-four-year-old Plummer sisters' home. Restoration, from the no-interest, deferred payment special needs program, made possible the almost complete rehabilitation of the elderly sisters' home.[35]

Although in its infancy, the restoration of the "total community" is well under way. Cheap in its costs and rich in its public and community relations, there is little doubt now that once crisis projects are completed, the DHPC can shift more resources and attention to the National Historic Landmark designated total community environment, thereby creating an atmosphere focused on the preservation of a historic legacy even at the costs of some private property rights. Given this move, the future of preservation in Deadwood is bright in spite of a western ethos of individualism, for the promise of tax benefits or even the real contribution of $500 is most likely less important to preserving the past than a "blood and sweat" commitment by local residents.

Historic Preservation: Conflicts and Resolutions

Given the nearly thirty-five-million-dollar investment of gaming revenues in Deadwood's preservation efforts, one would expect almost universal support for the decisions of the DHPC. But that is not necessarily the case. From day one of gaming, or perhaps preceding opening day, economic concerns (profit/cost issues) were in conflict with the principles of good historic preservation, the stated rationale for gaming in Deadwood. Immediately, the conflict between preservation of historic buildings, both externally and internally, gave way to economic concerns, with profits and the economics of gaming tourism gaining the upper hand. Total restoration gave way to facadism, where storefronts were retained at the expense of gutting historic interiors. Within the morass of rhetoric, arguments raged over the trivial, such as the location, size, and nature of signs, as well as the significant, such as the complete destruction of historic properties included in the National Historic Landmark designation in the name of maximizing economic return. Enmeshed in the various arguments was the apparent conflict between the public good and private enterprise.

The public good, according to Mark Wolfe, involved maintaining the integrity and ambience of the downtown historic district as well as the total National Historic Landmark designation. This commitment to historic purity placed him and the DHPC at loggerheads not only with private entrepreneurs but also with public entities such as the public library board members, who were less concerned with historical accuracy than with space for patrons, handicap access, and public restroom facilities. The library was constructed between 1903 and 1905 with $15,000 donated by Andrew Carnegie.[36] By the early 1990s graceful aging, technology (particularly the shift to electronic media), and space limitations pushed the library board into investigating alterations and renovations. In April 1993 the stage was set for an ongoing conflict between the Carnegie Library Board and the DHPC when the board applied for permission to build an addition on the rear of the building, to add an elevator, and to make minor modifications to the front of the building to allow additional patron parking. Based on an appraisal by the state preservation officer, Paul Putz, who noted that "any addition would have an adverse effect upon the historic quality of the building," permission was tabled.[37]

The petition was revived a week later, again on August 28, and again on October 13, 1993, when still no compromise was reached. Finally, at the November 15 meeting, the DHPC approved an addition that was five feet shorter than originally proposed but only for the rear of the building, and by June 1994 a bid of $209,209 was approved for actual construction to be paid from the $250,000 of bonded historic preservation funds.[38] Historic preservation funds, as approved, provided only partial funding of the estimated $730,073 total costs. Although taking more than half a year to reach a compromise and almost a year to review construction bids, the Carnegie Library project exemplified the process of negotiation needed to satisfy the needs of the library board and the requirements of the American Disabilities Act and still maintain historic integrity of the district. Although an agreement was reached on the addition to the library, Preservation Officer Wolfe expressed continued reservations: "I think that it's a shame. It's not the right thing to do. It was one of those political problems. The community seemed to want it. They didn't seem to care as much for the resources as for the function. I recognize the need for the function, and the importance of that, but I don't think it had to happen at the expense of the resource. Unfortunately it will."[39] This case reflected an uneasy compromise, but such compromises have been even less easily obtained with the private sector.

Signage. Greeted with less than universal enthusiasm after a two-year debate by business owners and the Historic Preservation Commission, new ordinances now regulate sign size (forty-five square feet), shape of nameplates, and calculated "total signage" and prohibit most external use of neon, with exceptions granted on a case-by-case basis, such as the Veterans of Foreign Wars, who retained their outdoor neon sign on the "grounds of its historic nature."[40] Originally a proposal for sign equations regulating square footage allowable per building controlled even the use of lights three feet inside buildings but was eventually reduced to one foot and excluded slot machines. Typical sign disputes occurred early in gaming when, in December 1990, building inspector Keith Umenthum noted that a tractor trailer had "recently arrived in town bearing the legend 'Deadwood Gulch Resort just ahead; Come play with us.' The trailer was parked on the motel's property near the highway. . . . We were told with a straight face this isn't a sign, it's a construction trailer for tool storage."[41] The DHPC noted that the trailer was out of compliance and would have to be moved. Mark Wolfe was adamant that Deadwood not look like Las Vegas.[42] It doesn't, at least from the street, and he has been willing to do battle with even Kevin Costner over the historically appropriate shape of the awnings on Costner's Midnight Star. Although variances were granted for "nonfunctional" shutters, the DHPC gave the Costners ninety days to replace the bubble-shaped awnings with a historically correct design. In making the decision, Commissioner John Gable commented on the commission getting bogged down in minutiae. "Minutiae are what makes a historic community," countered Preservation Officer Wolfe. "Little by little you can take away the historic integrity of Deadwood."[43]

Private Property Rights. More controversial are the conflicts the DHPC has had with a few business sites that proved unsuitable for gambling but are now valued at too high a rate for their old retail purpose. They are located within the National Historic Landmark District and are prohibited from being demolished. As gaming became the dominant industry in Deadwood, homeowners such as Ken and Erma Winkelman, with a log house at 617 Main Street, sought permits to demolish or move their building because of the misfit between residential and commercial property. Wolfe, opposing the request, noted, "It's a historic building in a historic district. Moving it would remove its historic designation." Wolfe continued, "The purpose of restoration is not just to repair and fix up but to retain in the original context."[44] Thus, early on, the line was contested between preserving the integrity of the historic district and individual rights to control private property: the "common good" versus "individual rights."

In May 1992 the owner of one of the three auto dealerships that went out of business with the advent of gambling asked for permission to demolish two twenty-by-twenty-foot stucco buildings, an office and a garage, situated on the lot used to display cars. While not contesting the new assessment of $190,000 on the 125-foot-wide lot or the $9,000 in taxes, businessman Pat Roberts said that he couldn't find a use for the land while the buildings were standing.[45] Roberts told the commission, "Those buildings are old and falling apart. I can't find any use for them. . . . We can't afford to pay for it, for folks to look at." Preservation Officer Wolfe responded that "economic hardship" was not a sufficient justification for demolishing buildings that were judged to be important to the architectural fabric of a historic community such as Deadwood. Built in 1927, the two buildings had housed a filling station owned by the Eagle Oil Company and were surrounded by a white picket fence against a wooded hillside. They represent the last of their kind in Deadwood and are presently being protected.[46] The commission gave preliminary approval to Roberts to convert the buildings into a pawn shop operation and ordered literature outlining creative uses of old filling stations, but five years later, after brief, unsuccessful retail experiments, the buildings remained empty and the lot unused.

In October 1992 another businessman, Roger Duba, began a long-term conflict with the DHPC when he hired a contractor to remove a concrete walk near a building formerly housing a pizza parlor and later used as a parking lot. Reportedly, when the concrete slab was removed, the prefab building constructed of porcelain and steel in 1939 slid off its foundation. The owner told the contractor to "do whatever you have to do to make it safe," and within fifteen minutes the building was demolished.[47] Since the building, within the historic district and governed by district ordinances, was destroyed without a permit, the commission directed its attorney to pursue full legal action and penalties against Duba, remedies including restoring the building on the site, not allowing any construction for three years except to replace the building, and a thousand-dollar-a-day fine until the building was reconstructed. The state commission on gaming threatened to take action against the license of Duba, who owned two gaming properties directly across the street. After almost two years of litigation the circuit court sided with Duba, noting that the one-thousand-dollar fine conflicted with state law, which limits such fines to $200 for "demolition by neglect," and, furthermore, that the two-hundred-dollar penalty is applicable only after an owner has been given thirty days' notice and access to a public hearing.[48]

A disastrous fire in December 1987 that destroyed the Syndicate Building provided fodder for additional conflicts, lawsuits, and resolution. Built in 1888, the Syndicate Building was a major element of the downtown historic district, as it housed F. L. Thorpe, manufacturer of "original" Black Hills gold jewelry. In April 1989, Achtien, owner of the property, was initially given a certificate of appropriateness to rebuild. When the certificate of appropriateness was later withdrawn because of a voting technicality, Achtien filed a 1.4-million-dollar suit against the city of Deadwood, Assistant State Attorney General Tom Harmon, and State Historic Preservation Officer Paul Putz for economic damages incurred as a result of their denial of his petition to build an eighty-foot-high, one-hundred-room, 6.8-million-dollar hotel that would have towered fifty feet above the space previously occupied by the Syndicate Building.[49] U.S. District Court Judge Richard Battey dismissed the suit in March 1993. In an effort to work with Achtien and in an effort to fill the hole left after the destruction of the Syndicate Building, the Historic Preservation Commission voted to allow construction of a building up to forty-three feet in height, an eight-foot variance over the present thirty-five-foot limit, but only if the new structure conformed to period architecture.[50] As of May

1997, no definite construction plans had been announced by Achtien, and the lot was for sale.

Finally, in a vain attempt to establish control over historic properties bordering the Deadwood historic district, the DHPC rejected a demolition request to raze the eighty-year-old Treber Ice House, a brick structure located at the edge of Deadwood on a narrow curve at the junction of Highways 85 and 385. Eighth Circuit Court Judge Timothy Johns ruled that the Ice House was outside of the Deadwood historic district.[51] The Historic Preservation Commission appealed to the South Dakota Supreme Court.[52] In 1997, the Ice House still stood in the curve of Highway 85.

These cases demonstrate the difficulty of providing tourist amenities other than gambling when property values escalate and historic preservation limits changes of physical structure. Moreover, these issues reflect the difficulty of the preservationist case in the face of "the independent attitude of the Westerner, and the region's strong tradition of property rights," in the words of William T. Frazier, director of the Western Regional Office of the National Trust.[53] As early as September 1993, Ron Island, in petitioning the demolition of a house at 121 Charles Street, reportedly stated, "I don't think you have a mandate from God that you can continue to take one of the major rights of property owners and continue to take this away from us. . . . There is a big perception out there that there is no balance."[54] Days later, Sam Shivers attacked Preservation Officer Wolfe by stating, "The City Commissioners should perform the duties they are elected to and not let Mark Wolfe run the town."[55] Obviously, "historic preservation" (the rationale for local option, limited stakes gaming) in fulfilling its mandate became a thorn to private enterprise; yet, through its rigorous interpretation of historic district ordinances and the Department of Interior guidelines for protecting historic properties, the DHPC also may have helped provide the competitive edge for Deadwood in the long run for the tourism market: that of historic integrity.

According to Michael Wallace, "Ada Louise Huxtable, architectural critic, argued that: 'Preservation is the job of finding ways to keep those original buildings that provide the city's character and continuity and of incorporating them into its living mainstream. Thus was born the doctrine of *adaptive reuse*. The exterior shell should be kept and the interior devoted to some profitable use.' "[56] Even with the best of historic intentions and a liberal interpretation of the idea of "adaptive reuse," the most that owners and historic preservation officers have been able to agree on or accomplish in Deadwood interiors are the retention of a few original tin ceilings, gigantic chandelier reproductions, some magnificent wooden bars, and

colorful Victorian carpeting. Otherwise, the uniformity of business enterprises—gambling, food, and drink—exhibits only minor variations in decor depending on the character celebrated (Calamity Jane, Wild Bill, Seth
Bullock) or the dream of winnings (Lucky Draw, Midnight Star, Golddiggers, etc.). There is nothing particularly historic about the slot machines
in Deadwood, except for one business that advertises historic slot machines. They are in a "museum" in the back of the building. No wonder,
then, that DHPC Officer Wolfe struggled with day-to-day minutiae, citizens' complaints about denial of rights, and the constant tug between
perceived individual profitability versus the common good found in preserving the historical context as well as particular buildings in Deadwood.

Colorado Preservation Efforts

Still, if in Deadwood gambling ironically facilitated the salvage of historically significant buildings yet contributed to the destruction of their
equally significant interiors, the South Dakota effort has been relatively
successful compared to the changes in the Colorado gaming towns. Substantial funds for historic preservation were made available in Central
City, Black Hawk, and Cripple Creek, but there are few mandates regarding their use. Facades in the business areas of Central City have been
restored, but only one bar, without gambling, has attempted real interior
historic preservation. In Black Hawk, most of the space is occupied by
new construction, some of it massive, as allowed by the wider canyon
along Clear Creek as opposed to the two narrow streets and steep side
hills of Central City.

As Deadwood was undergoing its transformation from being on the
National Park Service's "most endangered" list to receiving an award for
service in 1993, the three National Historic Landmarks in Colorado,
Central City, Black Hawk, and Cripple Creek, on the other hand, were
downgraded in 1992 by the National Park Service from a priority two to a
priority one. This designation places all three on the "most endangered"
list, because of the gutting and demolition of historic buildings and the
"incompatible new construction" in those towns with the advent of casino gambling.[57] Arguably, a case could be made that gaming was not the
culprit; rather, the existing disinvestment and deterioration associated
with aging communities caught them in the throes of economic and population decline. In 1992 then Central City Historic Preservation Officer
Alan Granruth made a strong case that the reclassification was based on
data preceding gaming, yet by late 1996 the towns' National Historic
Landmark designations were still in jeopardy.[58]

The intervening years witnessed the destruction of historic buildings (i.e., the Masonic Lodge and the Red Lantern in Cripple Creek),[59] the rehabilitation of some National Historic Landmark buildings (i.e., the schoolhouse in Black Hawk),[60] the restoration of facades (i.e., Harrah's in Central City), and the construction of elephantine "period" gaming casinos designed to look like turn-of-the-century mine and milling operations (i.e., Harvey's in Central City) or railroad stations (i.e., CCRR in Black Hawk). Preservation, at least of commercial properties, in these Colorado towns is best described by the rubric of facadism or what Wallace called "facadectomy or facadomy," referring to redevelopment that tears down old buildings entirely, except for their streetfront wall, leaving little more than a historic veneer.[61]

Colorado's preservation funding (unlike Deadwood's) deliberately excluded commercial properties, thereby resulting in owners' reliance on private capital for restoration, a legislative detail that encouraged facadism accompanied by new construction of greater magnitude than the razed structure. In fact, the *Rehabilitation Standards for the City of Black Hawk,* prepared by Nore V. Winter (1993), states that commercial buildings should "maintain the original size and shape of the storefront opening" along with exterior windows, recessed entries, if they exist, and kickplaces and transoms below and above display windows. There is no mention of interiors or the dimensions of the "reconstructed building." Incentives for facadism in both Black Hawk and Central City lie as well in

New "period" construction for Silver Hawk Casino in Black Hawk.

their prohibition against the use of historic preservation funds for interior restoration except for maintaining the integrity of the building (i.e., foundation stabilization work or replacement of electrical wiring that is a hazard to the safety of a historic building).[62]

Yet while Black Hawk and Central City endorsed rehabilitation guidelines that encouraged facadism, Cripple Creek Historic Preservation Officer Brian Levine, when queried about Cripple Creek losing its National Historic Landmark designation, noted, "I get defensive about this. . . . I think I've had enough I can take of being called a facadomizer." According to *Rocky Mountain News* reporter Mary Chandler, in discussing development versus preservation, "Preservation officials in the three gambling towns . . . begin a not-so-slow boil when their work is questioned. They say they have taken the heat from investors, developers, and architects for more than a year, holding the line as best they can against powerful development pressure from people who have no stake in the towns' history."[63]

Like Deadwood, Cripple Creek and Central City used historic preservation funds to improve existing and to develop new city infrastructures such as lighting, sidewalks, curbs, and municipal buildings and to restore and support local tourist attractions such as the Cripple Creek Museum and cemeteries in Cripple Creek and Central City. Black Hawk produced an hour-long video oral history of the town, including various

Creekside "mill" construction for Harvey's Casino, the largest hotel/casino in Central City with more than one thousand gaming devices.

views of current changes. Acting somewhat as a maverick, Black Hawk also opened its preservation funds to local citizens for restoration and preservation of private homes, requiring only a simple two-page application. Initially, grants were for a maximum of $10,000 per year per property with most funding for improvements to exteriors (some funds were allocated to bring interior electrical, plumbing, and heating up to city code).[64] By November 1994, excess preservation funds had led the city council to discuss raising the maximum to $20,000 per year per property. Thus far no private residence has been refused funding.[65] In order to reduce the prospect of speculation based on "free improvement to private real property," grants are subject to prorated payback based on improved valuation if the property is sold within five years.

In spite of all three communities having developed ordinances designed to protect their historic downtowns, what is not facadism tends to be fill-in, the construction of new buildings with period architecture, or what Black Hawk calls restoration: "one reproduces the appearance of a building exactly as it looked at a particular moment in time; to reproduce a pure style—either interior or exterior."[66]

True, historic preservation committees in all three communities have attempted to protect their National Historic Landmark District designations and have won occasional battles with developers in regard to maintaining facades, signage (inappropriate lights and signs), roof lines, and

Historic facades that front Harrah's Casino in Central City.

restoration of some interiors. Yet developers have appealed to legitimate concerns regarding "life safety" in aging, unkempt, uneconomical (in their former lives), deteriorating buildings with renovation and rehabilitation taking precedence over preservation. The difficulty of preserving the past when preservation confronts millions of dollars of investment funds for large-scale limited stakes gaming is attested to by the fact that of the three original historic preservation officers in the Colorado gambling towns, none is still directing historic preservation efforts. The longest lasting, Brian Levine of Cripple Creek, admitted to failures, including the razing of three historic Cripple Creek buildings: a turn-of-the-century meat market, the Masonic Lodge, and the Red Lantern (reportedly a black bordello of the late 1800s). More recently, historic preservationists were surprised when Canyon Casino in Black Hawk proposed moving the Carpenter Gothic Lace House Museum, a residence built in 1863 shortly after gold was discovered in Gregory Gulch, plus six other historic residences to a "historic village" to make room for a casino parking lot.[67]

Overall, preservation efforts in Colorado have taken a vastly different path from the one taken in Deadwood, partly because of earmarked legislative funds and laws regarding the number and location of gaming devices in Deadwood, and partly because of the lack of strong local ordinances and/or will to resist the juggernaut of economic growth based on large-scale casino gaming in Colorado. In an October 1990 editorial opposing Amendment 4, which would legalize gaming in three mountain towns, Clark Strickland, director of Denver's Mountains/Plains Regional Office of the National Trust for Historic Preservation, was clairvoyant in his prediction that "gaming will be permitted not only in historic buildings, but also in buildings that look historic." Authentic historic buildings could be demolished and replaced by new "pseudo-historic" structures that are more convenient for gaming tables and machines. He foresaw that Cripple Creek, Central City, and Black Hawk would "degenerate into collections of fake 'historic' buildings housing nothing but gambling operations."[68] Strickland's clear vision of the future, based partially on the tremendous economic changes that had occurred in Deadwood, if not the popularity of his stance on Amendment 4, proved fundamentally accurate.

Granted, the three Colorado gaming towns have received appreciable gaming revenues earmarked for historic preservation, have experienced ongoing conflicts between the economics of large-scale, limited stakes gaming and preservation of gold rush turn-of-the-century architecture and communities' structures, and have seen tremendous capital investments, both public and private. At least in regard to historic preservation, the real beneficiary of gaming has been the Colorado State Historical Association. The historical society receives 28.2 percent of the state revenues from gaming for statewide historic preservation projects. Dispersal of funds is based on a competitive grants program with a maximum grant of $75,000. The director of the grants project, Craig Hunter, noted that historic preservation in Colorado has been "sort of like insurance—someone has to die before you collect—with the state gaining the benefits while the three gaming communities died, at least in terms of historic preservation."[69] Hunter noted that by fiscal year 1993 the state had funded 467 different projects worth approximately $18 million involving 58 of 62 Colorado counties. Thus, enabling legislation provided substantial statewide funding of historic preservation at the expense of the historic integrity of the three gaming communities in Colorado, while in South Dakota the historic integrity of Deadwood has been emphasized at the expense of statewide historic preservation projects.

Conflicting Contentions in Central City

The conflicts between private profit associated with gaming and a commitment to civic pride, historic preservation of buildings, and the maintenance of the classical music tradition are exemplified by the Central City Opera House Association's (CCOHA) actions since gaming became legal. The CCOHA has felt trapped between the finances of gaming and its sixty-two-year-old mission to preserve the history of Central City, particularly the Opera House and its physical milieu. The transformation of CCOHA's initial ambivalence about gaming into its aggressive participation, albeit as a second party, is, if not a model, at least indicative of the economic and social structural changes taking place in all three Colorado towns.

Preceding the December 17, 1990, CCOHA panel vote concerning the possible conversion of the 118-year-old Teller Hotel into a casino, board chair Landis Martin noted that the association wanted to be supportive of the city's gaming effort. "We think some limited form of gambling would be in keeping with the character of that Western town that's had gambling many times over the years."[70] Incidental to the panel's investigation were the continual fifty-thousand-dollar annual deficits in maintaining the Teller House and its operations. The three-story Teller House and adjacent 756-seat Opera House are two of some thirty properties valued at $2,995,000 owned by the CCOHA. On January 24, 1991, the study panel submitted to all fifty board members a report favoring gaming, so long as it would be compatible with the summer opera festival. Landis Martin emphasized that gaming would supplement current activities at the Teller House and that the panel did not "want the gambling to be an annoyance to our opera patrons." The panel stressed the dual mission of CCOHA: the summer festival and historic preservation. Based on the panel's recommendation, Martin said, "We will only participate in any kind of gambling so long as it's consistent with those kinds of objectives (festival and preservation)."[71] They were strong words indeed, but not surprising given that Central City gambling had long been integral to the summer opera festival.

However, by July 10, 1991, CCOHA had signed a 31.5-year lease with JPC/Tivolino, a Swiss firm. JPC/Tivolino initially expected to spend at least $3 million to renovate the first floor as a gaming/bar area and the second floor as a restaurant and museum that would display artifacts of the Teller House.[72] Under the agreement JPC/Tivolino paid all expenses associated with gambling renovations plus a base rent and a piece of the gambling revenue to the CCOHA. By opening night, Teller House's "modest" gaming beginnings, complementary to its other activities, had mushroomed into a gigantic operation featuring more than 250 gaming devices. By fall 1992, the second floor buffet dining room had been gutted to expand the number of gaming devices to 442 slots, 6 blackjack tables, and 2 poker tables with total expenditures topping $7 million.[73]

By August 1993 the complicity and dependency of the CCOHA on gaming interests and revenues were made apparent through the two-million-dollar loan from the Teller House casino to help build a new rehearsal facility. Repayment, delayed until the completion of the facility, came in the form of rent reductions.[74] Thus, the Teller House moved from an annual $50,000 deficit to being a revenue producer and subsidizer of loans to benefit the opera festival. Ironically, as profitability became more assured, attendance at the festival dropped by 15 percent the first year of gaming and remained about 8 percent below peak seasons thereafter, returning only recently to pregaming attendance levels. Thus, despite tremendous increases in tourism, inconsistencies between opera festival activities and gaming continue.

States, Legislation, and Historic Preservation

There are very real limitations to historic preservation in the presence of low stakes gambling, which is defined most prominently and profitably by slot machines. The gaming devices, while intended to provide exciting variations on the business of dropping in coins and pulling a handle, are all essentially metal and plastic, with bright flashing lights, loud and repetitive musical jingles, and colorful moving parts.

Different rules about the number of slot machines permissible in an establishment have made the building of Las Vegas–style casinos much more possible and attractive in Colorado, where Harvey's, with its thousand-plus gaming devices, seems to be the specter of the future. While Deadwood limits the number of slot machines in each "building" to thirty, some establishments have been able to claim that they occupy more than one original building and therefore are entitled to as many as ninety devices (these limitations are imposed on owners, not buildings, by the state of South Dakota). Colorado regulations only limit slots to 35 percent of a building's total floor space or 50 percent of any one floor, not counting aisles, change booths, or even the stools patrons sit on. Therefore, new buildings with lower ceilings, balconies, and densely spaced machinery are a better investment than an old Victorian storefront.

As a result of differential state policies, in Deadwood one prime lot that had contained F. L. Thorpe, manufacturer of the original Black Hills gold jewelry, has remained empty since a fire in 1987 because the DHPC will not approve a plan for a six-story hotel in that part of the historic district. Central City and Black Hawk now have two Bullwhackers casinos, with 1,350 slot machines and 800 employees, one of them in a new three-story building. Harvey's in Central City, with its exploding mine shaft and arcade as entertainment for the family, advertises access to more than a thousand gaming devices. In Cripple Creek, expansion of the gold rush theme emphasizes the enormous. Essentially, the rule in Colorado gambling is "the bigger, the better."

Thus, divergent state gaming legislation has resulted in two different development patterns. The first, in Colorado, focuses on a few large casinos that have preserved the facade of the late 1800s while razing the remainder of the building to gain floor space; their main attraction is the contemporary gamble on the quick buck. The second, in Deadwood, involves legislation that restricts gaming to thirty devices per building, thereby encouraging gaming in many "limited" gaming establishments ("the more, the better"), yet with the same main attraction—the gamble for the quick buck. Although the attraction is identical, the means of enticing the gamers has differed.

The central question is, what difference do legislative mandates make for the gaming communities and their states? By 1997 involvement of state and local municipalities in the two states forced a reevaluation of Eisinger's model of state enterpreneurism. Obviously, in both states local governments have not only become dependent on gaming revenues but are active participants in touting gaming. As a consequence, endangered historic relics that stand to gain the most from economic development spin-offs from gaming are perhaps also most endangered by this benevolence. In confronting the unique boomtown growth offered by gaming, it is problematic to determine what, if anything, will remain of the historic integrity of the "boom" communities.

Barbara Pahl, the director of the National Trust's Mountains/Plains Regional Office, refers to gambling as a rapid-growth issue; "otherwise, people cannot deal rationally with the impacts because of all the money involved."[75] They are boomtowns, to be sure, but their rapid growth is characterized by economic units and revenues, not by the resident population increases that usually denote boomtowns. Rather, the population boom is temporal, composed of either daily commuters and gamers or short-term tourists whose commitment to the four communities is utilitarian. Gaming tourist impacts on the four communities are also seasonal, unlike boomtowns that experience rapid and permanent population growth. Even the gentrification of historic preservation takes an odd twist, for while downtown businesses that have undergone economic transformation are more profitable and more attractive on the surface, other permanent structural community components such as housing and schools have so far been mostly unaffected.

Evidence suggests that limited stakes, local option gambling has been successful beyond all expectations in attracting gamers, gaming action, gross gaming revenue, and taxes for state and local government. Gambling revenues provided the funds to rebuild deteriorating city infrastructures such as water and sewage systems; city streets, curbs, and gutters; and a newly restored courthouse in Deadwood. A new Gilpin County courthouse and Central City city hall were built in Colorado. In addition, historic preservation funds coupled with private investments in gaming parlors have generated over $80 million and $200 million in new and restoration construction in Deadwood and Colorado, respectively. Questions remain about what the towns will have gained by way of historic preservation and investment in infrastructure if this tourist hand plays out. In any case, they are the current big attraction in small towns of the Rocky Mountain West.

CHAPTER 6

Community Transformation in the Gamble

In September 1994, as Deadwood approached its fifth anniversary of legalized gambling, Jeffry Bloomberg, Lawrence County state's attorney, testified before a congressional hearing on the impacts this political and economic decision had imposed on his community and county. Telling the House Committee on Small Business that until November 1988 he had had no background or interest in the issues related to casino gambling, he had, subsequent to the legalization of gambling in Deadwood, been contacted by dozens of journalists, government officials, and private citizens seeking information on the effects of casino gambling on a small community. "Since that time, as I have traveled to various states which have been considering casino gambling, the promoters of gambling have uniformly made the same pitch, 'economic development, new jobs and lower taxes.' While these goals appear lofty, I believe that it is imperative that government leaders and citizens scrutinize these claims very closely before opening the Pandora's Box of gambling because as we have learned in Deadwood, once gambling is legalized it is virtually an irrevocable decision."[1] The contents of Pandora's box for various groups of citizens and for the social institutions in gambling communities provide the rubric for this chapter. The seemingly irreversible choice poses an even larger problem, which we explore as well.

The Human Consequences in Deadwood

Clearly, at least in Deadwood, many business property owners fared well for the most part. The bravest of entrepreneurs who took advantage of historic preservation programs that would hold their property taxes to the prerestoration valuation of their structures for eight years, those who could afford to invest some $55 million in private funds, and those whose businesses were on the central blocks of Main Street garnered enormous profits almost immediately. But not all did so well, and Bloomberg reported that while only a handful of casinos had closed in the first five years, over half still claimed that they were operating at a loss. On the other hand, those investors who combined ownership of multiple casinos appeared to be making handsome profits.

Retail Conveniences. Other business people, especially those who provided retail outlets or skilled trades, had a hard time holding on to the space from which to offer their wares or services. Even with huge investments in remodeling and building, the 1993 Deadwood-Lead Chamber of Commerce listed only one contractor from Lead and another from Rapid City, one electrician and one plumber from Deadwood, and two Deadwood hardware stores. In contrast, there were thirty-six restaurant members, some with Spearfish and Rapid City addresses, twenty-three of which were gaming establishments in Deadwood. Eight of the twenty-four hotel and motel members in Lead and Deadwood were also gaming establishments.[2] Of the six tourist attractions listed in Deadwood, four were tours, one was a wax museum, and the other was a reenactment of the trial of Jack McCall.

So Deadwood continued to be a tourist town, now one that not only drew a million tourists a year rather than the previous 250,000 but also attracted tourists who wanted primarily to eat, drink, and gamble. Sensitive to this image, on the fifth anniversary of legalized gaming, the Deadwood Tourist Bureau took the public relations position of "making steady progress." Eileen Haberling, marketing director, made the claim in the local newspaper that the town now had nearly three times as many nongaming activities and attractions than pregaming Deadwood had to offer.[3] However, in a follow-up telephone interview, Haberling mentioned not only the long-running production *The Trial of Jack McCall* and the Broken Boot Mine Tour at the edge of town but also the Homestake Mine tours in Lead and natural attractions, such as trout fishing and hiking, of the Black Hills area. Indeed, the only new nongaming recreation developed by the city was the "urban section" of the walking trail along Whitewood Creek, which joins the Mickelson Trail being developed the length of the Black Hills. "[Nongaming] recreation has not changed a lot," she admitted, "but we are trying to build on what we had."[4] One resort casino on the south edge of town had built a trailer park and campground and added a video arcade, miniature golf, bumper boats, and a go-cart track to its convention center, but the amusements at Gulches of Gold were closed for the winter, and there was no sign of recent convention activity there in mid-November 1996.

The official position of local gaming boosters was that before gambling "Deadwood was on its way to becoming a ghost town." Then-mayor Bruce Oberlander echoed that sentiment in explaining the fates of three auto dealerships.

> We lost some of our retail, but in my mind, and I think in a lot of people's minds, some of the retail was destined for history anyway. I didn't like seeing the Oldsmobile garage go from here because, you know, I'd drop my car off in the morning at eleven o'clock, it'd be serviced, and I'd go home. Now I've got to get somebody else to do it on a different schedule. Or if I need car parts or something, I've gotta go to Spearfish. But you know that business sold prior to gaming, and it was destined to head to Spearfish anyway. And the other two were family businesses; well, Ford was a family business, and it was going basically from hand to mouth. There was no debt service there, so they could afford to be in business in Deadwood. When gaming came it was obvious that they could afford it a lot better to get the money and run rather than try to maintain the business, and that's what they did.[5]

But if it's hard to find people who will argue about whether retail flight was inevitable, resignation didn't always come happily. One Deadwood employee remarked, "I get a big kick out of all these ads from the Chamber of Commerce that say, 'Shop at home; spend your money at home.' But there's no place to shop." And another: "Of course I don't like Rapid City. I'm not a mall shopper in the first place."[6] One of them recounted a recent inquiry by a potential western wear retailer with whom she had spoken, but all of the empty buildings she had suggested were either too small or too expensive for a business that might appeal to both local customers and the tourist trade. Another women's clothing boutique that had moved down from the troubled Twin City Mall in Lead had also closed down, and so had its successor.

Employment Opportunities. The positive perspective on gaming for working people derives from the increased availability of jobs. Initially, Michael Madden's report to the South Dakota Commission on Gaming had predicted as many as 1,500 new jobs, or 1,200 jobs in gaming plus 600 ancillary jobs, but by 1996 it was reporting 1,719 jobs.[7] But to talk of an employment boom that would rebuild Deadwood (or Lead) would be misleading, for in the first seven years of gaming there had been almost no net increase in housing in Deadwood or in the adjacent areas. So most of the workers were commuters from other parts of Lawrence and adjoining Meade, Butte, and Pennington Counties. Moreover, when the visitors bureau claimed that the new jobs "have replaced what used to be mainly seasonal work," it neglected all the evidence of cyclical gaming and consequent fluctuating employment. To point out seasonality does not make the employment without merit. Given the fact that most of the jobs are also part-time service jobs that do not require elaborate qualifications apart from a record that satisfies a security check and licensing procedures, many students from Black Hills State University, teachers from the Lead-Deadwood area, and early retirees from Homestake were able to fill those positions during the peak summer months. Mary Ticknor, principal of the Deadwood Middle School, said that nearly all her teachers worked in the casinos in the summer months.[8]

But gaming work is by no means "extra" work or "pin money" for many local residents. Some people have been working in Deadwood since legalized gambling began in 1989. Donna Franke, a lifelong resident of Lawrence County and someone who has done wage work for her entire adult life, is a blackjack dealer at one of Deadwood's fifty-three tables. Widely considered to be one of the best jobs in gambling, because dealers get tips in addition to their tuxedo costumes, which lend the aura of a real casino to Deadwood's gaming parlors, Donna Franke's work and that of her husband, Kenny, who also deals blackjack, has been professionally satisfying if not meteoric.[9]

Donna Franke began working in Deadwood in the booming summer period of July 1990 but was laid off the first October during the first seasonal downturn by employers with Nevada backing that soon pulled out. She found no more work in Deadwood until the next April, when she went to work for a local entrepreneur whose small casino was a bit too far down Main Street; not even lingerie shows as part of an early entertainment effort could sustain the business. Both the Nugget and Poker Alice's were early casualties of the initial economic shakedown. But by May 1991, Franke had found work at the newly refurbished Bullock Hotel in the old Ayres Building, opened by owner-manager Mary Schmit, who was also active on the Deadwood Historic Preservation Commission. Four and a half years later Donna and her husband still worked at the Bullock, finding meeting new people to be the most satisfying aspect of their positions and parking to be the worst.[10]

Vicky Hendrickson also grew up in the rural part of the county, graduated from Lead High School, and lived and worked in Deadwood as a young single mother. Her perspective on the transformation of Deadwood was even more complex. "Fifteen years ago, before I moved to

Colorado, I lived in Deadwood. I had a good job. I worked for [local attorney] Clinton Richards. I had the best job in town. I probably was making $5 an hour then. And I was raising four kids. . . . I had a four-bedroom apartment on Main Street that I paid $150 a month for. I tell you what: I come back; everybody is making $5 an hour. They're paying $450 a month rent. They're trying to make a car payment. They can't do it."[11]

Both women were reluctant to discuss wages directly, especially of people in other job categories, "because you know, that's a secret. We don't discuss wages." But they generally offered that many jobs depended on tips but that tips, even for blackjack dealers, did not exceed wages. Also, pay raises come early but stretch out after awhile. Few employees have insurance plans with fewer than three years' work. No one knew of employer-sponsored retirement programs other than Social Security.

Nevertheless, some creative benefits have appeared. Since most employees commute, one casino with backing by an oil company provided a tank of gas a week to at least some employees, and Hendrickson thought that was as good as a raise. Perhaps not all employees are as satisfied, however, as this business was the site of the first effort to unionize workers in 1995. Other casinos encouraged coworkers to choose an employee of the month, with a fifty- or one-hundred-dollar prize given to the winner and smaller prizes (dinner or $10) to other nominees and the nominators.

While generally positive about not only their own employment but how gambling has improved Deadwood "from a place that was just about boarded up," gaming workers face a peculiar set of working conditions. Some aspects are familiar to other service workers—most profitable hours are nighttimes and weekends; they spend lots of time on their feet; they have uniform dress requirements. Donna Franke resented a little that while costume expectations for her coworkers had been loosened to polo shirts and slacks, blackjack dealers still had to wear tuxedo shirts and bow ties, regardless of the weather. Most places other than the Midnight Star had stopped hiring cocktail waitresses for body type and willingness to wear Gay Nineties bar girl attire. But everybody works in the presence of cigarette smoke, depending on the quality of the filtration system, for few establishments have no-smoking sections, even in their restaurants. The biggest complaint is the continuous noise of the slot machines. Donna wished there could be an experiment to determine if a section with lower jingle levels would have fewer or more patrons. But she said, "The only time I hear that jangly noise is when I'm stressed. Pull your hair out, you know. Otherwise, it's just blocked out."[12]

But the relatively low pay of waitressing, bartending, and change-making positions also made dual worker families ubiquitous. The twenty-four-hour work day (since in the summer Deadwood casinos never close) plus the pattern of asking food service personnel to work split shifts put additional strains on families with small children. In 1996, Lead and Deadwood had only one licensed day-care center and only eight to ten registered day-care homes in the two towns, no more than in 1989, when gambling opened.[13]

Social Services. Casino workers reported, "A lot of people ask about babysitting services; why doesn't Deadwood have babysitting services for visitors?" But one thought it would be difficult for someone to run a business without a steady guaranteed clientele, with insurance and strict regulations about provider/client ratios. "How do you know if you're going to have twenty kids this hour and two the next?"[14] Reminded that one casino had a hawker outside shouting, "Do you know where your kids are?" and inviting them into a basement arcade, another worker responded that it was for "older kids, not for little kids." She did say that she sent a lot of people up there. The current casino solution is to impose an early evening curfew on children, even though there is nothing for them to do either inside or outside the gaming establishments.

Child Protection Services Director Lora Hawkins reported having more and more referrals when both parents were in the gaming industry. Hawkins thought part of the pattern was historical. Having been a supervisor in the area since 1980, she observed,

> We have a reputation for easy employment in the mines or gaming. . . . Lawrence County always had the highest DWI per capita in the state. We've always had our share of unusual people who chose to locate here. . . . It's an individualist's place, a cool place to go. After that we have people who don't fit other places: families who have had trouble with their relatives, those with poor employment records and work histories, people who have had trouble with the law, chemical dependency problems, folks who have struggled other places before they chose to come here. . . . We've always had the thing with the miners' "live for the day" attitude. On money, for instance. They've had healthy incomes, but because of very stressful and physically demanding work, they've always said, "Let's buy this. Don't have the money for it, but let's buy it." The difference now is that families have a new major economic stressor in gambling.[15]

Hawkins worried about problem gambling as well as problems in employment, but her view of the work climate in Deadwood was echoed by the Reverend Chuck Horner, pastor of the First Methodist Church in Deadwood (located just a block off the busiest intersection on Main

Street). By May 1992 he was ready to leave town. Having been an active guide in Alaska for twenty-four years, he was interested in the tourist industry but felt completely "frozen out" by the Chamber of Commerce and other community organizations. Part of the problem was undoubtedly his critical stance.

> Deadwood has sold its soul. . . . We've had some bad incidents late at night. And my wife is tired of it. We're only half a block off Main Street, and we get a lot of people who need a tank of gas to get back to Nebraska or whatever. And we're right between two Veterans Hospitals, one in Hot Springs and one in Sturgis. There are some very scary mental cases. I'm a pretty big guy and I'm not used to being intimidated, but I have been intimidated on my own front porch.
>
> The Ministerial Association has a good arrangement worked out with the police. They send people over for us to screen, we fill out the forms, and then they give them enough emergency assistance for rooms or meals or to get out of town.[16]

Then–Lawrence County sheriff Chuck Crotty confirmed the increase in "undesirables," in Deadwood, "transient people who think they'll make it rich, lose their money, and can't get out of town. We buy them a bus ticket or five dollars' worth of gas. They think they'll get rich for five dollars or fifty cents."[17]

Lucille Tracey, who in 1977 had helped start a food pantry called the Lord's Cupboard in the United Methodist Church in Lead, said that at the beginning the volunteers provided on average food for one family per month. Now the call comes from about 40 to 50 families per month, and in October through December 1992, 160 families had received food. Open from 9:00 A.M. to noon daily, Tracey said demands for assistance nearly doubled when gambling began. By May 1992 volunteers had to limit food distribution to once a month per family, even though the gaming houses provided some assistance, particularly turkeys at holidays. The Lord's Cupboard had made small loans as well—$300 to hire a tow truck and $210 to someone released from prison on a gambling debt charge and waiting for a Social Security check. That one had been paid back. Tracey reported requests from travelers from nearly every state, including Puerto Rico, and many from southern states but remembered no one from North Dakota or Minnesota. Some were families with as many as seven children. And she too offered that the local solution was "to provide help to get them out of state."[18]

Tracey's portrayal was of homeless transients who were not simply roving gamblers but people looking for work. She said the problem lay in advertisements in newspapers saying "gambling provides good work." But gambling jobs were not necessarily high paying, and those that required licensing also necessitated a waiting period for a security check. Tracey said men used to be able to find work at Homestake, but the company had experienced two big layoffs in the last decade. Many recent arrivals were unemployed and broke in their previous location. "They come here with nothing. If they do get work, many have brought in groceries to pay back their assistance."[19] It was difficult to accumulate very much cash. Tracey said that once gaming had arrived, rents went up from the past, when it was possible to rent an apartment with two bedrooms for $100 to $125 per month. In addition, vacant houses had been bought by gaming establishments to rent to their workers.

In reporting to the South Dakota governor on the impact of gambling on Lawrence County, county commission chair George Opitz cited the expenditure of $171,256.86 in services to indigent people in 1991, with $13,788 in rental assistance alone. He wrote, "Most applicants are people that have come to find work in Deadwood and need help with rent, utilities, etc., until they find a job. Then when gambling slows down in the winter months, they are back for assistance when they get laid off. These people usually do not have health insurance; thus it falls on the county's shoulders to pay medical bills."[20]

Senior Citizens. If gambling provided promise but no automatic opportunities for working people, it provided almost no advantages for elderly townsfolk. Retail outlets for men's and women's ready-to-wear had disappeared. In the words of the retiring sheriff, "I have to drive sixty miles to buy a pair of socks!" Only one grocery store in Deadwood remained, and some older people felt uncomfortable having to run the gauntlet of slot machines to get from the check-out stands to the door. Other forces seemed to have conspired against retail services in the Lead-Deadwood area, for a slow-moving landslide had made the Twin City Mall, constructed with Deadwood Urban Development Action Grant funds, uninhabitable. While the Alco discount store had moved into the Lead National Guard Armory (displacing the day-care center), the Sun Mart grocery simply closed its doors for many months. A damaged caselot-grocery had opened in one of the vacant Lead Main Street buildings, but the stairs and high curbs plus the necessity of crossing the street (which is also U.S. Highway 85) from the closest parking spaces made this inexpensive alternative difficult for senior citizens to reach. Many of the senior citizens in Deadwood had moved elsewhere. The inexpensive downtown walk-up apartments had either been turned into gaming establishment

Slot machines in the front aisle of Deckers Food Center, the only grocery store in Deadwood.

offices or were now renting for $450 to $500 per month, with no parking accommodations.[21]

For retirees, recreation was ironically one of the great losses from gambling. Deadwood had no senior center at all. The Lead Senior Center invited Deadwood residents to participate in its programs, but only those who could drive came up for an aerobics class or an occasional potluck dinner. Since the Lead-Deadwood shuttle bus had closed down, a cab ride cost four dollars each way.[22] Notably, the bowling alley in Deadwood had been torn down to make room for a casino. "These have always been bowling towns," said one woman. "I used to bowl three times a week. Now I have to drive clear to Spearfish to bowl. Now my husband, he don't bowl at all and I've gone once." Indeed, the Homestake Recreation Center, abandoned by the company in 1972, had featured a very popular bowling alley. Subsequently, a larger bowling venue had been opened where the Gulches of Fun video arcade (and casino) now stood between the two towns. No movie theaters were left in either town, although the seniors figured there were more video stores than anything else besides casinos. Rising rents meant that for the first time in the century there was no flower shop in Lead or Deadwood. Seniors missed that feature on holidays and when friends were ill. The fact that we were invited to interview the group following the afternoon bingo game spoke to their gambling inclinations.

Property Taxes. In addition, homeowners early on faced rising property taxes. Since South Dakota has no state income tax or major sources of revenue such as Wyoming's Mineral Severance Tax, property taxes had long been both relatively high and volatile. Deadwood homeowners first felt the impact of gambling when they received their 1991 property tax assessment. Although ostensibly a commercial real estate reassessment mandated by a statewide directive, anyone who lived along Main Street now found their property values based on transactions in the speculation boom of 1989 and 1990. Said Lyle Wendall, former head of the state Department of Revenue and currently of Statewide Real Estate Service, Inc., hired by Lawrence County for the reassessment, "Sales establish the market value, and the state constitution requires that property be assessed at market value. . . . Maybe it's overpriced," he responded to a startled homeowner whose appraised value on his house jumped from $15,000 to $177,000, "but we can't speculate on the future. We only have the past market to look at. If values start to fall the county will have to assess again. . . . We do have a property tax, and it does require market value appraisal."[23]

Not only were private and commercial property owners in Deadwood hit by rising taxes, agricultural property owners in the county discovered that regardless of their location, terrain, or principal enterprise, their land was suddenly regarded as potential development property, again based on a few land sales at high prices, increasing the taxes per acre by a factor of 2.5 (a potential increase of $20 million for the county). Meanwhile, the state had just dropped the commonly assessed value of utility property in the county by $20 million.[24] Several gold mines appealed their assessments, precipitating a suit by the Lead-Deadwood school district. The beneficiary of the largest portion of tax revenue, it was hurt not only by decreased utility assessments but, ironically, by increased local property assessments, which had the effect of decreasing its entitlement to state aid.[25]

As Deadwood's assessed valuation in 1988 increased from $12.9 to $91.3 million in 1995, its mill levy decreased from $24.4 to $8.2 million.[26] Thus, while assessed valuation increased more than sevenfold, mill levies decreased by two thirds. Virtually all of the increased valuation came from gaming investments.

So the increases in property values had complex interlocking effects on nearly all business people, homeowners, and even schoolchildren. A certain regional loyalty from people who had spent their lifetimes in Lead and Deadwood made some hopeful that a new, integrated community would eventually reemerge. Some even imagined it atop the slag dump arising from the expanding open pit mining in lower Lead, re-creating a town where Terraville had once been before pit mining, once again "with the best view in the Hills."[27]

Young People. Children were less sanguine. At the Deadwood Middle School, across the street from the Silverado Casino, about half thought they would leave the area when they could. This is not a significant proportion; most adolescents probably express dissatisfaction with their lot. But the most interesting division was between kids who liked being in Deadwood and Lead (the school district has been combined since 1976) primarily for the beautiful scenery and outdoor activities, including skiing, snowmobiling, and hunting in the winter and hiking and camping in the summer, and those who felt "there was nothing to do" in a community that had no malls, no theaters, and little recreation directed at teens, despite the fact that the Deadwood Recreation Center had just reopened after major restoration.[28]

Ironically, Principal Ticknor did not worry specifically about the casinos that faced the middle school and lined the street for five blocks to the north on Main Street. "There's no place for them to go besides school." She recounted an incident in which two students had a mid-morning appointment with someone on Main Street. Two different casino workers had called to say, "There are kids walking down the street." So she felt that gambling had not affected school attendance.[29] Children were, in effect, so alien to the gambling business that their lives were isolated from it. She thought school attendance was generally enhanced by the fact that there was nothing else to do in Deadwood. Ticknor recognized problems of a transient school population, where students "who were new three years ago were now all gone," but she also attributed them to a culture of "miners' kids," arguing that Lead and Deadwood had always been "tough places."

Virginia Eastmo, Lead High School chemistry teacher, and her husband, Ron, a former high school coach and now a vocational education teacher at the Deadwood Middle School, had slightly different takes on the impact of gambling on high school students in the district. They related how very easy it was for youth to get jobs in Deadwood, to make minimum wage plus tips in a lot of cases. That was pretty good pay for high school students. Virginia hated that they fell asleep in class because they had worked until eleven. Ron said, "The average kid worked more hours to pay for cars and insurance than the students in distributive education worked for credit." They thought the motivations for working were pretty widespread, but there was more opportunity in Deadwood, and, in fact, the casinos probably depended on it. During the summer of 1993 Ron himself worked ten hours a week tending bar and washing dishes at the Deadwood Gulch Resort. He's licensed to deal and did about three hands, he said.[30]

Lora Hawkins, director of Child Protection Services for Lawrence County, felt that there were children's issues all along, most of which were not adequately reflected in published statistics or in the reports of people who used them. When first interviewed in October 1991, referring to the second report written by Michael Madden, she said, "They never asked us about caseloads, about families with special education needs, or what is really going on with law enforcement. Neither Sheriff Crotty nor State's Attorney Bloomberg were interviewed by Madden, who only looked at AFDC and food stamps" (which had declined slightly).

Hawkins reported over the course of interviews in 1991, 1992, and 1994 that individual intervention was limited by the size of her staff, rather than the number of cases reported. A caseload of 289 in fiscal year 1990 had increased to 325 for 1991, and she estimated a substantial increase to 440 or 450 the following year. What was not counted with reliability were the referrals that came to the office. With only one additional social worker since gaming began, the staff of five professionals and a paraprofessional who did parenting work had to screen out more and more referrals, although about half the increase in caseload involved families who worked in the Deadwood gambling industry while the other half mostly involved mining families. Since gambling, the child protection team had screened more cases, investigated a smaller proportion of them, and closed many that normally would have been recommended for intervention, because they could not follow up adequately to provide placement in foster homes for any but the worst situations. "Our problem is that we get many more referrals than we are able to handle. The burnout rate is high. Staff turnover is like a revolving door," Hawkins reported to the Lawrence County Commission in March 1991. In response to her report that more than five hundred children in Lawrence County were victims of child abuse the previous year, the commissioners reported shock. "I thought your office was just helping families pay the rent and buy groceries. I never realized this was going on," said Commissioner Hank Frawley.[31]

In 1992 Hawkins had been working with the police chief to record cases of children left in cars while their parents either gambled or worked in gambling establishments without available child care. Reports were not filed by police in most of the cases. Hawkins knew of incidents where children, age six, three, and two, were left alone in a car while their mother was working downtown; when the father appeared about forty-five minutes after having been called, the police decided not to file a report. In February a teacher had reported kids in a car to police, but no record of the incident was made. On a cold March day children had been left in a car with the motor running while their parents gambled at a local resort and went out to check on them every thirty minutes or so; again, no police report was filed. Hawkins suggested that the sheriff's dispatch logs, which were centralized for all police units in Lawrence County, be inspected, but the sheriff allowed that lots of departments keep two sets of logs because "lots of things are no one's business," including "a lot of domestic violence since gambling has come in." He granted that there had always been substantial violence because it was a mining town. "Lots of trivial things happen, not trivial to the people involved, but not something you need to report."[32]

As a parent, Lora Hawkins had gotten in some hot water with the city when she and other parents in the PTA protested the opening of a casino directly across the street from the Deadwood Middle School. Mayor Oberlander reported that event as having "raised the ire of some people" and used it as an example of things they had not planned for. Ultimately the city decided that if a casino was to be located within two hundred feet of the main entrance of a school or medical facility, it had to come to the city for a conditional use permit. Oberlander was relatively unconcerned. "The gaming down there hasn't been a problem for the kids. It's probably less disruptive than a drugstore. No, it hasn't been a problem. Kids in Deadwood have walked past bars for a long time, prostitution on the way to school, and things like that. Nobody has made a big deal out of it, so it isn't a forbidden fruit."[33] Nevertheless, by 1996, there was public consideration of selling the school building and moving the middle school population to Lead.

Law Enforcement. If Oberlander's description of the town's comfort with a culture of vice replicates almost exactly Lowell Thomas's memories of brothels on the way to school in Victor in the 1920s,[34] other locals thought the scene had changed in ways that were costly at least. In a letter to Governor George Mickelson on March 3, 1992, George Opitz, chairman of the Lawrence County Commissioners, documented the increase in law enforcement requirements since the advent of gambling. Asking that the county allocation of gaming revenues be increased from 10 to 12 percent of the state tax on gaming, Opitz reported that

> Law Enforcement has been the hardest hit department and budget for Lawrence County. This county had two armed robberies in the ten years prior to gaming and never a bank robbery. Since gaming, we have seen a gaming related bank robbery, a casino robbery, and a drug store armed robbery all within the last year and a half. General calls for service from answering questions to responding to all non-crime-related calls is [*sic*] up over 100 percent. The Sheriff's Office did 9,170 fingerprintings in 1990 compared to none in 1989. Additional personnel added since 1989 have been four full-time jailers, two full-time dispatchers, one full-time office clerk, upgraded one bookkeeper from part-time to full-time and one deputy. Lawrence County's jail is the only jail in the county. The total Sheriff personnel budget has increased $372,270 from the 1990 to 1992 budgets. There has been a 100 percent turnover in dispatchers since gaming due to overwhelming workload. Also we find it hard to compete with the gaming industry in wages. A [University of South Dakota] study shows a need for seventeen deputies. We operate with seven.[35]

Although the percentage rate of increase with such small numbers is overly dramatic, the numbers that Opitz cited were reported in the *Denver Post* as adjacent Jefferson County Commissioners asked the state of Colorado to anticipate increased crime in Gilpin County when gambling began there.[36] The figures showed changes between 1989 and 1990 crime rates in Lawrence County, with rape up 600 percent, simple assault up 33 percent, burglary up 300 percent, theft of over $200 up 1,000 percent, petty theft up 200 percent, forgery up 480 percent, bad checks for no funds up 55 percent, bad checks from no account up 87 percent, criminal sexual contact up 75 percent, driving under the influence of alcohol up 225 percent, and public drunkenness up 100 percent.[37]

Deadwood Mayor Oberlander's response to queries about increased crime was that

> what they have to do is educate the owners of the businesses and their employees not to take [bad] checks. That would solve some of the problem. Now I'm sure they've done some of that. But again, they beef up their statistics. We have had a tremendous increase in the number of incidents. Those relate to every time a false alarm goes off, that's a number. We had not had statistics like that before 1989 because we had no alarm system. So now you've got, I bet there's an average of one a day. That comes out 365 more incidents that happen in a year's time. The county says we've got all this crime. You know, that's not crime, but it is a call that somebody responds to. And you know, traffic tickets, you've got more traffic. [If] you arrest the same percentage of speeders, you're gonna have more now than you had before because there is [*sic*] more of them. Literally, the problems are people problems. People go downtown and they get to drinking a little too much beer and there's a crowd, and they start bumping elbows and pretty soon you might have a pushing and shoving match. It's either simple assault or disturbing the peace, and it goes down as an incident. But it's not a murder. Talk about the increase in crime! I'm sure there's a lot of big cities that would like to have the crime problem we've got in Deadwood. One homicide in three years.[38]

But Opitz's letter also detailed increased county court filings of 64 percent in civil cases, 71 percent in criminal cases, and 61 percent increase of juvenile filings, reflecting numerical increases of 111 civil, 171 criminal, and 26 juvenile filings, respectively.

State's Attorney Jeffry Bloomberg also reported the overall increases in civil, criminal, and juvenile filings in his congressional testimony, showing increases from pregaming year 1988 to the end of 1993 of 42 percent in Class 2 cases, 109 percent in Class 1 cases, and 72 percent in felonies, for an overall increase from 4,297 cases to 6,495 cases, or a 51 percent increase over five years. Bloomberg's testimony argued:

> While it is true that any increase in visitors will statistically result in higher crime rates than before, I believe that the type of visitors we are attracting results in crime numbers higher than in a more family oriented tourist community. . . . [T]here is a second category of increase that is due to the nature of gambling itself. It is this group that I find particularly disturbing

for we have seen individuals who, prior to their exposure to gambling, had no criminal history, who were not junkies or alcoholics, many of whom had good jobs, who became hooked on slot-machines and after losing all their assets and running all credit resources to their maximums began committing some type of crime to support their addiction.[39]

Bloomberg cited the cases that he had prosecuted: the pizza restaurant manager who had a spotless record and then embezzled $45,000 from his employers, the gaming business bookkeeper who committed suicide after running up thousands of dollars in debt, and the USAF technical sergeant with an exemplary military career who murdered a casino operator in an attempt to retrieve $400 in bad checks he had written to the casino. He also reported an increase in the number of child abuse and neglect cases as a result of gambling. On the other hand, Bloomberg acknowledged that overall he had not seen an increase in DUI cases or evidence of prostitution. In addition, he believed that because of the extensive background investigations and regulation by the South Dakota Commission on Gaming, there was no evidence of any involvement by organized crime. He conjectured that the low bet limits authorized in South Dakota helped to minimize any efforts to launder illegal funds.[40]

Of more long-term importance was the 1995 legislation that limited the proportion of total tax revenue that could be returned to Lawrence County for mitigation and enforcement at $425,000 per year, even though the Sheriff's Department employees had increased to thirty-three by then. While the county's 10 percent of the total 8 percent tax collected on gross gaming revenues had about kept pace with rising enforcement and social service costs through 1994, according to county commissioners, Commissioner George Opitz worried that "if we get one homicide, it blows us out of the water."[41] Indeed, the county was still paying bills for appeals filed by the person convicted of murdering a Deadwood casino owner in 1990.

The Colorado Comparison

Colorado had had less time to encounter the effects of legal low stakes gambling, but the human impact appeared to be just as immediate and remarkably similar in form. Deadwood's experience had given Colorado a year before the gambling vote and nearly two years before gambling started to prepare for the ramifications of gambling, and Colorado newspapers gave widespread reporting of the concerns of various constituencies. Not only were Deadwood's crime statistics reported by the Gilpin County Sheriff's Department, but the Gilpin and Teller County Nursing Services testified to the state board of health about potential problems of tourist high altitude sickness and auto accidents; employee health care, domestic violence, and lack of housing; social services needs of transients; mental health and social services needs of displaced families and business owners; displacement of teenage workers; mental health needs of casino owners; greater demand for governmental services; traffic, air, and noise pollution; and stress on all residents.[42] While recognizing how hard it was to predict effects, the executive director of the Columbine Family Health Center in Black Hawk and the administrator of the Hilltop Community Clinic in Cripple Creek agreed that patient visits might triple by 1993, and both worried about their all-volunteer ambulance services, especially during the eighteen months after gambling began and before they would receive any gaming tax revenues. In 1995 a health care provider in Cripple Creek was turned down because the funding agency assumed Teller County did not need extra money, although the side effects of gambling had cost the county $800,000 annually, according to County Commissioner Carol Vayhinger.[43]

After the first year, when emergency services had, in fact, grown fivefold in Gilpin County, the parent corporation of the St. Anthony Hospitals in Denver helped to open four modular units to take care of the increased number of diabetic, cardiac, and respiratory problems, plus what had come to be known as the "Central City syndrome," in which people faint after traveling to the higher altitude, having a drink or two, and becoming excited by several hours of slot machine play. While the volunteer medical crews answered 24 calls in the pregambling month of July 1991, they had taken care of 129 in July 1992. On the other hand, Gilpin County had not faced Lawrence County's increase in services for indigent patients (they surmised because parking problems kept them away from the towns).[44]

The Perilous Road to Sin. The earliest social impact in the Colorado towns when gambling began resulted from their treacherous highways and shortage of overnight facilities. The Teller County jail in Cripple Creek was filled the first night of gaming with drunk driving, outstanding warrants, and reckless driving offenders.[45] Over the first three months, alcohol-related traffic accidents quintupled on the routes to Central City and Black Hawk. Drunk driving contributed to fifteen accidents on the winding canyon roads between October 1 and December 31, 1991, compared to three in 1990. Six people were killed in three separate accidents, while only one fatality had been recorded in the last quarter of 1990. Overall, traffic accidents in Colorado gambling counties about doubled, with forty-six crashes on routes to Central City and ninety-eight in Teller

County in the last three months of 1991, compared with twenty-six and forty-one the year before in Central City and Teller County, respectively.[46] The effects of the increased accidents were felt primarily by the fire districts down Colorado Highway 6, rather than in Gilpin County itself. Increasingly, the accidents involved gambling buses, including a head-on collision that rolled one bus into Clear Creek, killing three and injuring forty-one people, and another in which a boulder dislodged by spring rains crashed down atop a bus, injuring several and requiring several road closures.[47] Increased traffic volume resulted in the closure of one-lane Little Ike Tunnel on Highway 67 to Cripple Creek in December 1993, resulting in detours of four to eight miles while a new highway was built around the mountain through which the four-hundred-foot-long tunnel had been bored a hundred years earlier.[48] As with the year-long closure of U.S. Highway 85 to Deadwood, even highway improvements entailed inconveniences and dangers to employees as well as patrons of the gambling towns. Like Lawrence County, South Dakota, the Teller County Sheriff's Department would experience an enormous increase in responsibilities, with calls for service soaring from two thousand per year before gaming to nearly ten thousand in 1995, with the average number of prisoners jailed daily rising from eight to forty-five, and with the annual felony arrests increasing from about forty to nearly two hundred.[49]

At the other end of the cultural spectrum, the Methodist, Catholic, and Episcopal churches in Central City, all with congregations and buildings well over a hundred years old, found immediately that parishioners had to combat traffic, noise, construction, and lack of parking in order to get to Sunday services. In their role as voluntary social service organizations, the churches saw small children left unattended on Central City's streets within the first month of gambling and anticipated increased requests from the food bank as well as the need for day-care for the children of casino workers and visitors, counseling for adults addicted to alcohol and/or gambling, and a shortage of affordable worker housing. A year later St. Mary of the Assumption Catholic Church in Central City and the Evangelical Free Methodist Church in Black Hawk both found themselves surrounded by casinos and chose to cancel vacation Bible school because "people don't want to bring their kids here."[50]

Retail Flight. If anything, Central City, Black Hawk, and Cripple Creek became exaggerated versions of the single industry gambling town evolving in Deadwood. In Cripple Creek, fewer than ten of fifty retail businesses operating in 1990 survived to the end of 1995. In Central City/ Black Hawk, within a year nearly all retail businesses and services had disappeared. Ed and Shirley Smith converted their grocery-laundromat into a casino, sold it, and left town. Marko Lah leased his Conoco station to a casino and traded his tow truck for two Mercedes convertibles. The Kwik Mart, locally known as "an arm and a leg," was replaced by the enormous Bullwhackers casino. Longstanding bars and restaurants no longer served locals as venues for comfortable eating and conversation. Even one real estate agent who had prospered with the gambling specula- tion said, "There's a lack of small-town atmosphere. You can't just wan- der into Crook's for a beer and find anybody you know. . . . We're just another face in the crowd." Parking problems in Central City and Black Hawk, ameliorated for gamblers by huge lots on top of the mountain and shuttles back to town, did little to help local citizens go to the post office conveniently. One county commissioner waxed romantic about his sense of loss. "The love, the caring, and the closeness are all gone. There's no sense of community as I knew it. Now it's just hundreds of these new people hawking and begging you to come into their casinos."[51]

If Agnes Ayres of "Don't even ask [about buying my hardware store]" fame became the symbol of resistance in Deadwood, Black Hawk had its Norm Blake, who was perhaps as apt a representative as the town could produce. Living in the house his grandfather built in 1878 at the junction of the main thoroughfares to Central City and Black Hawk, Norm spent a

Cripple Creek Market, closed and for sale. Gambling eliminated all other retail opera- tions, even in the center of town.

good deal of the summer on a rocking chair on his porch under a sign that says "The Blakes," lest anyone wonder. Even before the Colorado vote, Blake announced his objections. "Gambling will just turn Black Hawk into a parking lot for people who are going to gamble in Central City; that's what it will do. I just don't think it's going to get started right. We can take the gambling, but nobody on the city council knows how to do it right." Like many people in Deadwood, Blake was nostalgic about the good old days when gambling was illegal but tolerated and benevolent. "It was all illegal, what we were doing up here. During the opera season there was wide-open gambling with roulette tables. But when the town needed money, it was matched. There wasn't a kid who went without a hot lunch."[52] And like many property owners and business people in Deadwood who were reluctant about the wholesale conversion to gambling, Norm Blake would sell major pieces of property to casinos, while protesting what gambling was doing to his town.

As in Deadwood, property owners in Colorado gambling towns found their property assessments skyrocketing. The explosion of casino development in Gilpin County would make it possible to build a new jail while cutting homeowners' taxes from the year before, but residents would pay more in taxes than they had been promised. Because of land speculation, property values increased 3.4 times their 1991 value. Although property

Bullwhackers, which replaced the Kwik Mart in Black Hawk.

tax rates were cut, casino owners paid double what they had the year before. Still, the high price and value of land was becoming a burden to private citizens who still owned property in the gaming districts of Central City and Black Hawk. Norm Blake appeared again. "You're forcing me to sell off my property because I can't pay the taxes on it. My properties are Superfund cleanup sites. Nobody's going to buy a Superfund site."[53] But that too became prime casino property.

A letter to the editor just a few days later argued, "Recent articles have focused on the greed involved in the gaming industry and the casino owners or the property owners have been the targets. No one has mentioned the government's greed." Citing an assessment that had doubled on land that had not been changed in any way, Joan Wiggs complained, "Because of the raise [sic] in property valuation, families and retired people can't afford to live where gambling is legal."[54]

Four years later the cost of living for residents in these towns had changed dramatically. The assessed valuations in Black Hawk had increased to $50.8 million from the pregambling 1990 figure of $2.1 million, and the mill levy had dropped to only .118 from the previous 10.46. Similar declines occurred in Central City, where mill levies went from 11.475 to .631 on an assessed valuation of $74.9 million, up from $4.3 million. And in Cripple Creek assessed valuations went from $5.6 million (mill levy at 16.481) to $47.6 million (mill levy at 1.61).[55]

Cultural Competitors. The Central City Opera House Association, the biggest property owner in Central City prior to gaming and long its major enterprise, tried to bridge the gaps between casino ownership, historic preservation, and high culture. Joan Ditmer, *Denver Post* society editor, had sounded a general warning earlier when she reported on a forum on gambling and historic preservation. But her July column at the beginning of the opera season explored much more specifically the relationship between casinos and the opera. Starting with a celebration of the opera's rescue of a "moribund mining town" in 1932 and bringing money and an unmatched sense of "rare class and an international reputation for quality" to the second-oldest opera in the nation, Ditmer wondered whether the opera could survive "tacky, tacky, tacky" gambling while recognizing its equally long relationship in Central City. Reporting the renewed interest in moving the opera to Georgetown or even to Estes Park, Ditmer noted the appropriateness of *Faust* as the opening night program. But her harshest words were for the Teller House, "once gracious and nostalgic, filled with antiques, now jammed with slots." In her own particular view of cultural offerings she asserted, "But even today's gambling hells of sleaze can't dim the magic of the opera, bringing exhilaration to the soul and joy to the spirit."[56]

However, not all opera goers were convinced. Ticket sales for the 1992 season had dropped 15 percent from the previous season and regained only about half the loss in the 1993 season. John Morairty, general director, blamed the decline on worries about parking and accommodations. On the other hand, gaming lease payments on the Teller House paid for $2 million of the $2.4 million spent on the new McFarlane Foundry Rehearsal Hall. But if the place of the opera remained relatively secure in Central City, it became singularly unappreciated a mile down the road in Black Hawk. Jack Kisling reported an incident from the summer 1994 season in which two veteran Central City Opera singers expressed satisfaction with their breakfast at a Black Hawk casino and subsequently sent some of their fellow vocalists down to try the food.

Manager: "Oh, you live here?"

Baritone: "Yes, we're with the opera company."

Manager: "The what?"

Tenor: "The opera company."

Manager: "Opera?"

Baritone: "Yes, the opera company. We're here for the summer."

Manager: "What opera company?"

Tenor: "The Central City Opera."

Manager: "You work for a casino?"

Baritone: "No, we work for the opera company. About 150 people work for the opera company."

Manager: "Oh."[57]

If the longstanding Central City Opera no longer seemed major or even identifiable to some Gilpin County workers, it may have been because casinos in Colorado directly employed 5,983 people in July 1996 (down from 6,450 the year before), not counting either the bus drivers who ferried gamblers to the mountain towns or the government officials who supervised them. But, as in Deadwood, the jobs were not necessarily lucrative. Help-wanted signs for parking lot attendants and waitresses were plentiful spring through fall, but a 1994 survey of four Cripple Creek casinos reported that 86 percent of the workers said they earned less than $23,100 annually.[58]

Political Instability. Norm Blake had predicted political incompetence, but one of the earliest and most enduring effects of gambling that would produce political turmoil in Colorado was the local ordinance requiring that civic leadership come from people uninvolved in gaming. In Deadwood political power was increasingly consolidated between the city council and the Historic Preservation Commission (not to mention the Deadwood Economic Development Corporation and the Deadwood Visitors Bureau, which funneled historic preservation monies and decisions to a wide range of civic enterprises). The Colorado towns continued to wrestle with authority between citizenry and the gambling joker. Within the first year, infighting over gambling led to the recall of one council member in Black Hawk and four in Cripple Creek because voters felt they were placing too many restrictions on gambling, while Central City attempted recalls of two more of its council members. Black Hawk and Central City ran through five mayors in the first year as former mayors chose to enter the gambling business, thereby becoming ineligible for civic office, according to local ordinances. Eventually even the mayor of Central City, who was content to run a mine tour and work as the county coroner and an EMT on the local ambulance, was recalled in the spring of 1994.[59]

And after three years of gambling, both towns fired their city managers on consecutive days in October 1994 following independent secret sessions. Jack Hidahl, who ascended from positions as manager of the Central City Opera House Association and Central City's town clerk in the 1970s to manager of a high-rolling casino town, was held largely responsible for the early moratorium on building and city taxes on slot machines almost double those in neighboring Black Hawk, which together were thought to have moved the city from first to third place in gaming revenues among Colorado gambling towns. Meanwhile the city budget had risen from $346,000 in 1990 to $5.4 million. Hidahl's salary had risen from $20,000 to $69,181 over three years, but casino owners and residents seemed even more upset by his use of expensive consultants, whom they felt covered for his deficiencies.[60] The day after Hidahl was fired, Boulder resident Linda Martin, in what was reported as an independent decision by the Black Hawk City Council, was forced to resign as Black Hawk city manager, with the only explanation being that the council and Martin were "at a crossroads" on policy.[61] Norm Blake volleyed another shot about the growth of city government via the gambling industry. "They brought in all the bigshots who don't care about us."[62]

Attitudes and Perceptions. If gambling is itself anonymous anomic behavior, early evidence suggested that residents themselves felt displaced and disoriented. Patrick Long of the University of Colorado's business school began looking at the gambling towns in March and April 1992, when he sent students in his tourism class to survey people in Cripple Creek, Central City, and Black Hawk. The early results were inconclusive, although Cripple Creek officials seemed happier with the social changes than those in Central City or Black Hawk, but teenagers seemed particularly disturbed by the loss of their hangouts. Anonymity registered as a threat to small-town residents, and they resented gambling visitors who had no respect for their town. "The people I see coming up to gamble head right for the machines and don't care if they're in Central City or Vegas." And while the Deadwood sheriff wanted to be able to buy socks, one Central City official told the survey interviewer, "You can't even buy an aspirin or a condom in this town anymore."[63]

Two years later, Long, along with Jo Clark and Derek Liston, released an attitudinal study that showed that while 42 percent of Deadwood's residents reported their community as "an ideal place to live," only 15 percent of Central City's residents, 36 percent of Black Hawk's residents, and 30 percent of Cripple Creek's residents agreed with this statement. The survey made no comparisons of attitudes before and after gambling, nor did it distinguish among different groups of citizens. However, it reflected that while most residents did not find gambling inappropriate for their towns, most did not feel that they personally gained either economic or social benefits from gambling. They also perceived gambling-related expansion responsible for 98 percent of the change in traffic congestion and 60 percent of the change in serious criminal activity in their respective towns. Nearly half of the residents in each community felt less able to influence local government decisions.[64]

As Wyoming, neighbor to both gambling states, was considering a local option gambling initiative in the November 1994 election, *Casper Star-Tribune* writer Dan Whipple sought out Central City residents for their less statistically homogenized, more personal views on changes in their communities. He started with Pat Taylor, a blackjack dealer and bartender at the Gregory Street Casino, "Black Hawk's smallest and friendliest casino." Taylor had lived in Gilpin County since 1984, moving there from Denver to get away from the congestion and city problems. "There has been a lot of employment created, but we have lost a lot of the lifestyle, the clean air. It's been overwhelming to the local people." At the Gilpin County school one of the teachers talked about sixty-thousand-dollar houses and lots suddenly selling for $300,000; his wife, who headed the local Chamber of Commerce, wanted to open a day-care facility but couldn't afford the rent. And students preparing a float for homecoming cut the rhetoric to the bone: "Don't do it! It sucks." They recounted how there was nothing for kids to do in Central City, with no movie theater in town and almost nowhere that people under twenty-one could enter. Even with increased traffic and parking problems, young people weren't even allowed on some casino shuttles, making it difficult for them to get around town. "The first day of gambling," Amanda Welihan said, "we were escorted by armed guards to the bus."[65]

The transformation of the four gambling communities came not simply in the dramatic turnover in wealth, dividing local winners and losers and with the biggest profits increasingly going to outside investors. Uncertain employment, limited housing, and necessary commuting all characterized this particular economic boom. More important, the towns had become "adult communities," with few places children were allowed to go and fewer things for them to do, changing not only the tourist clientele but the climate in which the next generation of citizens would grow up.

Infrastructure Overload and Reconstruction: The Deadwood Case

Given the fact that all four gaming communities hitched their fortunes to local option, limited stakes gambling based on their well-documented record of having economic difficulties with declines in retail and employment opportunities, it is no wonder that gaming arrived in towns with seriously deteriorated infrastructures. Antiquated, inadequate sewage and water systems were doubly affected by the surge of new tourists. Although sharing common structural problems, the communities, partially based on differential returns from gaming revenues as specified by state law, sought remedies in diverse ways. The infrastructures of all the towns improved immensely relative to pregaming standards. Ironically, infrastructures were overbuilt, since they were constructed to meet peak demand in the summer; therefore, given the cyclical nature of gaming, infrastructures remain underutilized much of the year, although they require year-round maintenance.

Deadwood may not have had the most inadequate physical infrastructure, but its deteriorated conditions were typical of the problems confronting all four communities. Its larger size as well as a longer investment period in the new gambling business has allowed a more elaborated redevelopment scheme. But most interesting are the innovative financing and political savvy employed to use gambling revenues to rebuild the community. Because minimal gaming revenues are returned to the city itself, Deadwood officials turned to creative financing to repair municipal water and sewer systems. During the first year of gaming, the city issued

$10 million in bonds guaranteed by historic preservation commission funds. In year two a second ten-million-dollar bond was issued, again supported by anticipated historic preservation funds. The magnitude of tourism's impact on severely deteriorated infrastructures required large-scale and immediate action that could not be tackled piecemeal with existing budgets. Although not a strategy, initially, to retain gambling revenues, it quickly became apparent that "every time we [the Deadwood Historic Preservation Commission] bond, we pledge that money as revenue to help pay back the bond; it makes it more difficult to take that revenue from you. That is exactly the reason the state doesn't want [us] to bond."[66]

A new Deadwood fire station, bonded with $750,000 of historic revenue funds (ostensibly to protect the historic district), was begun in 1992 and completed in 1993, making available the old train station depot, which had served as city hall and fire station since 1952. Historic preservation funds were used subsequently to restore and remodel the depot as a visitors center. One of the original waiting rooms restored as an exhibition room touts the history of Deadwood along with the successes of historic preservation. The other waiting room has retained its original function but with much improved accommodations. Here, people from tour buses examine artifacts from Deadwood's early days. According to Mark Wolfe, the station was "a natural. It serves the purpose it served originally: a terminus where people load and unload."[67] The fifteen newly installed informational signs scattered throughout the downtown historic district, beginning at the depot, made the remodeled train station ideal for self-guided tours of "historic" Deadwood.

In their rush to vacate the old depot, city government officials bypassed acquiring the more attractive neoclassical but partially occupied post office to refurbish the Fish and Hunter Warehouse, which is not as grandiose but which is a functional building ideally located next to the newly restored Lawrence County Courthouse and its annex. Here the historic and majestic gave way to the functional. Having been in cramped quarters since 1952 and more squeezed as gambling demands had forced the expansion of many municipal services, including a doubling of Deadwood's police force, the city understandably opted for a warehouse over an ornate building. The ordinariness of city hall was partially overcome by landscaping, Victorian street lighting, and dark brick paving.[68] It would have been difficult for the city to have made any other decision given the increased volume of local governmental activity; police offices and dispatching, the financial center, city planning offices, and, of course, the Historic Preservation Commission were all relocated to the rehabilitated warehouse.

Housing Improvement. Given the more than $80 million invested in private commercial enterprises and historic preservation, primarily in the downtown historic district, surprisingly little investment was directed at either the restoration of private homes or the construction of new housing in Deadwood. It is difficult to evaluate whether the lack of population growth, even with the tremendous economic boom, was due to the shortage of adequate housing or to people's preference to live elsewhere and commute to Deadwood for employment, a possibility indicated by Pat Long's study.[69] Other than a small development begun in 1990 and completed in 1991 and the restoration of the Gillmore for low- to moderate-income residents, housing has been one of the failures of Deadwood's revitalization.

Formed in 1991 and supported by historic preservation funds, the Deadwood Community Housing Organization (DCHO) was charged with the examination of possibilities for rehabilitation of existing housing and securing outside funds for new construction. In 1993 Deadwood, via its housing authority, qualified as a 501C3 organization, which enabled it to receive pass-through federal monies, $50,000 in 1993 alone.[70] In October 1994 the DCHO was accepted as the first (one of thirty in the entire country) South Dakota affiliate of the Neighborhood Reinvestment Corporation (NRC), a nonprofit corporation that helps communities provide affordable housing. The DCHO, under the direction of Joy McCracken, who is also the finance officer for the Deadwood Historic Preservation Commission, put together a twenty-seven-unit housing project at an estimated cost of $1,377,000, with funding to come jointly from South Dakota Housing Development Authority, Federal Home Loan Bank, American Housing Development Corporation, and private investors. Support from the city of Deadwood came in the form of the creation of a tax increment financing district (TIFD).[71] The Hills Apartment project, completed in 1997, was a first step toward achieving the eighty-four rental units and thirty-six homes projected to be needed in Deadwood by the year 2000. More important, the project would be reserved for low-income residents, "with 80 percent of the units for persons earning 50 percent of the county's median income ($37,700), and 20 percent earning 60 percent of the median."[72] Utilities included, a two-bedroom apartment would rent for about $280 per month.

The Center for the New West, based in Colorado, in 1993 provided for a time the best hope for the construction of new integrated housing in Deadwood. A project consisting of restoration of ten houses plus the construction of multifamily housing was proposed by the Center for the New West to be funded in conjunction with federal and private funds. As only one of a few communities, Deadwood was selected in 1994 as a showcase. The city of Deadwood, in an effort to increase the supply of housing, created another TIFD in August 1993 to assist Art and Sophie Olson in paying the estimated $650,000 needed to provide water and sewer connections for a forty-two-unit condominium project known as Four Aces Village. Albeit supported by tax incentives, the project was the first major housing development to be funded by private funds since 1990; however, it did not materialize. A proposed twenty-four-unit apartment project to be located near the top of Burnham Hill was turned down in 1994 after neighborhood protests about increased traffic on the steep street as well as residents' expressed preference for single-family homes.[73]

The Deadwood Historic Preservation Commission in 1994 allocated funds for both revolving funds ($200,000 for 1994) and paint projects ($20,000). As yet there seemed to be little private investment in housing, perhaps a reflection of the disparity between returns on private investment for housing versus profits from casinos. Obviously the economic boom was not to be translated into a permanent population boom.

Transportation Issues. In accordance with its aspirations to celebrate the past while ameliorating present problems, Deadwood early on purchased four dark green "historic" trolleys at $75,000 apiece to provide shuttle service within the city limits of Deadwood. In 1880 the trolleys were yellow horse-drawn vehicles, but commercial enterprises complained that yellow trolleys would look like school buses and wanted "exciting" red trolleys. In a compromise move, the Historic Preservation Commission argued for historic accuracy: the 1902 electric trolleys that had forced the yellow omnibuses out of business were green.[74] A great success, the trolley schedule quickly expanded from a twenty- to a twenty-four-hour schedule during the busy summer months. However, while summer saw the operation of all four trolleys, in the winter months the service was trimmed back to a single trolley running during the week and two operating on the busy weekends. Like water and sewer needs, the acquisition of four trolleys demonstrates the necessity of developing an infrastructure to meet peak demand and then owning a resource that remains underutilized eight months of the year. Even with the downturn in ridership during the fall, winter, and early spring months, the trolleys have maintained more than a quarter of a million riders per year, with about half of those paying a fifty-cent fare (seniors and casino employees ride free, an incentive provided to free up scarce parking spaces in the downtown district).[75]

However, the three miles separating Lead and Deadwood have seemed an abyss in regard to efforts to tie the two communities together with some form of public transportation. At least initially, a shuttle bus service provided a connection, tenuous though it was, between the two communities. In 1991 the bus service provided a cheap link (twenty-five cents per ride) between the two communities, particularly for seniors residing in Deadwood who because of the bus service had access to the Lead Senior Center and the Twin City Mall, also located in Lead. Residents of Lead working in the casinos also utilized the bus service, thereby reducing the impact on parking in Deadwood. First canceled in September 1991, protests from gaming hall employees and local residents led to revival of the service in February 1992. Deadwood Area Rapid Transit Employee Shuttle received a ninety-day contract that called for one-dollar rider fares along with a three-hundred-dollar-per-month subsidy from both Lead and Deadwood. But due to poor management or lack of ridership, the bus service was terminated in May 1992, once again cutting a slender tentacle between the two communities.[76] South Dakota Senator Larry Pressler revived hopes of a bus link between Deadwood and Lead in September 1993 with possible federal aid through the Resource Conservation and Development Act.[77] These funds failed to emerge, and, still without mass transportation, the communities remain physically and socially isolated from each other.

Although Lead's city government wanted to see some connection between the two communities, a Deadwood business in November 1994 opted for detachment by terminating the trolley service to its establishment. Deadwood Gulch Resort, located on the southeast edge of Deadwood, made its decision after noting that many of its motel visitors were using the trolley to ride to downtown Deadwood to gamble instead of gambling at the resort's casino. So in the interest of venture capital, there was one less trolley stop.[78]

Moreover, adamant that historic preservation funds could only be used within the landmark designation, Wolfe suggested that "if the city of Lead wanted to put some money in and we [the Deadwood Historic Preservation Commission] could take a nonhistoric trolley, you know, a bus, and run it back and forth and if it would be commercially funded through the revenues generated by historic trolleys, probably no one would have a problem with that."[79]

Railroad Revival. A ghost from the past arrived in 1992 along with the Costners' Dunbar proposal: a reconstruction of the long-abandoned Burlington Northern Railroad spur from Whitewood (on Interstate 90) to Deadwood and from I-90 to the Rapid City Regional Airport. The proposal included a petition to reintroduce authentic, historic rail passenger train service from the Rapid City Regional Airport to Whitewood, then up and over Deadwood Hill to the Dunbar Resort and on to downtown Deadwood and Lead. Envisioned were vintage 1880s trains loaded with tourists headed for Deadwood gaming establishments. Eager to tap into South Dakota's $2.6 million in federal transportation funds, the Costners hired Terry Krantz, along with an Omaha-based real estate and development firm, Dial Companies, to convince local residents of the need for a railroad authority. Krantz, in lobbying for the authority, noted that within three years the railroad could generate $5 million in revenue and add $300,000 a year to state sales tax revenues. Of course, the authority would have the power to tax and the right of eminent domain— a necessity if the long-abandoned railroad right-of-way were to be reclaimed.[80] Krantz optimistically noted that the sixty-three-mile rail would haul 140,000 passengers per year (one must assume that most would disembark at the future Dunbar resort).

With the great western tradition of individual claims to land and resources lingering in the background, not only Deadwood but also Lead city governments were early, eager participants in forming a railroad authority. Only the downhill residents of Whitewood, with little if anything to gain and much to lose, were opposed to the railroad authority. Even the Deadwood Historic Preservation Commission committed funds from the 1994 budget year to investigate the feasibility of running a rail line from downtown Deadwood to the top of Deadwood Hill, the site of the future Dunbar resort.

The key to participation was $2.6 million in federal money the state had to distribute. "There's going to be a scramble for that money. We'd like to be first in line."[81] Some commissioners even had the naive notion of supporting the authority as long as it did not have taxing authority, a novel revision of state law. In responding to local residents' concerns regarding taxing authority, Krantz noted that the railroad authority had the legal right to tax two mills, "but it had no intention nor desire to tax the people."[82] By September 10, 1994, both the Deadwood City Commission and the Lead City Commission had approved the formation of the Northern Hills Railroad Authority (NHRRA), but only after modifying the taxing capabilities of the authority. Under the approved authority, the NHRRA could impose a two-mill tax only if approved by a unanimous vote of all member bodies (i.e., Lead and Deadwood City Commissions). Yet the NHRRA did retain the right of eminent domain, promising only that property owners would be fairly reimbursed for their property.[83] Lead's participation hinged on the promise of a railroad loop from Deadwood up and around Lead back to Deadwood.

It turns out that legal and financial support for the Dunbar resort is much more than a scramble for federal money. Both the city of Deadwood and the state of South Dakota have made heavy investments, even as the resort's initial construction was being delayed more than a year due to "architectural difficulties." By October 1995, $1.3 million in public funds had been spent on the Costner Project (funneled through the city of Deadwood), and with loans, grants, and tax breaks, the total exceeded $13 million. Most conspicuous so far is the 5.7-mile widening (entailing a one-year closure) of U.S. Highway 85 over the top of Deadwood Hill immediately in front of the Dunbar site. The 6.4-million-dollar investment reflects the overall increase in traffic to Deadwood and is not included as a Dunbar cost;[84] nor was the reconstruction soon after completion of the highway of a tunnel between two portions of the proposed Dunbar golf course separated by Highway 85; nor is the permit allowing the resort to pump up to one million gallons of water per day from Whitewood Creek for irrigation of the eighty-five-acre golf course and ten-acre grounds.[85] The transplanting of two hundred full-size Ponderosa pines to excavations for the three Dunbar entrances was financed with $800,000 by a state Department of Transportation grant channeled through the city of Deadwood for landscaping of the rebuilt highway adjacent to the resort site. In addition, $1.6 million of the 1.98-million-dollar bid for the proposed thirty-two-hundred-seat amphitheater will come from a Governor's Office of Economic Development grant to the city of Deadwood.

Deadwood voters in 1993 approved a TIFD for water and sewer expansion to the resort that, with a city water tank addition atop Deadwood Hill, totaled $7.4 million in deferred property taxes. The state of South Dakota Board of Water and Natural Resources added a nearly one-million-dollar grant for eight thousand feet of water lines and six thousand feet of sewer lines up the hill from the lower end of Deadwood. An added incentive from the state of South Dakota was a 1994 legislative expansion of state tax rebates on capital investments after voters defeated gambling expansion legislation sought by the Costners in 1993. Construction project rebates come in phases, returning paid state sales tax, contractor's excise tax, and state use tax. For spending $20 to $30 million, the state returns one third of taxes paid. For $30 million to $40 million, two thirds of the taxes paid from the beginning of a project are returned. After $40 million are spent, all construction taxes are refunded. By November 1995, private investment in the Dunbar resort had surpassed $20 million, netting a $125,443 rebate on what was by then projected eventually to be a one-hundred-million-dollar construction project.[86]

Historic Parking Battles. The contest in all four gaming towns between residents and visitors for the right to park vehicles is reminiscent of the range wars between the cattlemen and the sheepmen. Deadwood encountered the quadrupling of tourism and the proliferation of its labor force early on. The city council confronted the installation of parking meters, a ban on employee parking downtown, the revival of trolley and bus service, and the possibility of constructing a multilevel parking garage; of course, decisions in response to these parking issues left nearly everyone unhappy. Bound by the geographical slope of steep hillsides and narrow creekbeds, land in Deadwood is scarce, particularly that suitable for parking. And with parking banned on historic Main Street, space is even more limited. In an effort to drive employees from on-street parking, the city council initiated the installation of parking meters that were not in the least historic but a purely utilitarian solution that did support a third of the budget for the "historic" trolley cars.

Within the first year of gaming rumors were floated about a two-million-dollar parking ramp designed to solve Deadwood's parking problems.[87] Although neither financially feasible nor historic in nature, the proposal defined the seriousness of parking. The proposal for a parking ramp arose again in December 1992 by Merrick and Company.[88] Yet the downturn in gambling during the winter months and the lack of historic precedent for parking facilities led to a decision to make no decision. Finally, by November 1995, the estimated price for a 429-stall parking garage had risen to $7 million, and the Deadwood Historic Preservation Commission agreed to spend up to $2 million itself. Knowing that explaining the use of historic preservation funds for a parking garage that does not yet exist would be difficult, Historic Preservation Officer Mark Wolfe pointed out that $1 million had already been spent on parking improvements in Deadwood under the need for "visitor management," a necessary part of historic preservation.[89] Attorney Jon Mattson, representing the members of the city's Business Improvement District, which pledged to make up through revenue bonds the balance of the seven-million-dollar cost, agreed that preservation-related costs such as a historic-looking facade on the concrete building are unlikely to total $2 million but found other familiar justifications for the expense in new infrastructure. "Let's say it's a million in hard costs, because of historic criteria. The other justification is protection of the downtown historic district."[90]

That would be the rationale again when, once construction began, the excavation of the hillside caused several residences on Williams Street above to crack and be declared structurally unsound and the street itself to sink five inches, requiring another $2 million in historic preservation bonding for a retaining wall to enable the parking garage project to proceed. Approval of the additional bonding came after "downtown business owners told the commission that completing work on the stalled parking project is essential to preserve the economic viability of the historic Main Street district that is Deadwood's chief tourist attraction."[91]

Private parking was an issue as well. While the historic Franklin Hotel's eleven city-controlled parking places were first rescinded and then re-granted, the new Mineral Palace Hotel was just beginning its quest for the holy grail of adequate parking. Hoping to open on March 1, 1993, but having only fifty-four of the required sixty-three spaces (one for each room) to acquire a certificate of occupancy, the Mineral Palace was in dire straits.[92] The remaining spaces, obtained by lease, remained a contentious question: could anyone lease parking in perpetuity? Trivial yet conspicuous by its presence in all four gaming towns, parking became a crucial issue in these boomtowns confronted by daily population shifts of workforce and patrons. The need to prepare for a peak population in the summer exaggerated the requirements.

Learning from Deadwood

Jeff Bloomberg's testimony to the House Committee on Small Business reported increased jobs, most of them seasonal and without benefits. The loss of retail business had not been offset by lowered taxes because rising property values increased assessments. Increases in gaming taxes to the county had been mostly consumed by increased administrative, law enforcement, and infrastructure costs. The criminal caseload had doubled, and child abuse and neglect cases had increased as a result of gaming. On the bright side, there had not been the predicted increases in drunk driving, prostitution, or organized crime, and the town had been physically rehabilitated. But ultimately, Bloomberg's greatest concern was that the economic development that took place may now have stalled because of the growth of gambling everywhere in the country; moreover, local and state governments were now dependent on gambling dollars.

> Probably most disturbing has been the growing dependence of local and state government on gambling dollars. Because government officials have been unwilling to make the politically difficult decisions to either raise taxes or cut services, they have turned to gambling as a supposedly "pain-

less" revenue source. The gaming industry in South Dakota, armed with large amounts of cash, has gone from being non-existent seven years ago to being one of the most powerful lobbying forces in our state capital and virtually every decision at city hall is made based upon what is best for the gaming industry. Government is hooked on the money generated by gambling and I believe in the long term the ramifications of this governmental addiction will be just as dire as for the individual who becomes addicted to gambling.[93]

CHAPTER 7

Mining Quarters

Settler Camps to Gambler Traps

If new western historians have contributed substantially to a social history of the West by attending much more scrupulously to the sociological variables of race, gender, and class, some have used those analyses to go so far as to question the existence of a distinct "West" at all, especially in looking at the urban West of the late twentieth century. When examining these contemporary Rocky Mountain gambling towns, we must now ask whether there is anything distinct about or common among their social and physical milieus beyond their dominant industry.

We characterized their beginnings as created from diverse ethnic populations of men and women, some to be squeezed out and some to settle in for the duration. But if gender, race, and class were important, we find them to represent agency as often as oppression.[1] Clearly, the wide-open early prospecting and entrepreneurship eventuated in much more concentrated economic power, but some unique characters emerged to provide variations on the wealthy elite of the Gilded Age.[2] Physically, the towns, all built and rebuilt in the latter third of the twentieth century after disasters of flood and fire, comfortably accommodated Victorian architecture on their steep hillsides and narrow gulches after they became more tourist destinations than mining and mill towns.

Residents of the towns are in the main pretty sure that they are "western," making them different from a lot of the rest of the country, freer and more independent than other Americans, according to their mythology. And the western theme is now used frequently, sometimes rigidly, to portray the gambling industry there as different from gambling elsewhere. Yet the reality is complex and sometimes paradoxical.

Social structural changes resulting from the gaming industry takeover test the boundaries of gender, class, and race relations in new ways. If there is anything left of the frontier analysis in the new urban West, it may be that expanding, uninstitutionalized opportunities, for a time at least, permit innovative participation by a wider range of citizens. Economic booms may create a more democratic mix or they may simply provide a "shakedown" period and a return to old arrangements. No contemporary examination should avoid these sociological categories of analysis as they become the currency of a wide range of disciplines. But what we end up with is not likely to be the essentialist western story. Rather, it is a set of what historian Richard White calls "ironic narratives" of contesting groups, different perceptions of and ambitions for land and resources, and dynamic structures of power.[3]

Gender Blurring

If the founding of the communities was typified as the days when all the miners were men (and most of the men were miners) and women could find employment almost exclusively in the entertainment business, the towns are now in a period when jobs are much less sex segregated, but everybody is to some extent in the entertainment business. Women have been among the early political organizers for legalizing gambling, as well

Bennett Avenue in Cripple Creek.

as the most successful campaigners against its expansion. Women have held posts and been fired along with their male counterparts as city managers in Colorado and now serve as mayors of Deadwood and Black Hawk. Women are among the most prosperous local entrepreneurs. And women work in county government, managing the taxation and law enforcement impact of gambling in Lawrence, Teller, and Gilpin Counties as well.

At the lower end of the pay scale, women work alongside men as food servers, cooks, change makers, card dealers, and bartenders. While it appears that there may be a slight disproportion of male bartenders and female "floorwalkers" who deliver drinks and change, bartending is not a high income position where most drinks are "complimentary," bartenders are not in a position to push drinks, and patrons are less likely to be in a position to say, "Keep the change." "Girls" on the floor are more likely to get tips for their service. Women's work in the second boom, if not always highly profitable or benefited, is at least for the most part legally protected rather than legally ignored. Women and men from the region are grateful for the employment, not so much because it is the best work around, but because it is "about the only work around."[4] The Victorian Era theme of the towns means that costumes have ranged from gender neutral tuxedos to flouncy dresses, but they rarely demand the amount of physical exposure found in Nevada or Atlantic City or the nineteenth-century brothels and appear to be migrating toward greater casual comfort for both sexes. Managers wear androgynous jackets over the standard uniform of the establishment.

The blackjack dealers interviewed in Deadwood were working for female owner/managers "for the first time in their lives."[5] Virginia Lewis would become one of the richest women in Colorado as the owner of the Gold Mine Casino in Black Hawk. Mary Schmit, the owner/manager of the Bullock Hotel, served at the same time as a member of the Historic Preservation Commission in Deadwood. While not necessarily reflecting full ownership of the gaming establishments in Deadwood, an equal number of owner/managers listed in the Chamber of Commerce membership directory of 1992 were represented by women as by men.[6]

"Notable" political figures in the various gaming campaigns have included women as well as men. Campaigns for the legalization of gambling were led by Linda Blair in Deadwood and Freda Poundstone in Colorado; the statewide campaign to challenge the expansion of gambling in South Dakota was initiated and organized by the venerable JoDean Joy (she would be supported from time to time by early gambling advocate

Bill Walsh of Deadwood). A Florida-based expert, Nancy Todd, was flown in to Colorado in November 1995 to talk about how to persuade Colorado voters to increase the state's limits on bets and games.[7] If Child Protection Services Director Lora Hawkins had long raised questions about the effects of gambling on the children and families of Lawrence County, the spokesperson who worried aloud to a congressional committee (and had his life threatened, albeit "jokingly") was Lawrence County State's Attorney Jeff Bloomberg.

The 1990s provided opportunities for women as well as men to speak for issues related to gambling, just as early writers, philanthropists, and public characters had represented both sexes. But ultimately gender/class relations may not have changed all that much overall. The new frontier of gambling in the gaming communities allowed local entrepreneurs who were in a position to take advantage of new markets and new investments to become the nouveau riche, while women and men who preferred old retailing and service work were mainly squeezed out or drawn reluctantly into gambling enterprises.

Mary Schmit, one of the success stories, has lived in Deadwood less than a decade, but her current connections run back to the very founding of Deadwood. In October 1989, just a month before the third and finally successful try to legalize gambling in Deadwood, Schmit, disillusioned by the activities of a Denver business partner, drove to Deadwood. She bought the building that was originally the Bullock Hotel, opened by Seth Bullock, Deadwood's first sheriff, and that had housed Ayres Hardware from 1904 until 1976, when Agnes and Albro Ayres moved the business across the street to a smaller, 1,250-square-foot building.

Despite its very short list of proprietors, the Ayres Building had deteriorated before Mary Schmit bought it. The second and third floors were no longer operating as a hotel and had been partially gutted, the debris being deposited in the basement. The main floor had been turned into a Mexican and Chinese restaurant, featuring a Chinese junk floating in a pool with a circulating waterfall over the large doors into the rear bar portion of the building. Unfortunately, the pool leaked, and the twelve-inch beams that formed the floor joists were rotted to within four inches in some places, a fact not apparent until the basement was cleaned out.

But regardless of the outcome of the gambling initiative, Mary Schmit thought she could at least turn the place into a bed and breakfast inn, and because she had had experience in Denver "taking really dilapidated properties and fixing them up," including a recent project that covered two city blocks, the appearance of the building didn't bother her. The striped sandstone front of the building was spectacular. There was a wonderful open stairway on the second and third floors, the third-floor skylights were really special, and the rest of the building was in excellent shape. In terms of the foundation, she could see no settling. In fact, when the floor joists were raised back up, "there was almost a sigh and the building literally sprang back into shape," and the remaining plaster tumbled off the walls. "It had to go anyway."[8]

Gambling was approved, and the first floor became a casino, restaurant, bar, and hotel lobby, with as much of the original woodwork as possible. To say that the rooms on the second and third floors were all refurbished diminishes the complexity of the process. With some of the loan money—$327,000—from the Historic Preservation Commission, Schmit hired Spencer Ruff of Sioux Falls, who had been on the National Advisory Board for Historic Preservation for years as her architect. Still, negotiating among the various agencies involved in the restoration of Deadwood properties proved complicated, especially since she appeared very early in the game.

After eventually reaching a compromise on keeping the open stairwell despite its initially being deemed a fire hazard and combining some hotel rooms to make them big enough to be attractive by 1990 standards, thereby reducing the number of rooms from thirty-six to twenty-eight, Schmit added eight more rooms across the street at the Branch, whose executive suites are decorated in arts and crafts style, suited to the poured concrete building, which was originally a cold storage plant. This building, which has no gambling, includes a meeting room, beauty shop, and weight room in the basement and a retail shop next door. The project was financed in part with another $350,000 from the Historic Preservation Commission revolving loan fund on a 1.6-million-dollar investment, an amount almost equivalent to that spent on the Bullock.

While she herself was on the Historic Preservation Commission for three years, as well as the Deadwood Visitors Bureau, the Long-Range Planning Commission, and later the Special Events Committee, Schmit is now just concentrating on business, remaining only on the Long-Range Planning Commission and Special Events Committee. But there is no doubt that she is still an important player in decision making in Deadwood. Very recently when the city and the planning commission were putting heavy pressure on historic preservation to grant a height variance for a six-story, hundred-room hotel in an empty lot that was gutted by fire a dozen years ago, she and fellow businesswoman/hotelier Melodee Nelson appeared with their lawyer, outlining what would be an inevitable lawsuit if this project, "completely out of context with the rest of the town," were allowed in the middle of downtown Deadwood. The city council eventually unanimously voted not to grant the height variance.

Schmit's counterpart in Colorado is Virginia Lewis, who turned a rough childhood and an early and abusive marriage into a forty-million-dollar business when she became owner of the Gold Mine and Jazz Alley Casinos in Black Hawk. She started her new career as a single parent working as a camera girl in the Riviera Hotel in Las Vegas, but she began to accumulate capital by buying, repairing, and selling rundown houses. With a second husband, she opened the Gold Mine Casino in Black Hawk on October 1, 1991, the first day that gaming was allowed in Colorado, and for three months the Gold Mine was one of the few casinos in Black Hawk as entrepreneurial attention focused on Central City. Jazz Alley was bought out from co-owners. Her eleven-year second marriage foundered on another gambling venture, the Royal River Casino on the Flandreau Santee Sioux Reservation in South Dakota, where the Lewises had become the nation's first casino operators under the U.S. Indian Gaming Act and faced contract renegotiation a year into the venture.

It is not altogether clear how different an owner/manager Lewis is from the corporate investors, but she reported in August 1995 wanting to purchase property in Golden to offer a day-care enterprise free rent in exchange for discounted day-care for her employees. She also said she had given money to the Gilpin County day-care summer program, bought a computer and a baseball pitching machine for one of the schools, and replaced money that was stolen from the high school pancake breakfast. When the Gilpin County Chamber of Commerce faced closure because of lack of funds, Lewis paid staff salaries for a time. "I've been fortunate, but I've been in the position to be needy," she said. "I could have been broke. I feel it's important to give back to the community."[9] Whether as a gesture of class or gender consciousness, she eventually gave up her limousine for a Grand Cherokee and decided to live with her former limo driver. In any case her philanthropic sentiment seems rare, according to Patricia Stowkowski, who says that "most gaming business people have invested in the community on the basis of favorable economic conditions—not to save a community, but to secure a profit."[10]

Capital Concentration

Many of Deadwood's early gambling ventures were also undercapitalized, and after five years' time, with the attempted limit on outside investment disallowed by the courts in South Dakota, more and more transactions have occurred between large outside corporations. Golddiggers, opened in 1991 by Casino Magic, a Minnesota corporation that also operated casinos in Mississippi, Argentina, and Greece, was sold to a California-based Royal Casino Group that also had a riverboat casino project in Missouri. Principals in the company had been in the gaming industry for twenty-five years, and Royal Casino and Casino Magic had worked together in the past on gambling projects.[11] The largest of the early Deadwood gambling complexes, Deadwood Gulch Resort, founded by former Deadwood mayor Tom Blair, went from a merger between Full House Resorts, Inc., of Deadwood and a company owned by Lee Iacocca in early 1995 to being put up for sale a year later. Full House was also working on casinos with four Michigan Indian tribes and another tribal casino at Coos Bay, Oregon. Company chief executive officer and board chairman Allen Paulson (also America's largest thoroughbred horse breeder and founder of Gulfstream Aerospace) explained that "while we are pleased with our operation and personnel at Deadwood Gulch Resort, this operation is not in keeping with our company focus."[12] Meanwhile, more local entrepreneurs proposed an additional twenty-six-million-dollar resort complex across the highway from the Costners' Dunbar Resort. Super G. Investments Co., planning the Gold Mine Resort, also owned the Silverado Casino on Deadwood's Main Street. It listed ten Rapid City men in the company with state gambling licenses.[13]

The most expansive project in downtown Deadwood is the Wild West Winners Club, which spans seven buildings stretching more than half a block on lower Main Street in Deadwood. The Olympia Gaming Group, Inc., with headquarters in Wheeling, Illinois, was also involved in U.S. and overseas gaming ventures, including midwestern riverboats and a Greek casino. Glenn K. Seidenfiled Jr., president and chief executive officer, was a former vice president and general counsel for Bally Manufacturing, which had developed the largest hotel project in the world in Atlantic City, N.J., at the time.

But Olympia decided to "stake a claim in Deadwood because of its western heritage and the complement of other attractions in the Black Hills." Like Buffalo Bill's Wild West Show, Wild West Winners hopes to represent various Deadwood constituencies in a "walk through time," according to Spencer Ruff, the same architect who renovated the Bullock Hotel. In the former Eagle Bar, a six-by-eight-foot mural depicts the 1876 shooting of Wild Bill Hickok, followed in the next six buildings by decor portraying cowboy life in 1880, the cattle drives of 1885, a western saloon in 1890, the railroad days in 1894, the bordellos of 1900, and the "gentlemen cowboys" of 1905. The 18,000 square feet of ground-floor space include the rebuilt replicas of two buildings razed after a 1982 fire and the original site of Pam's Purple Door brothel. The only contemporary woman named in the project is Marla Friedman, who will paint the Wild Bill mural.[14]

From the beginning the new gambling frontiers in Colorado more closely resembled the antebellum economics or Gilded Age of capital investment that had produced their first booms, with big money (if not necessarily old money) coming from outsiders to dominate the gambling towns of Colorado from 1990 on. There Harrah's, Harvey's, and Hemmeter's Bullwhackers became the primary players. Women have not been among the corporate giants of Las Vegas or European gambling ventures, and they appear infrequently among Colorado gambling investors. Hemmeter Enterprises filed for Chapter 11 bankruptcy reorganization after a major casino in New Orleans foundered and reemerged as Colorado Gaming and Entertainment, the largest employer in Gilpin County. Both Bullwhackers and the Silver Hawk were sold to a U.S. subsidiary of the British gaming firm Ladbroke Group PLC in July 1997. Harrah's became Canyon Casino, owned by Denver-based Eagle Gaming, which is planning a parking lot for a ninety-million-dollar casino hotel on the site of the historic Lace House. But the award for the most anomalous enterprise in Black Hawk must go to the Isle of Capri casino, under construction by a Biloxi, Mississippi, firm.[15]

In Deadwood, the outsiders of note had been, conspicuously, Kevin and Dan Costner. They rode into town early on, having just made nearby Spearfish Canyon internationally famous in the last touching winter scene of the Hollywood production of *Dances with Wolves*, the lyrical portrayal of Plains people that Costner produced, directed, and starred in, to win seven Academy Awards and gross $500 million worldwide, netting Costner himself $60 million. Kevin Costner was not only the most famous actor to spend time in the Black Hills in decades, but his brother Dan obligingly purchased a house locally to comply first with the law and then with the spirit of local ownership. The town embraced the notoriety, as it had for more than a century. And even when Costner's character, "Dunbar," metamorphosed into a giant hotel resort project on the scale of things talked about if not yet materialized in Colorado, townspeople continued to argue that "people who come to Costner's resort to stay would be big spenders who would want to come downtown to gamble." The city obliged the project with a Tax Increment Finance District for water lines, sewer lines, clearance for the railroad project, as well as a golf course that required tunneling under the newly rebuilt U.S. Highway 85 just months after it reopened from a year's construction closure, even though JoDean Joy had prevented (at least for a time) the expansion of gambling bet limits the Costners wanted.

New Indian Wars

Then, in a replay of old animosities, the American Indians who had welcomed Costner and for the most part lauded his use of native people and the Lakota language in *Dances with Wolves* came to wonder if this outsider would be a compatible neighbor over the long run. When Costner first lobbied the state legislature for the higher bet limits and larger allowable numbers of slot machines, several Pine Ridge Sioux (Lakota) tribal leaders sought his support on behalf of their own gambling ventures and felt spurned in the process. The arguments in the capital all connected gambling expansion to hotel investments that the tribal leaders thought were beyond their means.

The bigger issue was about land. The U.S. Supreme Court in 1980 had awarded eight Sioux tribes what is now $400 million compensation for the Black Hills in a judgment that found that "a more ripe and rank case of dishonorable dealing will never, in all probability, be found in our history," but the tribes had rejected the decision and compensation, claiming that they wanted the 1.3 million acres of land back instead. Now the hero whose film a tribal elder had described by saying "Never has the knife in the heart of the Lakota people been depicted so graphically" himself wanted to trade 584 acres of private land for 564 acres of Black Hills National Forest on which to place the golf course and railroad. Mike Jandreau, chairman of the Lower Brule Sioux tribe, spoke in measured terms: "I feel a great sense of distrust and anxiety. We are being passed by as resources that we hold sacred are being bartered over. A native American group would be turned down if we asked to trade land on a reservation for land in the Black Hills." But his sense of betrayal was apparent. "If in making the movie, Mr. Costner and his brother did not come to a recognition of the real emotion of the Sioux people towards the Black Hills, then a great deal had already been lost."

Terry Krantz, director of acquisition and development for the Costners' Dunbar Corporation, was less eloquent. "The U.S. Supreme Court has decided in favour of the white guys. The reality is that the land belongs to the people who won it. I don't know why Kevin should establish himself as something better than the law of the land. After all, who does the land really belong to? The Sioux or the cliff-dwellers that were there before? Or us? Isn't this land sacred to us, too, in some way?" Krantz's sense of obligation to help Indian tribes build casinos was expressed in a disbelieving question. "Because Kevin's a friend of the Indian people he's supposed to penalize himself financially? Why should that money go back to them? What have they done for that money? The fact is that people begrudge him his success. These people want him to write out a check because he's successful and they're not. If they would like to be employed at the Dunbar they can come and fill out applications like anyone else."[16]

Although the land claim issue was covered almost exclusively by the *Times* of London and *Indian Country Today*, Indian tribes nevertheless promise to be serious competitors for gambling dollars, as tribal sovereignty arguments and development initiatives to stabilize tribal economies pose the strongest cases against new taxation of tribal casino profits at the same rates states and cities collect on legalized gambling.[17] By 1995 eight of the nine tribal governments in South Dakota operated gambling casinos, and the Santee Sioux of eastern South Dakota had used profits to purchase 127.5 acres of land in the Black Hills within twenty miles of Deadwood.[18] When South Dakota voters turned down expanded gambling in September 1993, both legislative Republicans and tribal leaders thought that racism might have played a role. Bill Walsh, a partner in the historic Franklin Hotel in Deadwood, House Majority Leader Larry Gabriel, and Paul Valandra, a state senator from Rosebud all thought the vote reflected a backlash against Indian gambling.[19] Colorado too has reservation gambling, but in the far southwestern corner of the state on the Ute Mountain Reservation near Mesa Verde, and it has not generally been perceived as a direct competitor with the gold town gambling near the large metropolitan areas of Denver and Colorado Springs.[20]

So if gambling provides a new frontier, an entrepreneurial opportunity in which women, working-class people, and Indians can participate, much as William Chafe described in colonial New England as well as in the nineteenth-century West, initial opportunities might not necessarily translate into radically different social structures.[21] Will women soon be seen only as moral entrepreneurs rather than economic ones? Will local millionaires be bought out by syndicates from Los Angeles and Las Vegas? And will the tax and political advantage that Indian casinos currently enjoy be subsumed by the advertising advantage of a Hollywood-based resort?

Gambling Facades: Decorated Historic Victorian Sheds

If the ironic narratives of gender, class, and race in the new gambling boom reflect social structural conditions, the physical structures provide their own ironies when compared to other gambling venues. Chapter 5 examined the process of historic preservation, the rationale that provided political success for local option gambling in both South Dakota and Colorado. While historic preservation to accommodate slot machines creates its own ironies, another more fundamental architectural characteristic constrains the Rocky Mountain mining towns as gambling venues.

No analysis of physical structures and architecture of a gambling town can ignore the pioneering work of Robert Venturi, Denise Scott Brown, and Steven Izenour, who in *Learning from Las Vegas* not only took seriously for the first time a modern American gambling town but in an appreciation of popular culture called into question the sacrosanct field of modern architectural design.[22] Although the title is so mellifluous as to be irresistible to contemporary analysts of the gambling business, it is also striking how little attention has actually been given to the arguments the Yale architects and their students were making nearly thirty years ago.[23] A. Alvarez doesn't mention the original volume at all in an article that uses its name. Robert Goodman dismisses the Venturi message on architecture as simply "to loosen up and enjoy yourselves."[24] The world of architecture gave the work a good deal more attention, even if much of it was negative. Stanislaus von Moos argued that in the early 1970s "showing sympathy for the Venturis [*sic*] was tantamount to belonging to a forbidden sect," but the architects also "opened a generation's eyes to the reality of popular American everyday culture and to the echoes of an authentic visual tradition it contains."[25] The task here is not to evaluate their architectural designs or even their assessment of Las Vegas architecture but to learn from their analysis of that preeminent gambling town, built essentially for the business of gambling, in order to reflect on the structures that gambling occupies in Deadwood, Central City, Black Hawk, and Cripple Creek.

The fundamental concept from Venturi and Scott Brown was of the "decorated shed." Arguing for the previously dismissed architectural value of the Las Vegas Strip, they insisted that the "simple and commonsense functional organization which meets the needs of the sensibilities in an automotive environment of big spaces and fast movement must not be discounted."[26] This meant wide streets with increasingly huge moving neon signs that directed traffic into parking lots fronting wide, low, windowless buildings where time and location would be forgotten under mirrored ceilings and walls of what would appear to be endless gambling opportunities. In celebrating the "ugly and ordinary" (originally from an epithet with regard to their work from Philip Johnson) over the "heroic and original," Venturi and Scott Brown illustrated the ways in which the layout of Las Vegas was itself a communication system of commercial persuasion. The symbol in space had precedence over form in space.

The Rocky Mountain gambling towns are now in the business of commercial persuasion as single-minded as anything Las Vegas has ever been. Indeed, one could argue that there is much more commercial and economic diversity in the booming city of Las Vegas than in Deadwood,

Central City, Black Hawk, or Cripple Creek. But the spaces they occupy are a huge contrast to the image of Las Vegas as the perfect gambling mecca. To begin, none of the Rocky Mountain towns was designed for cars. Indeed, only Cripple Creek has streets wide enough to even accommodate them very easily, but parking has remained a preeminent problem for both visitors and employees in all four locations. Second, in Deadwood, because of the mandate for historical accuracy, the use of neon was for the most part prohibited, and the restriction on signage continues as a limiting factor in the context of competitive "persuasion" to gamble in a particular place.

But beyond that, Venturi and Scott Brown might argue that the tall, narrow, Victorian buildings of the historic Main Streets are exactly the wrong shape for gambling enterprises. The huge windows allow a clear view of the passage of time and, not insignificantly, the changes in the weather. With floor space functioning primarily as a place to put slot machines, the narrow high-ceilinged historic buildings are characterized mainly as having much "wasted space." This is less an issue in Deadwood, which restricts enterprises to thirty devices per "building," unless other "buildings" can be found or imagined. But in Colorado, governed by percentage of floor space, the beautiful old buildings that long attracted historically minded tourists to Central City are not nearly as functional as the brand new nineteenth-century-"style" warehouses that Black Hawk has built. These are in fact the decorated sheds of nineteenth-century industrial architecture that Venturi and Scott Brown celebrated and architects of the modern movement ignored.[27] But that has happened not only because of differences in terrain but because Black Hawk has been able to stretch the idea of "historic" far beyond what the other towns have allowed. So the tension between the attraction to "historicity" and the gambling prototype continues despite protests that these places are "not Las Vegas."

An examination of what owners call their casinos is another way to measure this tension. Obviously the images of the heyday of gold mining provided a convenient theme to lure gamblers to get rich quick, as many of the original founders of the communities reputedly had. But in Colorado, larger and larger casinos with direct Las Vegas connections and the names that had already made them famous as gambling oases crowded out mom-and-pop operations built on earlier gold-mining lore. So Harrah's and Harvey's joined Hemmeter's vaguely western Bullwhackers as the early big players.

Early losers in the gambling game had names like Miner's Pick in Central City and Claim Jumpers in Black Hawk, both of which closed within three months of opening. Two months later the original Silver Hawk in Black Hawk and Narrow Gauge in Cripple Creek closed. Within a year the Crystal Carousel, Gold Star, Molly's, Red Horse, Calamity Jo's, Madam June's, Turf Club, and Grubstake followed. Seemingly, if you wanted to use the gold-mining theme, the grittier aspects of it were not especially appealing.[28] Even longstanding reputations could not save some enterprises. The Toll Gate Saloon and Gambling Hall, one of the town's longest-lived entertainment emporiums, became the thirteenth casino in Central City to close by midsummer of 1993. In the words of gaming analyst Steve Grogan, "Putting it simply, the Toll Gate was a honky tonk cowboy saloon. The problem with the Toll Gate is that they maximized the gaming and lost all the old-time flavor that made it a very strong place for the locals."[29]

In Deadwood, where the use of historical names for businesses is directly encouraged, the gold theme is still vivid, with a First Gold, Golddiggers, Gold Dust, Gold Nugget, and Gold Coin, if the Gold Rush and Gold Street have disappeared. Anaconda is gone, but Silverado remains. The Nugget is closed, but there is a Lucky Miner along with a Lucky Wrangler and Lady Luck. Again gritty characters seem not to have carried the day. Poker Alice's was one of the first to close, and Calamity Jane's became the French Quarter early on. More recently, Carrie Nation's and Cousin Jack's have disappeared while Hickok's, Miss Kitty's Chinatown, Wild Bill's Bar, Butch Cassidy and the Sundance Kid Gaming Parlor (transformed from the Wildflower), and the Deadwood Dick Saloon survive. The Dakota Territory has weathered the shakedown and so has the Wilderness Edge, but the Prairie Edge and the adjacent Eagle Bar were closed and vacant for nearly two years, until they became part of the Wild West Winner complex. Capitalizing on the town's longstanding lodging accommodations, Deadwood's historic hotels have kept their names (the Franklin, the Fairmont, the Bullock), and the new Mineral Palace came from a nineteenth-century establishment, even if the Costners' proposed Dunbar Resort comes directly out of Hollywood.

What do we make of the imagery projected and transformed: the mythical West versus the historical West? Apparently, if the real West of the new gambling towns is one that challenges to some extent at least the proper place of women, of entrepreneurs, and of Indians, with lines of gender, class, and race blurred on many issues, the images of the towns are, if anything, more rarified than their real past or present. The towns are looking prettier and prettier and more and more alike in their "historic" false fronts and uniform slot-filled interiors. If Claim Jumpers, Narrow Gauge, Madam June's, Calamity Jo's, Calamity Jane's, Poker

Alice's, Carrie Nation's, and Cousin Jack's did not carry the appropriate imagery of the good life come easy, almost anything gold is good, and characters with Hollywood name recognition draw well also.

Does that suggest that the towns are becoming more like Las Vegas or will have to in order to compete? Space restrictions make the absence of live entertainment a distinct difference. Other than a few western bands, the mining town gambling joints have little in the way of professional performers, certainly not the names that billboards feature in Las Vegas, and certainly not the showgirls that make it even more famous. But as Las Vegas has moved more toward theme park entertainment in the last decade, perhaps the various venues will converge in what Robert Goodman has called "McGambling."[30]

Even if they do, we should not assume that the convergence is about family entertainment. Even the chairman of the Mirage Resorts, which built and promoted Treasure Island with ads that include dolphins and a child, now says, "We never said this was a family place, not me. We never knowingly build anything for kids. We don't think this is a proper place for children. This is an adult experience. I did the dolphins for the child in me and in everyone else."[31] The portion of Las Vegas visitors under twenty-one years of age is only 8 percent, up from about 5 percent historically (while Los Angeles says about 17 percent of its 22 million visitors are under age eighteen). Moreover, some in the industry argue that many of the 2.26 million visitors under twenty-one are in fact between eighteen and twenty-one and are not really children at all. While families with and without children spend similar amounts on shopping, entertainment, and food, according to the Las Vegas Convention Bureau, gamblers who come with children spend 30 to 40 percent less at the slots and card tables than those without children.[32] Even the new seventy-million-dollar light show on "Glitter Gulch" (the old Fremont Street gambling strip) functions as a 50 percent sun break during the day and an explosive computerized common exterior lobby of 2.1 million lights for the downtown casinos at night to better compete with the megajoints on the Strip.[33] This is not kids' entertainment either.

But the issue is not that children have never entered the casinos; in Deadwood and Colorado their presence has been not forbidden, only their touching the "devices" is. *Denver Post* staff writer Ann Schrader reported seeing large number of kids amid the cigarette smoke, alcohol, and din of the slots watching Mike Tyson's return to the boxing ring on a casino big-screen television. But most of the children were in strollers, their bottles dumped over the side, and one remarkable woman at a horizontal slot machine was breastfeeding her baby.[34] By May 1996 the

Colorado legislature had passed a bill restricting people younger than twenty-one from lingering in gaming areas of casinos but allowing them to pass through to adjacent restaurants or other "family-oriented" parts of the buildings. One legislator, an avid gambler, said, "This bill sends a clear message that gaming is an adult activity . . . and gaming areas are no place for children."[35] Whatever the historical aspects these towns are preserving, they do not, for the most part, constitute history most would think it important for youth to learn. Indeed, it is the sort of romanticized and simplified history most historians now abhor.

Structural Ironies

While the old quarters of prospectors, mining laborers, and local business people have become locales for mining the quarters of the retired, the freespending, the unimaginative, and the desperate, economic similarities remain. Put in the national context (in the next chapter), local option gambling still mines depletable resources, requires enormous investment for short-term profits, and, like mine tailings, leaves an enormous residue of costs.

But ironies extend beyond the mining metaphor. There is no expectation of rekindling the Great Sioux Wars, but Anglo prosperity in Deadwood's gaming business faces challenges on both land rights and bet limits by Sioux tribes who run their own casinos and return an even larger proportion of profits to their communities. The profits that casinos garnered as regional monopolies are threatened by ubiquitous competitors.

The second major premise, that of historic preservation, becomes more and more of a sham as big new buildings squeeze out vertical slices of Victorian architecture and historic preservation monies are funneled into concrete parking garages. Local economic development comes at the price of losing the amenities that construct a community. Tax relief is a reality only if your property is convertible to gaming income, preferably with "historic restoration."

Finally, these old towns, which spent nearly a century trying to foster identities as communities, have become places where few children live and those who visit are objects of moral opprobrium. Individual citizens also embody the contradictions of the new gambling boom. Bill Walsh, member of the original Deadwood You Bet Committee and owner of the Franklin Hotel and Casino, was featured prominently in a *New York Times* article in November 1995, saying that the 1989 vote on gambling in Deadwood would probably have come out differently had he and others known more about how gambling would change the character of the town. "In many ways, it's been 180 degrees different from what we sold the state when we fought for this."[36] Yet two months later, he was working on a proposed ballot measure to raise Deadwood bet limits to $25. He argued for a low profile campaign centered on "old fashioned grass roots" political efforts at local events such as county fairs. "Our gaming industry is flat and no one has any money to spend on a campaign; we know this going in," said Walsh.[37] And if consistency helps explain contradiction, Marcie Hepner, owner of the Gold Camp Mercantile in Cripple Creek, said she would "vote no in a heartbeat" if the election to legalize gambling were held today. She complained that people used to want to know about the history of Cripple Creek. Now they only want to know where the hot machines are. Still, she would support raising bet limits, because they would "bring in people with more money."[38]

CHAPTER 8

Legalized Gambling as a Community Development Quick Fix

Beginning in the 1970s and accelerating in the 1980s, the dismantling of the welfare state found Washington, D.C., reducing federal revenues that had reached all fifty states through a complex pipeline of federal programs. With defunding came the disassembling of the pipeline itself. Taxpayer rebellions against higher taxes and even demands for tax cuts, however, paradoxically coexpanded with increased budget requirements for mandated expenditures such as debt payments, Social Security, and politically mandated funding for the military. Responding to a perceived political necessity for tax cuts, the federal government resorted to middle-class tax breaks coupled with a new program of federalism that shifted programs such as urban development, welfare, and health care to state governments.

State governments, confronting their own contradictory taxpayer rebellions and the continued demands of citizens for quality services, rallied to the call for local control, of course, coupled with local fiscal responsibility. Thus, both local and state governments were confronted with the unenviable position of financing mandated federal programs, state and local services, as well as optional services requested of the citizenry in a time of taxpayer revolt. Calls for additional taxes fell on deaf ears. Creative financing seemed the logical answer.

In an unusual seizure of opportunity, states turned to "painless" sources of revenue. Revenue enhancements that looked like recreation rather than taxation became the solution for at least forty-eight of the fifty states that turned to games of chance such as horse racing, lotto, scratch tickets, casino gambling, or some other "get-rich-quick" schemes to supplement and, in some cases, eventually to drive state finances. What were the sources of this initiative? What is its likely conclusion?

The Third Wave: Learning from Cyclical Histories of Vice

Most likely because of its English history, the United States, even as a confederation of states, relied on games of chance to support government.[1] The Continental Army relied on lotteries, although they were mismanaged and not as lucrative as were the games of chance that helped to support the early founding and operations of Dartmouth, Harvard, and Princeton. Yet gambling had come into disfavor on the East Coast by the early 1800s, and what became the first-wave games of chance, including numerous gambling enterprises such as card games, roulette, and keno, along with other less civilized forms of entertainment such as prostitution, alcohol, and drugs, spread west and south along the Mississippi River. Whether reflecting the rise of fundamentalist religious groups, the activist "civilizing" influence of women, or the extensiveness of dishonest games, legal games of chance largely disappeared east of the Mississippi by the early 1830s. The risk of a toss of the dice or a shuffle of cards was replaced by the everyday risks of physical labor and capital investments. Riverboat casinos, dockside saloons, and cribs were gradually replaced by churches, fraternal organizations, and retail and wholesale enterprises as the eastern portion of the United States went about the daily chore of doing the business of America. What had been seen as recreation became viewed as vice, soon to be regulated and then made illegal. By the first half of the 1800s the United States east of the Mississippi, particularly the deep South (perhaps excluding a "friendly" wager on a horse), became a model of propriety with regard to gambling.

The second wave of America's involvement with "vice" coincided with westward expansion, particularly the settlement of California after the discovery of gold and silver in 1848 and the penetration of the railroads into and across the Rocky Mountains. During the second half of the nineteenth century the Rocky Mountains and the territory west of them were dotted with hundreds of boomtowns that owed their existence to reported claims of gold. Thousands of adventurers risked their lives and their fortunes to find the elusive mother lode, while thousands more risked their fortunes, if not their lives, to provide the daily necessities of food, shelter, clothing, and recreation. Often these necessities included liquor, gambling, and prostitution. The landscape, now strewn with tens of dozens of abandoned mining sites or mining ghost towns, attests to the magnitude of this risk taking. Those towns, whose mineral reserves were sufficient to establish enduring, viable towns that survived into the late 1900s, are steeped in colorful histories that have in many cases today provided a source of livelihood in tourism.

Early on in these mining towns, few if any prohibitions were placed on individual behavior. Providers of liquor, gambling, and even prostitution were often leading capitalists in the community. The gamble on the fast buck, whether it be prospecting for ore or betting at tables of chance, was seen as commonplace, even admirable, although the results were often financial ruin. Even as communities became "settled," excesses of moral turpitude were generally regulated rather than prohibited, and local communities gleaned substantial revenues from fees imposed on saloons, dance halls, and "boarding houses." By the beginning of the twentieth century, however, excessive liquor, games of chance, and prostitution were no longer defined, at least publicly, as recreation but again as vice to be controlled and if possible eliminated.

Of course, all three continued to exist, but they were now not only moral improprieties but also illegal activities subject to periodic, discretionary control by local and state authorities. Even after 1900 some Rocky Mountain towns were famous for their toleration of "illegal" vice, as noted by the notoriety given to Cripple Creek's red-light district, Central City's opera festival, which included gambling for Denver's elite, and Deadwood's prostitution and backhall gambling, all enduring well into the second half of the twentieth century, despite intermittent legal interventions.

But in the main, by the early 1900s reformers in concert with captains of industry had pushed for moral restraints, with states passing legislation restricting games of chance and in some cases alcohol, while local ordinances placed constraints on prostitution. Except for the maverick state of Nevada, these legal barriers remained intact until 1976, when New Jersey made possible large scale casino gambling in Atlantic City under the guise of economic development. The aims of this legalization were laudatory: to revitalize the "boardwalk" in an effort to keep it from fading into American folklore and to benefit the total community of Atlantic City. (There are those who question the success of either goal.) Of course, small inroads on restrictions on gambling had already been made by pari-mutuel betting on horses and dogs in some states, by New Hampshire's return to a state lottery in 1964, and by states allowing charities and fraternal organizations to engage in games of chance, primarily bingo and an occasional "casino night."

While other states climbed on the gambling bandwagon with lotteries and diverse scratch card games, access to casino-style gambling remained limited until 1988, when the state of South Dakota via a state referendum authorized Deadwood to begin limited stakes casino gambling in the form of slot machines, poker, and blackjack, thereby emphasizing the tone of the third and perhaps most expansive leap into gambling in the country's history. With the third wave of gambling, a curious wedding of state and private efforts established gambling enterprises supported by private capital, regulated by one state agency and sponsored by another. These were strange bedfellows indeed.

The New Beginnings

November 1, 1989, marked the end of an eleven-year hiatus since the opening of Atlantic City's casino-style gambling in 1978. Although modest in scope (five-dollar limits, action restricted to slot machines, poker, and blackjack, and only thirty gaming devices per building), opening day signaled a return to casino gambling outlawed in South Dakota since 1881. Gambling would not only help fill state coffers but would primarily be used for the morally upright purpose of restoring the declining mining and tourist town to its late-nineteenth-century heyday with the intent of creating a "family tourist destination" where gambling would be an aside.

But an examination of the recent history of legal gambling in the United States shows that the late 1980s was also a federal legislative turning point. In 1988, in response to the Supreme Court decision of *State of California v. Cabazon Band of Mission Indians,* Congress had passed the Indian Gaming Regulatory Act (PL 100-497), which established three categories of gambling. Class I games primarily involve social and traditional Indian games and are not regulated; Class II games, bingo and grandfathered Indian casinos, are regulated by the National Indian Gaming Commission at the federal level; and Class III games, including casinos, race tracks, off-track betting parlors, and lotteries, are regulated according to compacts entered into jointly by the Indian tribe and the state. Essentially, the 1988 legislation allows federally recognized tribes to negotiate casino agreements in any state where casino-style gambling is allowed, even for limited charity purposes.[2] The extent and nature of that gambling was to be negotiated in "good faith" by the states and Indian tribes. To prevent foot dragging by states, the legislation provides a six-month grace period for states to commence negotiations. If states fail to negotiate in good faith, then the affected tribe has recourse to federal courts, where an impartial mediator will devise a compact.

Minnesota was the first state to negotiate agreements to establish casinos on Indian reservations and by 1993 reported that five thousand jobs had been created at a dozen reservation gambling sites.[3] Generally, as was the case in Atlantic City and Deadwood, arguments for gambling centered on economic development, primarily job creation. However, new schools, housing, roads, and hospitals, as well as per capita payments, in some cases resulted from gambling windfalls.[4] Unlike gaming in Nevada, Atlantic City, and Deadwood, gaming revenues on reservations were subject to neither federal nor state taxation, a bone of contention to be brought to federal court in April 1993 when Donald Trump filed a complaint charging reservation gambling with unfair interstate competition.[5] Irrespective of Trump's legal challenge, Vegas-type gambling on Indian reservations had spread by 1996 to include 131 compacts in 115 of the 557 federally recognized tribes in 23 states, a number that changes monthly.[6] To emphasize the success of gambling in creating jobs and revenues, some Indian leaders and writers now refer to gambling as the "new buffalo."

Preeminent among the success stories is Foxwoods, operated by the Mashantucket Pequot Indians in Connecticut. By 1995 Foxwoods was the largest casino in the United States in number of gambling devices, square footage, and profitability.[7] The fifty-five-million-dollar investment in 1991 proved successful beyond imagination. Located within the population corridor of New York and Boston, the Pequot Reservation, which began only with table games, negotiated a deal with Connecticut's governor Lowell P. Weicker to pay the state a yearly minimum of $100 million for the exclusive right to casino gambling in Connecticut and for the right to operate slot machines,[8] an agreement that netted Connecticut $137 million in 1994, making the Pequots the largest single contributors of revenue to state government.[9] Estimates in early 1994 suggested that Foxwoods had grossed a million dollars or more per day, had created some ten thousand jobs (for a tribe of fewer than three hundred), and had begun to diversify the Pequot economy.[10] The compact between the Pequots and the state of Connecticut provides a fascinating example of two governments reaching agreement on a gambling issue for the good of both entities.

As Indian gambling spread, numerous states began to question the advisability of Indian gambling. The ex-governor of Arizona, Fife Symington, attempted to limit Indian gambling to bingo, but, when confronted with legal action, he negotiated in "good faith" for casinos with a limit of 250 devices, primarily because a number of charities engaged in casino nights as fund-raisers. When other tribes sought federal intervention regarding the device limitations and won the right to have up to 2,600 devices, the governor promptly abolished all casino games and thereby deprived charities of a source of revenue and eliminated the basis for the Indian appeal.[11] New Mexico quietly followed suit and became embroiled in a similar dispute regarding Indian gaming, which in the spring of 1997 was still in federal court.[12] Colorado likewise negotiated a limited stakes gaming pact with its Indian nations based on the restrictions imposed on

Cripple Creek, Black Hawk, and Central City. While abiding by the five-dollar limit and space limitations, tribes filed federal suits to remove the restraints. Thus, as the nebulous working of "negotiations in good faith" proved achievable in some cases but contentious in others, pressure mounted on Congress to modify the 1988 legislation to give states more control over gambling within their state boundaries, thereby setting up additional confrontations regarding sovereignty issues.[13] These conflicts represent basic issues of competition for the gambling dollar, in the form of Indian gambling vying with local option gambling, as is the case in Colorado and South Dakota, or with state lotteries, as is the case in Arizona, New Mexico, South Dakota, and Colorado.

The Spread and Entrenchment of Gambling

If 1988 marked the beginning of casino gambling's third cycle, then 1990 was a benchmark. That year saw the state of Colorado, after a successful referendum petition, approve local option, limited stakes gambling in the three mountain communities of Cripple Creek, Black Hawk, and Central City, as well as the state of Iowa approving riverboat gambling for the first time in over a hundred years. Of the two, Iowa's decision to revamp the economies of communities by gambling was probably the more dramatic in terms of its impact on other states. Iowa's decision to legalize the "vice" of gambling led to a "new" form of gambling: that of floating casinos. With a revival of activities from over a hundred years past, Iowans might have been pathbreakers, but they were at first not very adventurous in their commitment to gambling. In solving the moral conflict between sin (gambling as vice) and economic development, gambling was approved but with only a five-dollar bet limit and only on turn-of-the-century, "authentic" riverboats while afloat and for forty-five minutes after docking, with a maximum loss of $200 dollars per gambler. Furthermore, specific docking sites had to be approved by local voters in a countywide referendum. In compliance with the notion of economic development, Iowa products were to be available for purchase on all riverboats. Finally, in the name of wholesome family entertainment, a section of each boat had to be reserved for children.[14] These restrictions revealed the tentative commitment Iowans made to gambling and strongly emphasized the notion that gambling should be a form of recreation, thereby easing religious objections. The official shift of gambling from an immoral vice to a form of "harmless" recreation with numerous beneficial side effects was under way in the Heartland.

Being first allowed Iowa to capture six riverboats by 1991. Initially riverboats created jobs, but riverboat owners also cajoled various local

188 / *Chapter 8*

governments, in their competition for riverboats, to invest in infrastructures to accommodate large mobile floating casinos. Communities such as Davenport and Fort Madison invested $10 million and $2.6 million, respectively, in dockside facilities and adjoining tourist amenities.[15] While an initial success in terms of visitors, riverboat gambling under Iowa's restrictions proved unprofitable when other states (Illinois, Mississippi, and Louisiana and later Missouri, Indiana, and Washington) legalized riverboat gambling in rapid succession.[16] In a feverish competition to outbid one another, states quickly dropped restraints on riverboat gambling, including bet limits and maximum losses, and, in the case of Mississippi, removed all pretense of "off-shore" gaming through the creation of what would be called land-based riverboat gambling, in which boats are not expected to leave dockside.

Ironically, in re-creating riverboat gambling Iowa provided the avenue for its own demise by establishing a model for other states to follow in their search for painless revenues and community revitalization. Iowa's mandate that boats float for at least two hours ensured that they were seaworthy, thereby facilitating their mobility. Therefore, when Mississippi passed legislation in 1990 enabling riverboat gambling with neither bet limits nor loss totals, three of the six Iowa boats simply pulled anchor and departed downriver. The marketplace and free capital left Iowa cities with long-term bond issues and high unemployment. As Fort Madison, the first Iowa community to begin riverboat gambling, discovered, a pact with the devil can indeed be injurious. In 1992 the *Emerald Lady* departed for Biloxi, resulting in a loss of 350 jobs and increased property taxes to cover debt payment on a new, empty dock, leaving Mayor Arlene J. Carlson to wax optimistic on the prospects of another, though smaller, boat arriving by 1994.[17]

Iowa's first claim to gambling on riverboats was quickly relegated to the position of minor player by state legislatures in Louisiana, Mississippi, and Illinois. Mississippi's legislation authorized casinos to stimulate its tourism industry, which was in serious decline. Given the "no holds barred" law—with no bet limits, low taxation (8 percent at the state level plus up to 4 percent at the local level), no requirements regarding losses or time spent gambling, no need for seaworthy vessels since gaming was now a dockside enterprise, and almost unlimited access to Las Vegas–style gaming—it was little wonder that by 1992 Mississippi's coast was dotted with thirty riverboat casinos.[18] All pretense of gaming being a family activity was dropped since riverboats were not required to devote any space to child care or to activities for children. Likewise nary a Mississippi handicraft was to be seen. The business of Mississippi gaming was simply gambling.

Tunica County, Mississippi, once one of the nation's poorest, became the industry's showcase. Prior to legalized casino gambling, Tunica County was known as a place where the indicators of social pathology, including unemployment, welfare caseloads, substandard housing, and rates of family disruption, were among the highest in the nation. After the advent of gaming Tunica County was touted as an example of community transformation par excellence. With a "flotilla" of ten riverboats, Tunica County boasted twenty thousand new jobs, an increased tax base, and low rates of unemployment. Yet despite the heralded economic success, by 1995 the *Lady Luck* had left Tunica, and Treasure Bay Casinos located in both Gulfport and Tunica had filed for Chapter 11 bankruptcy.[19]

The entry of Louisiana and Illinois in 1992 into riverboat casino gaming might help explain the volatility in the riverboat gaming industry. Louisiana legislation provided for fifteen riverboat licenses plus one land-based casino to be located in New Orleans. The legislation pushed by then-governor Edwards provided unlimited stakes gaming along the Red River while the land-based casino was awarded to Harrah's Jazz Co. and Hemmeter Enterprises, Inc., after much controversy. The almost half-billion-dollar project ran into financial and locational problems almost immediately. By December 1995 the half-finished project was placed under bankruptcy proceedings. The fifteen riverboat permits that were granted came under investigation by the FBI on the basis of allegations that Governor Edwards's relatives and friends received millions in kickbacks in the form of "consulting fees."[20] Obviously the riverboat gaming business had created jobs in Shreveport, Baton Rouge, and New Orleans, but these transformations were accompanied by allegations of graft. The city of New Orleans was left with a half-finished building and a twenty-seven-million-dollar gap in the city budget created by the anticipated taxes that would now not be paid.

Illinois, on the other hand, also entered into riverboat gambling in 1992 but did so with some constraints on the enterprises. Applicants for the ten state licenses had to provide $50,000 up front for the opportunity to apply for a license and for background checks; if successful, they then had to pay yearly fees of $25,000 plus a 20 percent tax on profits. Furthermore, like Iowa, Illinois required riverboats to maintain either a nineteenth-century architectural design or a modern cruise ship motif. As riverboats were limited to twelve hundred gaming devices per boat, one could argue that these restrictions were primarily safeguards for the existing gambling enterprises centered around horse racing and the profitable state lottery.[21]

In Illinois, the available licenses were allocated to create regional gambling centers or, seen from a different perspective, economic development nodes. One such node, Joliet, has undertaken an eighteen-million-dollar downtown infrastructure repair, including renovation of the train station and library, new brick sidewalks, and improvements to a riverside park.[22] Riverboats supplied about 20 percent of the city's 1994 budget ($27 million) and were by January 1996 the largest employer in the city with an estimated thirty-nine hundred employees.[23] As is the case in other gambling communities, there was little evidence to suggest that the success of riverboat gambling has spread to other retail business, and there were no indications of how deep and long-lasting the economic transformations of Joliet would be.

Gambling as Economic Development

The work of Peter K. Eisinger, in *The Rise of the Entrepreneurial State*,[24] showed that beginning in the 1960s and 1970s a number of communities undergoing economic stress entertained numerous and diverse economic development schemes. (See chapter 3 for a detailed overview.) Contradictory to the accepted model of free capitalism, in which individual entrepreneurs risked their capital with the expectation of substantial returns (or losses), these development schemes involved direct federal, state, and/or local government intervention. (More recently, a similar proposal involving state lotteries to support a small business fund was suggested by Robert Goodman in a chapter titled "The Good Gamble.")[25] According to Eisinger, laissez-faire principles to support small businesses confronting national and even international competition or to support local municipal or county government were abandoned. Essentially, government intervention would be directed at generating supply incentives, including infrastructural enhancements such as industrial parks, tax incentives such as abatements, and financial incentives in the form of outright grants to encourage companies to relocate in a given community.

Eisinger saw that supply incentives resulted in local governments engaging in cutthroat competition amongst themselves for scarce capital investments, with long-term financial disaster resulting. The alternative, the stimulation of demand, forces local communities to rely on some unique advantage such as environmental amenities (location, minerals, or visual perspective), local historical events, or unusual population characteristics (university towns, technical schools). Here, government emphasis on uniqueness creates an attraction for capital, including "natural" tourist attractions. This development model suggested that Deadwood, South Dakota, and Cripple Creek, Black Hawk, and Central City, Colorado, all steeped in the coarse history of the late 1800s mining ethos and all designated as historic landmarks, would be successful demand markets.

Efforts by all four communities to market such demand characteristics in the 1960s, 1970s, and 1980s had met with limited seasonal success, drawing many tourists in the summer and almost none in the winter. All four communities turned to legalized gambling in the 1990s to ameliorate that cycle, but the gambling was pitched as entertainment steeped in historical integrity. Eisinger's model of the entrepreneurial state suggested that the most effective use of resources was to focus on local assets within a demand model that would be jump-started by federal revenues. Yet, unlike the Eisinger model, Deadwood, followed closely by the three Colorado communities, focused on demand but without initial governmental support. This was possible because the monopolies created by enabling legislation at the state levels resulted in dramatic opportunities for economic development. Variations in gambling investment patterns and revenue dispersal between South Dakota and Colorado emerged; nevertheless, major similarities and difficulties in terms of community transformations prevailed. Analysis of these differences and similarities is informative for future community development.

With the rapid infusion of capital the four communities underwent substantial community transformations. In both states, local retail and wholesale stores were cannibalized by gaming operations. By the end of year one of gambling in Deadwood, seventy-eight retail/wholesale businesses had been converted to casinos. With gaming and the potential for high profits, land speculation resulted in escalated land values and property tax liabilities. Many store owners sold to the highest bidders; others who saw potential profit in gaming quickly converted grocery stores, clothing stores, T-shirt shops, and even local drive-ins into gaming halls. Similar transformations occurred in Colorado, whose towns had fewer retail businesses to begin with.

The four communities became boomtowns, with rapidly expanding economies and dramatic increases in temporary visiting populations. In Colorado the lack of motels and hotels (most had been converted into gaming casinos) meant that most gamblers were day visitors. Over four million visitors, a fourfold increase in tourism, came to the Colorado gambling towns every year. In Deadwood, which has more than six hundred rooms, many visitors were able to stay for a couple of days. Still, few of Deadwood's more than one million visitors (also a fourfold increase in tourism) made any commitment to the community. Tourism, in addition to quadrupling in all four communities, changed in nature, shifting from families to adults, since gambling by law is an adult-centered activity. There was now little for teenagers or young children to do in the communities and not even many places for them to be. Opera patrons in Central

City had to compete for parking space and confront street congestion at the peak of the gambling season. Furthermore, in all four communities, gambling crested in June, July, August, and September, requiring the towns to develop infrastructures to accommodate that population. But newly developed water and sewage facilities remained underutilized much of the year. Also, service personnel requirements such as police needed to be available for the period of greatest demand.

Although there was little growth in the permanent population in any of the communities, all reversed the steady economic decline they had experienced from the 1920s to the 1940s, all made major improvements in city infrastructures, and all saw the renovation of the facades of some "historic" buildings. Also, all experienced increased criminal and civil offenses, and all have residents that complain about a loss of the sense of community and ability to participate in decisions about it.[26] The ultimate irony can be found in Black Hawk, the poor sister of the gambling towns whose creekside advantage of scale made it the leader in Colorado gambling. In four years' time its once stable population of 250 people dwindled to 125 because the town's homes were too close to the gaming district and the idling diesel tour buses. But as *Denver Post* staff writer Steve Garnaas pointed out, "Even without people, Black Hawk has prospered. Municipal revenues went from $120,000 in 1990 . . . to $12.6 million five years later."[27]

Finally, to support the expanded personnel and infrastructure, the four communities essentially became hooked on the large volume of gambling revenue, as have the states in which they are located. When in 1993 a constitutional question temporarily shut down video lottery in South Dakota until a voter referendum could revive it, Governor William Janklow threatened to close state libraries, shut down public radio and public television, and raise college tuition unless voters supported the continuation of the lottery. Some constituents thought the targets were specifically chosen to blackmail those who questioned gambling as a basic source of state revenues. The more specific campaign in the gambling towns has been to raise the bet limits in order to compete with Nevada, Atlantic City, and Indian casinos, as well as the unrestricted midwestern riverboats.

Whether or not bet limits are raised, pressures from economies of scale shape profits and tax revenues in both Deadwood and Colorado. Deadwood's gross revenues began falling behind the equivalent months of the previous year for the first time in September 1995 and continued through the winter and spring months.[28] Deadwood Gaming Association President Mike Rodman expressed fear especially for the smaller operations, those with thirty or fewer gaming devices and without a hotel/motel or other amenities.[29] Despite Deadwood's creative counting of buildings to permit more than thirty devices, the issue of scale is reflected even more dramatically in Colorado. By January 1996 Colorado casinos' monthly revenues in Black Hawk, Central City, and Cripple Creek had all fallen below their level of a year earlier for the first time ever. However, while revenues dropped, state taxes rose as more casinos entered higher tax brackets because of the Colorado progressive tax structure. Casinos paid $3.25 million in gaming taxes in January 1996, compared to $3.17 million in January 1995, so the state profited while Central City faced a budget reduction, the cutback of six city workers, the closure of one casino with six hundred devices, and the decrease by three hundred in another.[30]

Rocky Mountain Gambling in the National Context

With forty-eight states involved in some type of gambling (Utah and Hawaii abstaining) and twenty-five involved in riverboat casinos, Las Vegas–style casinos, Indian gambling, or video gambling, the crest of the gambling third wave is yet to come. Americans wagered more than $400 billion in 1995, and the gambling industry garnered profits exceeding $40 billion,[31] a tripling of revenues since 1982. As gambling revenues continue to escalate, America's former moral qualms about gaming seem to have faded. A 1993 survey by Home Testing Institute found that for the first time more than half of American adults have gambled in casinos at some point in their lives, and, of these, one in five had gambled in the past year.[32] The proliferation of riverboat gambling from six in 1991 to more than seventy by 1996, most centered in the deep South, signaled the Bible Belt's acceptance of gambling and a redefinition of gambling from vice to entertainment, the latter definition bolstered by accompanying activities of dining and live shows.

Acceptance of gambling is reinforced by the constant barrage of gambling industry promotional materials touting jobs created and investments made, while government agencies directly benefiting from gambling revenue in the form of taxes and fees focus on millions of dollars generated for general funds. An Associated Press article exemplifies this optimistic viewpoint by reporting data from Sean McGuinness, Mississippi's gaming commission compliance director, showing $285 million in casino revenues, with the state's take at around $25 million just for the first year of legalized gambling.[33] Likewise, Indian reservations highlight job creation such as the more than 10,000 employed by the expanded Foxwoods, or the 257 employed in Montezuma County by the Ute Mountain Casino in Colorado; but Indians also discuss the possibility of gaming revenues providing an avenue for financial independence from the federal government. At the same time, other Indian tribes have avoided all forms of gambling because of the real fear of a loss of tribal community. And, though smaller in scale than riverboat gambling or Indian gambling, casino gambling for four Rocky Mountain towns brought substantial economic revival of their economies along with dramatic changes in the social and structural fabric of their communities.

But the issue of scale alongside the proliferation of gambling raises important questions for the Rocky Mountain gambling communities in the contemporary context. While Solomon Brothers estimated that gambling revenues at casinos would rise to $18 billion in 1996, from $16.1 billion in 1995 and $14.1 billion in 1994, most analysts predicted that the more moderate growth would help only the biggest companies, not the dozens of smaller gambling concerns that had gone public in recent years. Gamblers need a new thrill, and so the companies would have to erect ever larger casinos. That would happen in Las Vegas, the fastest growing city in the United States, with three new enormous casino-hotels. But it is not clear that Deadwood, Central City, Black Hawk, and Cripple Creek would, on the whole, benefit from this growth. "Nineteen ninety-six," said Scott M. Renner, an analyst at Solomon Brothers, "is going to be the year when the rich get richer."[34]

Indeed, while gambling grew overall in the United States in 1996, the wealth was not evenly divided. Deadwood's casinos lost more than $1.16 million during 1996, after profits of $3.7 million on 1995 and $4.16 million in 1994. And of the fifty-one different ownerships in Deadwood, twenty showed profits, while thirty-one experienced losses; thirteen closed and five others reopened under new ownership.[35] And 1997 figures were even worse.

If Deadwood, like Iowa, had been the model of truly limited recreational gaming, in terms of size of operations, bet limits, and loss limits, Deadwood followed Iowa in hitting the wall of expanding opportunities. Iowa's riverboats had the choice to leave, and Deadwood's clientele could also make other choices. As Mike Rodman, general manager of the Silverado Casino and president of the newly merged Deadwood Chamber of Commerce/Deadwood Visitors Bureau, would observe, "Nearly everyone in America today lives within a hundred miles of a gaming opportunity."[36]

Colorado casinos continued to experience winter doldrums; however, the growth of large-scale casinos allowed Colorado to experience in March 1997 their second best month in five and a half years of gaming. Adjusted gross proceeds of $30.9 million in December 1996 were eclipsed by $38.7 million in March 1997, trailing only the $39.5 million recorded in the peak month of August 1996. Black Hawk continued its newfound dominance with more profits than Central City and Cripple Creek combined.[37] The town that had lost much of its tiny population now housed the largest corporate enterprises, poignantly raising the question of whether "community" development had taken place or not.

The ever accelerating movement by states to engage in more and more diverse gambling activities as a form of painless taxation raises the important question of when a saturation point will be reached. When will the American public realize that gambling is an inefficient form of taxation that cannibalizes other businesses, particularly those dependent on discretionary spending? Expert I. Nelson Rose, professor at Whittier Law School, "sees the bubble bursting, but not until the year 2020, give or take a few years."[38] Jerome Skolnick, author of *House of Cards,* cautions, "As the casino industry expands, there is always the danger that the golden goose will run out of eggs."[39] But who will bet on it?

Why is gambling preferable to taxation? What happens to state agencies when gambling revenue is earmarked for specific uses? How do towns that depend on the seasonal service jobs associated with making change and serving food and drink organize stable social institutions? What is their civic relationship to surrounding communities? What happens when slot machines become ubiquitous, and when do players notice that they all sound and operate alike? What long-run social and economic costs are likely to cause a turnaround in the social legitimacy as well as the legal operation of gaming industries?

Unfortunately, the choice of limited stakes gambling does not imply temporary stakes, for many of the decisions that support gambling and the seasonal demands for infrastructure in the old mining towns are nearly irrevocable. The towns are heavily bonded to support the improvements they have made, and their expanded budgets are highly dependent on gambling income. The return of retail business remains severely disadvantaged by the tax structure, so the city governments are in the trap of having to demand ever expanded rather than more limited gambling, which would allow more diversified economies.

The examples of the Rocky Mountain towns, whose entire histories are characterized by booms and busts, demonstrate a transformation from mining and recreation communities that always encompassed gambling in some forms to recreation sites defined almost exclusively by gambling. Other civic entities should consider whether gambling in the present context can have limited impact or if, in fact, the stakes are low. And citizens should question the complicity of government agencies in disguising recreation as taxation that may serve to destroy the communities they are meant to protect.

N O T E S

Abbreviations

BHP	Black Hills Pioneer
CCDR	Central City Daily Register
DP	Denver Post
DT	Denver Times
LCC	Lawrence County Centennial
LCN	Lawrence County Newspapers
LDB	Laramie Daily Boomerang
NYT	New York Times
QCM	Queen City Mail (Spearfish)
RCJ	Rapid City Journal
RMN	Rocky Mountain News
VCCDP	Victor and Cripple Creek Daily Press
WSJ	Wall Street Journal

Chapter 1. The Drive for the Legalization of Gambling

1. Although the land is currently claimed as sacred territory by the Dakota tribes (called Sioux by the French and U.S. governments), these peoples were part of a succession of native groups that have occupied the Black Hills, including the Kiowas, Crows, and Cheyenne.

2. Watson Parker, *Deadwood: The Golden Years* (Lincoln: University of Nebraska Press, 1981), 14–18.

3. "Mill Creek Resort Plans Move Forward," *LCC*, March 5, 1994.

4. Donald Toms, ed., *The Gold Belt Cities: Deadwood and Environs, a Photographic History* (Lead: G.O.L.D. Unlimited, 1988), 5.

5. Parker, *Deadwood*, 64–74.

6. Edith Eudora Kohl, *Land of the Burnt Thigh* (Funk & Wagnalls, 1938), republished by the Minnesota Historical Society Press (Saint Paul, 1986), 80–81.

7. Duane A. Smith, *Rocky Mountain Mining Camps: The Urban Frontier* (Lincoln: University of Nebraska Press, 1967), 225.

8. "Lightning Gambling Raid Closes Tables," *Lead Daily Call*, June 30, 1947. In 1946, the county prosecutor and sheriff's department had decided to enforce the 1881 law outlawing gambling, gaming halls, brothels, and "other disorderly houses and practices." Karen Hansen and Megan Seacord, "A Twentieth Century Gold Rush," *State Legislatures* (March 1991): 15.

9. Scott Randolph, "With State Constitution Change, Gaming Returns to Deadwood," *LCN*, November 1, 1989.

10. Michael Trump, "Raiding Tradition: A History of Governmental Assaults on Deadwood's Beloved Brothels," master's thesis, Department of History, University of Wyoming, July 1994, 33, citing *RCJ*, June 15, 1980.

11. *Deadwood Pioneer Times*, May 21, 1981.

12. Randolph, "Gaming Returns."

13. Ibid.

14. Ibid.

15. Ibid.

16. Larry A. Weirs, "Limited Gambling for Deadwood on the Horizon: You Bet Committee Gears up for Active Year," *LCN*, March 26, 1988.

17. Ibid.

18. Randolph, "Gaming Returns."

19. Scott Randolph, "Deadwood Votes 'Yes' to Gambling; Runoff Set April 25 to Elect Mayor," *LCC*, April 12, 1989; Heidi Bell, "November 1, 1989--Deadwood You Bet," *LCC*, November 1, 1989.

20. Bill Park, "High Noon Finally Arrives in Deadwood," and Heidi Bell, "Legalized Gambling Begins with a Bang," *LCC*, November 4, 1989.

21. Steve Garnaas, "Stakes High for Gambling Petitions," *DP*, July 29, 1990.

22. Sam Lusky, "1503 Slot Machines," *RMN*, February 5, 1948.

23. "Central City Takes Wraps off Gambling," *DP*, July 21, 1948.

24. Ibid.

25. "Teller County Levies Slot Machine Fines," *DP*, November 30, 1948; "Gambling Still Rife despite Crackdown by Teller County Law," *DP*, December 6, 1948.

26. "Gaiety, Gambling Back at Central City," "Strauss, Dice Vie at Festival," "Tinkle of Opera, Jingle of Gambling Cash—It's Central City Season," " 'First-Nighter' Parties Hail Opera Season," "Audience Lauds 'Die Fledermaus' on Opening Night in Central City," *DP*, July 3, 1949.

27. "DA Clamps Lid on Central City Gambling," *RMN*, July 8, 1949.

28. "Lid Clamped on Gambling in Central City," *DP*, July 8, 1949; "DA Clamps Lid."

29. "It's Law versus Law as Scrappy JP Wars on Central Gamblers," *RMN*, August 7, 1949; "Raid Fails, Central City Slots Hidden," *DP*, August 10, 1949.

30. Edward Lehman, "Central City's Elite Hit in Slots Purge: Warrants Served on 37 in Gambling Crackdown," "Crusading J.P. Hopes to Jail Central Citizens," "Mayor among Those Named in Warrants," *DP*, August 11, 1949.

31. "Woman Jailed, Feted in Slot Machine War," *DP*, August 12, 1949.

32. "Stone Walls Do Not a Prison Make," *DP*, August 15, 1949.

33. "Central City Jail's Lone Occupant Visits Restaurant," *DP*, August 12, 1949.

34. Eva Hodges, "Jailed Organist Who Spurns Bail Becomes 'Toast of Central City,' " *DP*, August 12, 1949; Sam Lusky, "Anti-Gambling Drive Folds in Central City," *RMN*, August 15, 1949.

35. "Central City Gambling Row," *DP*, August 12, 1949; Lusky, "Anti-Gambling Drive"; "Witnesses Balk, Slots Row Eases," *DP*, August 15, 1949.

36. Sam Lusky, "Central Maps Plan to Be 'Little Reno' with Legal Gaming," *RMN*, August 21, 1949.

37. "No Gambling without Corruption," editorial, *RMN*, August 23, 1949.

38. Ibid.

39. Al Nakkula, "Gambling Ban Asked of Knous," *DP*, clipping file, Denver Public Library, n.d.

40. "D.A.'s Oppose State Gambling Law Repeal," *DP*, August 28, 1949.

41. "Central's 'Martyr' Quits Jail," *DP*, August 27, 1949.

42. "Central City Gambling Plan Seen outside Law," *DP*, June 7, 1950.

43. " 'Kingdom' of Gilpin Isn't Sovereign, Attorney Says," *DP,* June 7, 1950.

44. "Gambling for Revenue? No!" editorial, *RMN,* March 14, 1951.

45. "Crackdown on Gambling in Churches Here Hinted," *DP,* July 28, 1953.

46. Robert Tonsing and Pat Carrico, "Gaming Lodge at Black Hawk Raided; 12 Held," *DP,* August 19, 1959; Bob Tonsing, "Miamians Ran Thorn Lake," *DP,* August 25, 1959; Charles Roach, "Thorn Lake Gamblers Linked to National Crime Syndicate," *RMN,* August 26, 1959; Robert Tonsing, "Fixed Dice Cache Found in Bushes," *DP,* August 27, 1959.

47. John M. Findlay, *People of Chance* (New York: Oxford University Press, 1986), 111–135.

48. Dick Prouty, "State-Banned Gaming Devices Pay 'Dividend' to U.S.," *DP,* November 20, 1966.

49. Steve Garnaas, "Backers of 3 Initiatives Work to Get Proposal on the November Ballot," *DP,* July 29, 1990.

50. Steve Garnaas, "Poundstone Places Winning Bet," *DP,* November 7, 1990.

51. Steve Garnaas, "Proponents' Appeal to Voters Is Low-Key," *DP,* September 30, 1990.

52. Steve Garnaas, "Odds Have Improved for Casino Gambling," *DP,* September 30, 1990.

53. Richard Salmonson, personal interview, May 21, 1992.

54. Steve Garnaas, "Church Plea to Fight Gambling Disputed," *DP,* November 2, 1990.

55. Jennifer Gavin, "Gambling Bill Chips on Table," *DP,* April 6, 1991; idem, "Small-Stakes Gambling Specifics Win Initial Approval in House," *DP,* April 12, 1991; Eric Anderson, "Gaming Bill Gains Initial OK in Senate," *DP,* April 16, 1991; Jennifer Gavin, "Gambling Bill Wins Initial OK in House," *DP,* May 2, 1991.

Chapter 2. Race, Gender, and Class in the Legacy of the Gamble

1. Reverend Peter Rosen, *Pa-Ha-Sa-Pah; or, the Black Hills of Dakota* (Saint Louis: Nixon-Jones Printing Co., 1895), 304. Gold had apparently been found in the Hills as early as 1834 by a party who had left a message carved in a rock as they were being attacked and killed by Indians. Geologist Ferdinand Hayden made trips to the Hills in 1859 and 1866 and reported the finding of gold to the American Philosophical Society in 1869. Ironically, it was Custer's military expedition to set up an outpost to manage native peoples' excursions outside the reservation that spurred the encroachment of white settlers on the land.

2. Watson Parker, *Deadwood: The Golden Years* (Lincoln: University of Nebraska Press, 1981), 51–53.

3. Ibid.

4. *Dakota Register,* July 22, 1882.

5. *Black Hills Daily Times,* May 23, 1896.

6. Joe Sulentic, *Deadwood Gulch, the Last Chinatown* (Deadwood: 1975), 16.

7. Greg Nedved, "Deadwood's Wong," *South Dakota Magazine* (November–December 1989): 49–51.

8. Parker, *Deadwood,* 146–148.

9. *LCC,* February 6, 1994.

10. Helen Rezatto, *Mount Moriah: "Kill a Man, Start a Cemetery"* (Aberdeen: Northern Plains Press, 1980), 211.

11. Michael S. Trump, "Raiding Tradition: A History of Governmental Assaults on Deadwood's Beloved Brothels," master's thesis, Department of History, University of Wyoming, July 1994.

12. Annie Donna Fraser Tallent, *The Black Hills; or, The Last Hunting Grounds of the Dakotahs* (Saint Louis: Nixon-Jones Printing Co., 1899); Estelline Bennett, *Old Deadwood Days* (New York: J. H. Sear and Co., 1928). The assessment of Bennett's contribution is included in Watson Parker's history of Deadwood.

13. Clarence Kravig, "Mining in Lawrence County," in Lawrence County Historical Society, *Some History of Lawrence County* (Pierre: State Publishing Co., 1981), 551.

14. Ibid., 569.

15. Parker, *Deadwood*, 66.

16. Albert Gushurst, "Manuel, Fred and Mose, and Their Niece Josie," in Lawrence County Historical Society, *Some History of Lawrence County*, 2–9.

17. Pauline Rankin and Irma Klock, "W. E. Adams Family," in ibid., 13.

18. "Fish and Hunter Inc.," in ibid., 540.

19. Phyllis Guenin, "The Lead-Deadwood Gas Light and Fuel Company," in ibid., 554–556.

20. "Ayres Hardware Store," in ibid., 524.

21. Parker, *Deadwood*, 73–76.

22. Figures from Robert E. Driscoll, *Seventy Years of Banking in the Black Hills* (Rapid City: First National Bank of the Black Hills, 1948), 13, quoted in ibid., 65.

23. Scott Randolph, "Stopping Deadwood Gaming . . . 'To Dream the Impossible Dream,'" *LCC*, November 1, 1989.

24. *RCJ*, June 9, 1980.

25. Joseph C. Cash, *Working the Homestake* (Ames: Iowa State University Press, 1973), 14–19.

26. U.S. Department of Commerce, U.S. Census of Population, 1880, 1890, and 1910.

27. Cash, *Working the Homestake*, 77. Phoebe Hearst later also made a substantial contribution to the Carnegie Library in Deadwood.

28. Donald Toms, William J. Stone, and Gretchen Motchenbacker, eds., *The Gold Belt Cities: Lead and Homestake (a Photographic History)* (Lead: G.O.L.D. Unlimited, 1988).

29. Donald Toms, *Ethnic Heritage, Lead, S.D.*, vols. 1–3 (South Dakota Historic Preservation Society, 1989).

30. Toms, Stone, and Motchenbacker, *The Gold Belt Cities*, 112; Jeanette Larson, "City of Lead, 1876 to 1981," in Lawrence County Historical Society, *Some History of Lawrence County*, 581–582.

31. Cash, *Working the Homestake*, 19, 64.

32. Toms, Stone, and Motchenbacker, *The Gold Belt Cities*. Larson in "City of Lead" describes Lead as an "open" town, with gambling houses that used gold coins as currency, two famous houses of prostitution at the turn of the century, and even, at one time, thirty opium dens (in Lawrence County Historical Society, *Some History of Lawrence County*, 583).

33. Caroline Bancroft, *Gulches of Gold: A History of Central City, Colorado* (Denver: Sage Books, 1958), 250.

34. "Cherry Creek Emigrant's Song," *RMN*, June 18, 1859, cited in Duane Smith, *Rocky Mountain Mining Camps: The Urban Frontier* (Lincoln: University of Nebraska Press, 1967), 14.

35. Bancroft, *Gulches of Gold*, 146.

36. "A Young Rebel's Diary of Central City—1865," published in the *New Mexico Sentinel* in 1938 and found in a Gilpin County cabin in 1922.

37. *CCDR*, October 18, 1864, October 19, 1864, November 24, 1868, December 6, 1868, January 29, 1870, February 20, 1871.

38. Bancroft, *Gulches of Gold*, 42.

39. Ibid., 249.

40. Smith, *Rocky Mountain Mining Camps,* 35.

41. H. William Axford, *Gilpin County Gold: Peter McFarlane, 1848–1929, Mining Entrepreneur in Central City, Colorado* (Denver: Sage Books, 1976), 60.

42. Central City clipping file, Denver Public Library, Western History collection.

43. Caroline Bancroft, *Six Racy Madames of Colorado* (Boulder: Johnson Publishing Co., 1965), 5, 42; idem, *Guide to Central City* (Denver: World Press, 1946), 6.

44. Grace Greenwood (Sara J. Lippincott), *New Life in New Lands* (New York: J. B. Ford, 1873), 76–77, cited in Smith, *Rocky Mountain Mining Camps,* 49.

45. *CCDR,* May 23, 1874, cited in Axford, *Gilpin County Gold,* 61.

46. Frank R. Hollenback, *Central City and Black Hawk, Colorado: Then and Now* (Denver: Sage Books, 1961), 90.

47. Axford, *Gilpin County Gold,* 118–120.

48. Ibid., 117.

49. *DT,* February 6, 1900.

50. Betsy Jameson, "Imperfect Unions: Class and Gender in Cripple Creek 1894–1904," *Frontiers* (Spring 1976): 89–117.

51. *DT,* February 6, 1900.

52. *DT,* February 9, 1900.

53. *DT,* February 14, 1900.

54. *DP,* April 13, 1900.

55. *DT,* May 27, 1900.

56. *DT,* May 23, 1900.

57. *DT,* May 27, 1900, May 29, 1900, June 7, 1900, June 23, 1900. Jameson said that municipal revenues included a more stratified set of monthly fines: $16 for madams, $6 for parlor house prostitutes, $4 for crib women and dance hall workers. All prostitutes had to pay, in addition, for periodic physicals ("All That Glitters" [unpublished manuscript, 1991], 282).

58. *DT,* June 3, 1900.

59. Jameson, "All That Glitters," 245.

60. *Denver Sunday Times,* June 11, 1900.

61. Jameson, "All That Glitters," 256.

62. Ibid., 219.

63. Ibid., 225.

64. "Regulate It," *VCCDP,* August 24, 1899.

65. Jameson, "All That Glitters," 258, citing "A Strike in Dance Hall," *VCCDP,* April 23, 1902, and "Labor Notes," *VCCDP,* April 27, 1902.

66. These are U.S. census figures. City directories and other local histories show much larger figures, totaling over 55,000. See, for instance, Fred M. and Jo Mazzula, *Cripple Creek and the Pikes Peak Region: The First 100 Years* (Denver: A. B. Hirschfeld Press, 1956), which shows photographs of Cripple Creek, claiming a population of 35,000 in 1908, and Victor with more than 17,000.

67. Robert Guilford Taylor, *Cripple Creek* (Bloomington: Indiana University Press, 1966), 123–128.

68. Jameson, "All That Glitters," 61.

69. Ibid., 66.

70. Leland Feitz, *Cripple Creek! A Quick History of the World's Greatest Gold Camp* (Colorado Springs: Dentan-Berkeland Printing Co., 1967), 42.

71. Taylor, *Cripple Creek,* 139.

72. Bancroft, *Six Racy Madames,* 54–59; Leland Feitz, *Myers Avenue: A Quick History of Cripple Creek's Red-Light District* (Colorado Springs: Dentan-Berkeland Printing Co., 1967).

73. Marshall Sprague, *Money Mountain: The Story of Cripple Creek Gold* (Boston: Little, Brown and Co., 1953), 278–284; Julian Street, "Colorado Springs and Cripple Creek," *Collier's*, November 21, 1914.

74. Lowell Thomas, foreword to Mabel Barbee Lee's *Cripple Creek Days* (Garden City: Doubleday & Co., 1958), xii–xiii.

Chapter 3. Stagnation and Decay in Retrospect

1. In 1975 the fixed price of gold at $35 per ounce was allowed to float on the commodity market. Heap leaching of low-grade gold ore began in the district in the 1970s, whereby a diluted solution of cyanide was pumped over the ore on an impermeable floor, removing the metal by carbon adsorption coupled with hot caustic/cyanide stripping on an electronic process called electro winning. Rich Moritz and Ed Hunter, "Going for the Gold: Recovery Methods in the Cripple Creek Mining District," in *Cripple Creek, Colorado,* Commemorative Centennial Program (Chamber of Commerce, 1992), 81–86.

2. Indeed, since the 1990 census does not report communities of less than 1,000 population in its hard copy, these communities had all but disappeared statistically.

3. Gene Summers, *Technology and Social Change in Rural Areas* (Boulder: Westview Press, 1983).

4. Warren L. Trock, Thomas A. Miller, and S. Lee Gray, "Impacts of Financial Stress in Agriculture," ANRE Working Paper WP:86-2 (Fort Collins: Department of Agricultural and Natural Resource Economics, 1986); Russell C. Youmans, *Sustaining American Farm-Ranch Family Income: The Land Grant Institutions Can Help,* WRDC #27 (Corvallis, Oregon, 1985).

5. Daniel T. Lichter, Glenn V. Fuguitt, and Tim B. Heaton, "Components of Nonmetropolitan Population Change: The Contribution of Rural Areas," *Rural Sociology* 50 (1985): 88–98.

6. Peter K. Eisinger, *The Rise of the Entrepreneurial State* (Madison: University of Wisconsin Press, 1988).

7. Daniel T. Lichter and Glenn V. Fuguitt, "Demographic Response to Transportation Innovation: The Case of the Interstate Highway," *Social Forces* 59 (December 1980): 492–512.

8. Calvin L. Beale, "Rural Development: Population and Settlement Prospects," *Journal of Soil and Water Conservation* 29 (1974): 23–27; idem, "The Revival of Population Growth in Nonmetropolitan America," ERS-605 (U.S. Department of Agriculture, 1975).

9. G. F. Summers and K. Branch, "Economic Development and Community Social Change," *Annual Review of Sociology* 10 (1984): 141–166.

10. Joseph Schumpeter (1962), as quoted by Eisinger, *Rise of the Entrepreneurial State,* 8.

11. Ibid., 121.

12. Beale, "The Revival of Population Growth"; Kenneth L. Deavers and David L. Brown, "The Rural Population Turnaround: Research and National Public Policy," in *New Directions in Urban-Rural Migration* (Boulder: Westview Press, 1980), 51–65; John M. Wardwell and David L. Brown, "Population Redistribution in the United States during the 1970s," in ibid., 5–35; and John M. Wardwell, "Employment Deconcentration in the Nonmetropolitan Migration Turnaround," *Demography* 17 (1980): 145–158.

13. Richard A. Engles and Richard L. Forstall, "Metropolitan Areas Dominate Growth Again," *American Demographic* 7 (1985): 23–35, 45.

14. Jeanette Larson, "City of Lead, 1876 to 1981," in Lawrence County Historical Society, *Some History of Lawrence County* (Pierre: State Publishing Co., 1981), 583.

15. Marjorie Pontius, "Pine Crest Tourist Park," in ibid., 574–576.

16. Deadwood-Lead Chamber of Commerce data, telephone interview, September 1993.

17. F. B. DeChaine, "Colorado Mountain Theater: A History of Theatrical Festivals at Central City, Colorado, from 1932 to 1960," vol. 2, Ph.D. dissertation, University of Michigan, 1966, 268–278.

18. Bill Wood, "Move Opera to Red Rocks? Discord Tears Central City," *RMN*, August 12, 1948.

19. Ibid.

20. "Central City Backs Opera by 9–1 Margin," *DP,* August 15, 1948, 22.

21. "Quarter Million Visit Historic Central City," *DP,* August 9, 1951 (based on highway patrol car count multiplied by a three-and-one-half-persons-per-car average).

22. Jack Riddle, no title, *DP Sunday Empire,* June 18, 1961, 2.

23. "He Looks toward 'Old' Central City," *DP,* June 22, 1971.

24. Marshall Sprague, *Money Mountain: The Story of Cripple Creek Gold* (Boston: Little, Brown, 1953), 253.

25. Dorothy Mackin, "Gold Is Where You Find It: Tourism Is Cripple Creek," *Cripple Creek, Colorado,* Commemorative Centennial Program (Chamber of Commerce, 1992), 67–72.

26. Fred Baker, "New Gold Rush of Tourists Goal in Cripple Creek," *DP,* December 26, 1951.

27. Ibid.

28. Bill Brenneman, "Deluge of Tourists Hints New Boom," *RMN,* June 8, 1954.

29. Willie Columbine, "Cripple Creek–Victor Area Proves Mecca for Visitors," *RMN,* October 3, 1953.

30. "Remodeling of Central Hotel OK'd," *DP,* January 11, 1950.

31. Eudora Kohl, "The City That Wouldn't Die," *Rocky Mountain Empire Magazine,* July 2, 1950, 4–5.

32. "$35,000 Donated by Mrs. Penrose for Historic Site," *DP,* January 31, 1954.

33. Marjorie Barrett, "Williamsburg Approach for Central City," *RMN,* November 21, 1970. Marjorie Barrett, "Central City Establishes Plan for Restoration," *RMN,* May 11, 1973.

34. Joanne Ditmer, "After Years of Neglect, 'Lace House' Gets a Needed Face Lift," *DP,* June 8, 1977; Frances Melrose, "Lace House Restoration Planned in Black Hawk," *RMN,* June 28, 1976.

35. J. Sebastian Sinisi, "Lace House to Stay Put: 1976 Contract May Avert Move," *DP,* July 30, 1997.

36. Marjorie Barrett, "Discussion on Central City's Future," *RMN,* February 12, 1972.

37. Ibid.

38. Sharon Sherman, "Black Hawk Forges Community Spirit," *DP,* December 7, 1977.

39. Harley Lux, personal interview, October 30, 1991.

40. Ibid.

41. Banner Associates, Inc., *Mining Area Clearance and Buffer Zone Development Plan* (Rapid City, S.D., 1989).

42. John M. Findlay, *People of Chance* (New York: Oxford University Press, 1986), 109.

Chapter 4. Gold Rush Returns

1. Russell Stubbles, "The Deadwood Tradition: Putting Gambling before Planning in South Dakota," *Small Town* 20 (1990): 20–27.

2. George Ledbetter, "Deadwood Property Owners Shocked," *LCC*, March 23, 1991.

3. State of South Dakota Commission on Gaming, monthly summary, September 1991. All subsequent data on gaming revenues, taxes, gaming devices, and number of casinos come from monthly summaries or annual reports, 1989–1996.

4. Valerie Goodman, "Promote Deadwood: Drive up Your Profits," *LCC*, December 15, 1990.

5. Peter K. Eisinger, *The Rise of the Entrepreneurial State* (Madison: University of Wisconsin Press, 1988).

6. Ibid., 245.

7. In Colorado, Central City, Black Hawk, and Cripple Creek city governments each contributed $10,000 to support the petition. Victor chose not to join the campaign and therefore was excluded from local option gaming.

8. Steve Garnaas, "Betting Changes S. Dakota Town," *DP,* October 14, 1990.

9. Steve Garnaas, "Gaming Czars Check out Digs in Deadwood," *DP,* August 13, 1991.

10. Ibid.

11. "Marketing Notes," *Deadwood Historic Preservation Progress Report* 2, no. 1 (January 1992): 13; Jeff Zieger, personal interview, October 1992; William R. Cissell, "C.A.S.T. Study: Colorado Gaming Shows No Impact on Deadwood," *QCM*, December 10, 1991.

12. "Surveys Look for Deadwood Gamblers," *LDB*, July 28, 1991. Rapid City marketing consultant Jody Severson reported these findings to the state gaming commission, based in part on a telephone survey by Jim Robinson Associates of Sioux Falls in which 91 questions were asked of 1,130 people in 10 major television markets; overall, 65 percent of the respondents did not know about Deadwood gambling.

13. "Gambling Was News in 1991," *RCJ*, December 29, 1991.

14. Patrick O'Driscoll, "Folks Wagering on Land in Colorado Towns," *DP,* October 14, 1990.

15. Steve Garnaas, "Gambling Spurs 2nd Gold Rush in Central City," *DP,* November 12, 1990.

16. Steve Garnaas, "Central City, Black Hawk Land Sales Soar; Investors Put Chips on Property," *DP,* March 28, 1991; idem, "$1.3 Million Deal Cut in Black Hawk," *DP,* May 11, 1991.

17. Steve Garnaas, "Casino Developers Rarin' to Get Started," *DP,* April 16, 1991. Properties ready to be renovated and their 1991 purchases prices follow: the Silver Slipper (formerly the Chandelier House), $2.9 million; Annie Oakley's (formerly the Gilpin Jail Exhibit), $1.45 million; the Grubstake (formerly the Grubstake Restaurant), $1.275 million; the Glitter Gulch Saloon (formerly Old Chicago's Restaurant), $1.2 million; Molly's (formerly Sweet Aspen Ice Cream), $675,000; the Gregory Diggins (formerly Sheriff Weezie Anderle's), $215,000; the Prospector (formerly the Prospector's Cafe), $200,000; and an unnamed casino in the former Arcade Building, $235,000. The Gold Coin was about to close at $3.9 million; the Glory Hole at $1.7 million; the Gold Dust Inn at $750,000; and the Gaslight Inn at $500,000. In May Central City's Golden Rose Hotel was to be sold for $5 million and the Toll Gate Saloon for $4 million.

18. Steve Garnaas, "Gaming to Evict Trailer Residents," *DP,* April 11, 1991; idem, "$1.3 Million Deal Cut in Black Hawk," *DP,* May 11, 1991.

19. Steve Garnaas, "Black Hawk Families Offered $1200 to Move," *DP,* June 18, 1991.

20. Steve Garnaas, "Casino Developers Ready to Roll," *DP,* April 11, 1991.

21. "Colorado Group Prepared to Build Casino," *LDB*, August 10, 1991.

22. Frank Scandale, "Gambling Towns Stalk Financing," *DP,* April 28, 1991.

23. Paul Hutchinson, "Bet on an Old Theater Nets $9.9 Million," *DP,* July 25, 1991.

24. Jana Miller, "Casinos Bring Investors, Rancor to Small Towns," *USA Today,* September 11, 1991.

25. Ibid.

26. Steve Garnaas, "Sore Owner Won't Sell Out—Yet," *DP,* September 15, 1991.

27. Steve Garnaas, "Central City Old-Timer Holds Ace," *DP,* September 15, 1991.

28. Steve Garnaas, "School Board Negotiating Casino Deal," *DP,* October 19, 1991.

29. Ibid.; idem, "Casino Deal Could Be Lucky for Gilpin Schools," *DP,* February 23, 1992.

30. Steve Garnaas, "Gaming May Kick County in Seat," *DP,* May 6, 1991.

31. "High-Staked Bet Involved in Conversion of Casinos," *DP,* May 26, 1991.

32. Claire Martin, "Let the Games Begin: Fabled Teller House Ready to Start a New Life," *DP,* October 1, 1991; J. Sebastian Sinisi, "Slots of Fate: Tears, Cheers," *DP,* October 2, 1991.

33. Colorado Department of Revenue, Division of Gaming, "Gaming Update," September 30, 1992; subsequent gaming data for Colorado, including revenues, distribution of revenue from taxes, and numbers of gaming devices and casinos, all come from *Gaming in Colorado: Fact Book and Abstract* for 1992–1996.

34. Steve Garnaas, "Casinos Rushing to Open on Time," *DP,* September 29, 1991.

35. Steve Garnaas and Jim Gibney, "Casino Owners Race to Finish," *DP,* October 1, 1991. The authors confirmed the newspaper accounts through personal observations in the towns and on the highway leading into Central City and Black Hawk.

36. J. Sebastian Sinisi, "It's No Vegas, but Even Losers Smiled," *DP,* October 2, 1991.

37. Steve Garnaas, "New Gold Rush Hits Central City Area," *DP,* October 2, 1991.

38. Blevins and Jensen were in Cripple Creek the day before opening and in Central City the day before that (September 29–30, 1991).

39. Michael Booth and Jim Gibney, "Bang Unfurls Buck in Cripple Creek," *DP,* October 1, 1991.

40. Michael Booth and Jim Gibney, "Cripple Creek Hoping for New Gold Rush," *DP,* October 2, 1991; Steve Garnaas and Michael Booth, "Weekend to Be Towns' Big Test," *DP,* October 3, 1991.

41. George Lane and Steve Garnaas, "Casinos Change Tune, Roll out Carpet," *DP,* October 4, 1991.

42. Ibid.

43. Steve Garnaas, "Casinos Expect Full House," *DP,* December 31, 1991; idem, "Crowd Light at Casinos," *DP,* January 1, 1992; "Gambling Crowds Didn't Materialize as Expected," *LDB,* January 2, 1992; Judith Brimberg, "Full Houses Not in the Cards for All Casinos," *DP,* January 2, 1992.

44. Steve Garnaas, "Slow and Steady Black Hawk's Way," *DP,* October 27, 1991.

45. "Gambling Future Looks Bright for Slow-Starting Black Hawk," *DP,* October 27, 1991.

46. Steve Garnaas, "Gambling Far Exceeds Original Concept," *DP,* November 4, 1991.

47. Steve Garnaas, "A Black Hawk Bonanza," *DP,* November 5, 1991.

48. "Colorado's Largest Gambling Hall to Open in Central City in May," *LDB,* March 19, 1992.

49. "Investors Plan State's Largest Casino," *DP,* March 22, 1992; "Glory Hole Expanding," *DP,* March 28, 1992.

50. Steve Garnaas, "Ex-Owner Claims Casino Land Swindle," *DP,* March 29, 1992.

51. Steve Garnaas, "Casino Backer Bows Out," *DP,* April 18, 1992.

52. Tustin Amole, "Building Moratorium in Central City Upheld," *RMN,* April 24, 1992; Steve Garnaas, "Central City Freeze Puts Deals in Limbo," *DP,* April 19, 1992; idem, "Casino Moratorium in Doubt," *DP,* April 21, 1992.

53. Steve Garnaas, "Casino Ruling Coming Soon," *DP,* April 22, 1992; idem, "Central City Casino Moratorium Upheld," *DP,* April 24, 1992.

54. Patricia A. Stowkowski, "The Colorado Gambling Boom: An Experiment in Rural Community Development," *Small Town* (May–June 1992): 13.

55. Steve Garnaas, "Casino Towns' Feud Hindering Joint Planning?" *DP,* April 26, 1992.

56. Steve Garnaas, "Developer Plans Casino with Day Care, Arcade," *DP,* February 19, 1992; Dan Whipple, "Gambling on the Heart of Colorado," *Casper Star-Tribune,* October 21, 1994. In 1997 a casino franchise day-care, "Kid Quest," opened at Bullwhackers in Black Hawk following the passage of a law in 1996 banning anyone under twenty-one in the gaming areas of casinos (George Lane, "Cops: Kid-Casino Law Works," *DP,* July 14, 1997).

57. Steve Caulk, "Casinos Grow, Crowds Thin Out," *RMN,* September 27, 1992.

58. Steve Garnaas, "Limited Mom-and-Pops Gave Birth to Giant," *DP,* September 27, 1992.

59. Steve Caulk, "Casinos Grow," *RMN,* September 27, 1992.

60. Steve Caulk, "Gambling's Early Days Created False Expectations, Official Says," *RMN,* September 25, 1992.

61. Weather, it turned out, was a convenient excuse either way. When crowds were below expectations the weekend of September 7, both good weather and the Broncos were used as explanations ("Slow Weekend at Colorado Gambling Towns," *LDB,* September 8, 1992).

62. Caulk, "Casinos Grow."

63. Audie Blevins and Katherine Jensen, "Gambling as a Community Development Quick Fix," *Annals of the American Association of Political and Social Science* 556 (1998): 109–123. Colorado reports data in terms of adjusted gross profits, while South Dakota shows gross revenues. While there are small accounting differences, these data are essentially comparable.

64. M. K. Madden, "Gaming in South Dakota: A Statistical Description. An Analysis of Its Socioeconomic Impacts," Business Research Bureau, University of South Dakota, 1991.

65. Don Aaker, South Dakota Job Service, Lawrence County office, personal interview, October 1, 1993.

66. Stephen Keating, "Gaming Panel May Cut Casino Taxes," *DP,* September 29, 1994.

67. John Sanko, "Eight Counties Get Cut of Gambling Tax," *RMN,* August 29, 1992.

68. Colorado, unlike South Dakota, allows businesses to take machines out of service during slack gaming periods; therefore, these December figures will be lower than for the summer months.

69. Jim Gibney, "Manitou Getting Gambling Fever," *DP,* April 4, 1991; Steve Garnaas, "Backer of Gambling Will Oppose New Bills," *DP,* December 1, 1990; Jennifer Gavin, "House Says No Dice to Gambling Bill," *DP,* April 24, 1991.

70. Eric Anderson and Steve Garnaas, "Gaming Bandwagon Gets Crowded," *DP,* January 19, 1992; Jennifer Gavin, "Proposed Gambling Moratorium Dies on House Floor," *DP,* February 11, 1992; Woody Mitchell, "Gambling Proposal Bitterly Protested," *DP,* February 18, 1992; Eric Anderson, "Bill Would Give Local Voters Say on Gambling," *DP,* March 2, 1992; Jennifer Gavin, "Local Gambling Vote OK'd," *DP,* April 22, 1992.

71. Steve Garnaas, "Legal Challenges Up Stakes for New Gambling Initiatives," *DP,* March 17, 1992; Eric Anderson, "Gambling Proposed for LoDo," *DP,* March 26, 1992; "Gambling Town Being Sought near Morrison," *DP,* May 15, 1992.

72. Dick Kreck, "LoDo Gambling an Idea Whose Time Came and Went in '45," *DP,* March 27, 1992.

73. Alan Katz, "Gambling Foes Come up Snake Eyes," *DP,* June 2, 1992; John Sanko, "Petitions Filed for Seven More Potential Ballot Questions," *RMN,* August 4, 1992; Steve Garnaas, "Pro, Con Gaming Strategies Forming," *DP,* August 25, 1992; John Sanko, "Towns Rolling the Dice, Gambling on the Future," *RMN,* September 1, 1992; Peter Sleeth, "Confusing Gaming Proposals a Real Gamble for Coloradans," *DP,* October 18, 1992.

74. Joe Garner, "Casino Owners Try to Stop Rapid Expansion of Colorado Gambling," *RMN,* September 27, 1992.

75. Peter Sleeth, "Experts Don't Back Expanded Gambling," *DP,* October 18, 1992; Steve Garnaas, "Experts: Expansion May Doom Gaming," *DP,* September 24, 1992.

76. Kevin Simpson, "Real Gambling Ballot Issue: How Short Is Your Memory?" *DP,* September 20, 1992; "Readers Forum," *DP,* September 20, 1992; Steve Garnaas, "Two Towns' Anti-Gambling Votes Assessed," *DP,* October 1, 1992; Dick Kreck, "Look Past the Razzle-Dazzle Side Show; It's Still Gambling," *DP,* October 2, 1992; editorial, "Time to Clamp a Moratorium on More Colorado Casinos," *DP,* October 23, 1992; "Readers Forum," *DP,* November 1, 1992; Steve Garnaas, "Gambling Short of Winning Numbers" (gambling amendment vote totals by precinct), *DP,* November 4, 1992.

77. George Ledbetter, "Out-of-State Casino Ownership Ban Ruled Unconstitutional," *LCC,* December 25, 1991.

78. "Costner Group Considers New Hotel," *QCM,* December 3, 1991; George Ledbetter, "Costner's [*sic*] Have New Idea for Deadwood Hill Development," *LCC,* December 4, 1991.

79. Kevin Woster, "Chances Slim for Deadwood Bet-Limit Increase," *RCJ,* December 28, 1991; "Deadwood Wants Gambling Ante Upped," *DP,* February 4, 1992; Kevin Woster, "State Eyes Bigger Gaming Cut," *RCJ,* February 22, 1992; George Ledbetter, "Deadwood Gambling Bill Put on Hold," *LCC,* February 29, 1992.

80. Kevin Woster, "Maverick Walsh Opposes Deadwood Gambling Bills," *RCJ,* February 27, 1992; Pat Dobbs, "Gambling Backers Go One-on-One," *RCJ,* March 10, 1992.

81. Kevin Woster, "Bet Limits to Stand," *RCJ,* March 12, 1992.

82. Joni Lee Martin, "Deadwood's Gaming Industry Looks toward Pierre," *LCC,* November 14, 1992.

83. Joni Lee Martin, "Proposed Gaming Changes: Impact Higher Limits, More Devices Discussed," *LCC,* December 19, 1992.

84. Joni Lee Martin, "Proposed Gaming Changes," *LCC,* December 19, 1992.

85. Scott Randolph, "Questions Raised about Impact of Costner Project," *BHP,* November 14, 1992.

86. Joni Lee Martin, "TIFD Opposition Sees Referral Vote as Tax Fairness Issue," *LCC,* January 9, 1993.

87. George Ledbetter, "Rapid City Firm Picked for Costner Project," *LCC,* February 19, 1993.

88. Shane L. Mott, "Mickelson Supports Costners' Project; but Not All of Deadwood's Casino Owners Do," *LCC,* February 6, 1993.

89. Shane L. Mott, "Costners Say Expansion Can Be 'a Dream Come True,'" *LCC,* February 20, 1993.

90. Shane L. Mott, "11th Hour Deal Nets Costner Bill," *LCC,* March 3, 1993.

91. Vince Coyle, editorial, *LCC,* March 24, 1993.

92. Kent Meyers, "Referendum a Democratic Right and Responsibility," *LCC,* May 22, 1993.

93. Bob Mercer, "Joy Delivers Signatures," *RCJ,* June 22, 1993; Joe Case, "'Vote Yes' Opens Its Campaign Headquarters," *LCC,* July 4, 1993; Hugh O'Gara, "Joy Prepares for Campaign," *RCJ,* July 31, 1993.

94. Bob Mercer, "Defeat Illustrates S.D. Polarity," *RCJ*, September 16, 1993.

95. Matt Kelly, "Did Anti-Gambling Vote Reveal Racism?" *RCJ*, September 17, 1993.

96. Ned Martel, "Little Big Fink," *Outside* (September 1993): 21, 22.

97. "More Action, More Fun," *LCC*, April 3, 1993.

98. George Ledbetter, "Four Casinos Declared Multiple Buildings," *LCC*, June 15, 1994.

99. George Ledbetter, "Gaming Commission to Consider Multiple Buildings," *LCC*, October 5, 1994; idem, "Gaming Commission Increases Deadwood Building County by 4," *LCC*, October 8, 1994.

100. George Ledbetter, "Two-in-One Casino Approved," *LCC*, March 25, 1995.

101. Kay Lorenz, "Casino Owners: Romer Doesn't Rule Gaming Commission," *DP*, October 1994.

Chapter 5. Historic Preservation, Facadism, and the Fast Buck

1. "Deadwood Will Receive National Award July 4th," *LCC*, June 23, 1993.

2. Shane L. Mott, "Deadwood's Landmark Status Is Conditional," *LCC*, April 14, 1993.

3. "Deadwood-Lead Fourth of July Plans Additional Features," *LCC*, July 3, 1993.

4. "Deadwood Will Receive National Award July 4th," *LCC*, June 23, 1993.

5. William J. Murtagh, *Keeping Time: The History and Theory of Preservation in America* (Pittstown, N.J.: Main Street Press, 1988), 66.

6. Ibid., 74.

7. J. Myrick Howard, "Using a Revolving Fund for Downtown Preservation," *Historic Preservation Forum* (Summer 1989): 1–7.

8. Alan Van Ormer, "Historic Preservation Is 'for the People,' " *LCC*, July 10, 1993, 1.

9. Murtagh, *Keeping Time*, 167.

10. Joni Lee Martin, "Lawrence County Prepares for a Grand Dedication," *LCC*, March 28, 1992.

11. Barbara Ordahl, "Renovation Combines Old and New," *RCJ*, August 25, 1991.

12. Joni Lee Martin, "Bricks Glisten on Deadwood's Main Street," *LCC*, July 4, 1992.

13. Char Martin, "Railroad Engine House Restoration to Begin," *LCC*, August 31, 1994; Joe Case, "Commission Approves Trolley Station Design," *LCC*, September 7, 1994.

14. George Ledbetter, "Deadwood Rec Center and Days of '76 Grandstands in Desperate Need of Repair," *LCC*, March 23, 1991.

15. "Brighter Future Looms on Horizon for the Historic Gilmore [*sic*]," *LCC* (entertainment guide), January 1991.

16. Barbara Ordahl, "Deadwood Pulls Together for Gillmore Restoration," *RCJ*, July 27, 1991.

17. Joni Lee Martin, "Gillmore Restoration Completes Life Cycle of Former Hotel," *LCC*, August 15, 1992.

18. "Developer Who Renovated Gillmore Receives Award," *LCC*, October 29, 1994.

19. Joni Lee Martin, "Adams House Fate in Question," *LCC*, September 23, 1992.

20. J. Myrick Howard, "Using a Revolving Loan Fund," *Historic Preservation Forum* (Summer 1989): 1–7; Chris Hunfel, Deadwood Historic Preservation, personal interview, January 25, 1997.

21. Shane L. Mott, " 'Buried' Collections, New Programs Spark Renewed Adams Museum," *LCC*, March 20, 1993.

22. Vince Coyle, "Kroger Brothers Help Restore the Glory that Was Deadwood," *LCC*, July 22, 1992.

23. George Ledbetter, "Extra $50,000 Approved for Deadwood's Adams Museum," *LCC*, June 6, 1992.

24. Mott, " 'Buried' Collections."

25. Joni Lee Martin, "Grant Program Helps Preserve Deadwood's History," *LCC*, September 9, 1992.

26. Joni Lee Martin, "Preservation Commission Awards $247,318 in Grants," *LCC*, November 18, 1992.

27. Alan Van Ormer, "Historic Preservation Commission Conducts Marathon Meeting," *LCC*, June 2, 1993.

28. "Revolving Loan Fund's First Project Complete," *Deadwood Historic Preservation Project* (September–October 1991): 4.

29. Joni Lee Martin, "Deadwood Restoration Continues as Bank Takes on Former Look," *BHP*, December 8, 1990.

30. George Ledbetter, "Costner to Raise the Roof in Deadwood," *LCC*, March 23, 1991.

31. Mark Wolfe, personal interview, October 29, 1991.

32. Ibid.

33. Joni Lee Martin, "Deadwood's Revolving Loan Fund Continues to Help Restoration," *LCC*, June 27, 1992.

34. Mark Wolfe, personal interview, November 19, 1993.

35. George Ledbetter, "Community Programs Help Rebuild Deadwood House," *LCC*, September 14, 1994.

36. Deb Timm, "Deadwood Carnegie Library Builds for the Future," *BHP*, August 15, 1994.

37. Shane L. Mott, "Beck's Approved; Library Tabled," *LCC*, April 7, 1993.

38. George Ledbetter, "Deadwood Approves Library Bid," *LCC*, June 22, 1994.

39. Mark Wolfe, interview, November 19, 1993.

40. George Ledbetter, "Sign Committee Extends Deadline for Comments," *LCC*, December 5, 1990.

41. Joni Lee Martin, "Deadwood Finally Adopts a New Sign Ordinance," *LCC*, October 28, 1992.

42. Mark Wolfe, interview, October 29, 1991.

43. George Ledbetter, "Preservation Commission Debates 'Minutiae' of Midnight Star Awning," *LCC*, October 26, 1991.

44. George Ledbetter, "Preservation Commission Wrestles Tough Decisions," *LCC*, December 12, 1990.

45. Pat Dobbs, "Historic Building No Asset," *RCJ*, May 21, 1992.

46. George Ledbetter, "Demo Request Meets Cool Reception, Trail Plan Advances," *LCC*, May 23, 1992.

47. Joni Lee Martin, "Preservation Commission and Building Owner Square Off," *LCC*, October 31, 1992.

48. George Ledbetter, "Dismissal of Lawsuit on 1992 Gas Station Demolition Upheld," *LCC*, August 27, 1994.

49. George Ledbetter, "Achtien Lawsuit Dismissed," *LCC*, March 3, 1993.

50. Joe Case, "Achtien Gets 43-Foot Variance; Broadway to Be One-Way Street," *LCC*, October 27, 1993.

51. "Judge Rules against Preservation Commission," *LCC*, January 12, 1994.

52. George Ledbetter, "Supreme Court Will Review Ice House Demolition Decision," *LCC*, August 10, 1994.

53. Randolph Delahanty, foreword, *Preserving the West: California, Arizona, Nevada, Utah, Idaho, Oregon, Washington* (New York: Pantheon Books, 1985), vii.

54. Char Martin, "To Preserve, or Not to Preserve," *LCC*, September 29, 1993.

55. Joe Case, "Gaming Employee Questions Historic Preservation's Power," *LCC*, October 23, 1993.

56. Michael Wallace, "Reflections on the History of Historic Preservation," in Susan Porter Benson, Stephen Brier, and Rob Rosenzweigh, eds., *Presenting the Past: Essays on the Historic and the Public* (Philadelphia: Temple University Press, 1986), 117.

57. "Landmark Designation Threatened," *DP,* August 11, 1992.

58. Alan Granruth, "Gambling Is Not Destroying Our History," *DP,* August 30, 1992.

59. Brian Levine, Cripple Creek Historic Preservation officer, personal interview, July 12, 1994.

60. Craig Hunter, program administrator, Colorado Historical Society, and Sharon Holmes, deputy clerk of the city of Black Hawk, personal interviews, December 1, 1994.

61. Wallace, "Reflections," 195.

62. Nore V. Winter, *Rehabilitation Standards for the City of Black Hawk* (1993), 5, 8–9.

63. Mary Voelz Chandler, "Historic Landmarks Losing Their Luster," *RMN*, September 27, 1993, 121. Similar information was reflected in a personal interview, July 12, 1994.

64. Hunter and Holmes, personal interviews, December 1, 1994; "Black Hawk Waltz: Tales of a Rocky Mountain Town" (City of Black Hawk, 1996).

65. Larry Cook, personal interview, December 2, 1994.

66. Nore V. Winter, *Design Standards for the Rehabilitation of Historic Buildings in the City of Black Hawk* (1993), 2.

67. Levine, personal interview, July 12, 1994; Dave Curtin, "Cripple Creek Official Prowls Casinos as He Looks for Blatant Historic-Snatchers," *Colorado Springs Gazette Telegraph,* August 30, 1992; "Moving Historic House Dicey Idea in Black Hawk," *DP,* April 20, 1997.

68. Clark Strickland, "No, Gambling Could Destroy Colorado's Historic Mining Towns," *DP,* October 20, 1990, editorial page.

69. Hunter, interview, December 1, 1994.

70. Steve Garnaas, "Teller Hotel May Be Ante in Gambling," *DP,* November 29, 1990.

71. Steve Garnaas, "Opera Panel Says Yes to Gambling in Teller House," *DP,* December 18, 1990.

72. Steve Garnaas, "Swiss to Rejigger Teller House," *DP,* July 11, 1991.

73. Steve Garnaas, "Teller House's Gambling Trimmed," *DP,* December 1, 1992.

74. Janet Day, "Teller House Offering Loan for Rehearsal Hall," *DP,* August 1993.

75. Ellen Ittleson, "Gambling Boom or Bust for Preservation," *Historic Preservation Forum* 5, no. 6 (November–December 1991): 11–19.

Chapter 6. Community Transformation in the Gamble

1. Testimony of Honorable Jeffry L. Bloomberg, State's Attorney, Lawrence County, South Dakota, before a Hearing of the House Committee on Small Business, Concerning the National Impact of Casino Gambling Proliferation in the United States, Federal News Service, September 21, 1994.

2. "1993 Deadwood-Lead Chamber of Commerce Membership Directory (as of October 1, 1992)," 32–53.

3. "Five Years of Gambling Gives Deadwood New Life," *LCC*, November 2, 1994.

4. Eileen Haberling, marketing director, Deadwood Visitors Bureau, telephone interview, November 21, 1994.

5. Bruce Oberlander, mayor of Deadwood, personal interview, November 19, 1993.

6. Donna Franke and Vicky Hendrickson, personal interview, October 28, 1995.

7. South Dakota Commission on Gaming, "1996 Deadwood Gaming Abstract."

8. Don Aaker, Lawrence County director, South Dakota Job Service, Spearfish, personal interview, October 1, 1993; Ron and Virginia Eastmo, teachers at Lead High School, personal interview, October 3, 1993; Mary Ticknor, principal, Deadwood Middle School, personal interview, October 1, 1993.

9. Franke and Hendrickson, interviews, October 28, 1995.

10. Actually, considered a supervisor, Donna Franke had parking adjacent to the building, but other employees do not.

11. Hendrickson, interview, October 28, 1995.

12. Franke, interview, October 28, 1995.

13. Lora Hawkins, director, Child Protection Services, Lawrence County, personal interview, October 29, 1991. The day-care center had originally been housed in a defunct parochial school, then moved to the larger space of the former National Guard Armory, to be displaced to the basement of the adjacent Lutheran church.

14. Franke, interview, October 28, 1995.

15. Hawkins, interview, October 29, 1991.

16. Reverend Chuck Horner, pastor, First Methodist Church, Deadwood, personal interview, May 21, 1992.

17. Chuck Crotty, Lawrence County sheriff, personal interview, May 22, 1992.

18. Lucille Tracey, coordinator, Lord's Cupboard, personal interview, May 21, 1992; Joni Lee Martin, "Lord's Cupboard Helps Fill Hungry Stomachs," *LCC*, February 10, 1993.

19. Tracey, interview, May 21, 1992.

20. George Opitz, chairman, Lawrence County Commissioners, letter to Honorable George S. Mickelson, governor of South Dakota, March 3, 1992.

21. Hendrickson, interview, October 28, 1995.

22. Group interview with thirteen senior citizens, Lead Senior Center, November 19, 1993.

23. George Ledbetter, "Deadwood Property Owners Shocked," *LCC*, March 23, 1991.

24. George Ledbetter, "Homeowner's Group Formed to Challenge Ag Assessments," *LCC*, September 14, 1991; idem, "County Puts Budget Reading on Temporary Hold," *LCC*, September 1, 1991.

25. Joni Lee Martin, "Lead-Deadwood School Board to Appeal Mining Assessment," *LCC*, May 23, 1992.

26. South Dakota Division of Revenue and Taxation (microfiche), 1996.

27. Lead Senior Center, group interview, November 19, 1993.

28. Ticknor, interview, October 1, 1993; Deb Thorp, Eighth Grade Gifted and Talented Program, and two eighth-grade classes, October 1, 1993.

29. Ticknor, interview, October 1, 1993.

30. Eastmo, interview, October 3, 1993.

31. Marguerite Mullaney, "More than 500 Child Abuse Victims in Lawrence County," *LCC*, March 16, 1991; Hawkins, interview, May 22, 1992; Hawkins, telephone interview, November 21, 1994.

32. Crotty, interview, May 22, 1992.

33. Oberlander, interview, November 19, 1993.

34. Lowell Thomas, foreword to Mabel Barbee Lee, *Cripple Creek Days* (Garden City: Doubleday & Co., 1958), xii–xiii.

35. Opitz, letter, March 3, 1992.

36. Madonna Kukay, "Jeffco Wants Cut of Gambling Cash to Offset Its Problems," *DP,* April 25, 1991.

37. Opitz, letter, March 3, 1992; Gilpin County Sheriff's Department, reported in *DP*, April 25, 1991.

38. Oberlander, interview, November 19, 1993.

39. Bloomberg, testimony, September 21, 1994.

40. Ibid.

41. Senate Bill 235 (1995), in George Ledbetter, "County against Gaming Tax Redistribution," *RCJ*, April 9, 1995.

42. Ann Schrader, "Gambling to Strain Public," *DP*, August 22, 1991.

43. Ann Schrader, "Medical Services Gird for Added Load," *DP*, September 22, 1991; Alex Berenson, "Cripple Creek Has Its Doubts," *DP*, November 6, 1995.

44. Ann Schrader, "Black Hawk Health Center Gets Shot in Arm," *DP*, December 15, 1992.

45. Michael Booth, "Teller County Jail Full after 1st Gaming Day," *DP*, October 3, 1991.

46. Mary George, "Poor Bet: Gambler's One for the Road," *DP*, March 19, 1992.

47. Maureen Harrington, "Witnesses to Bus-Van Crash Sought," *DP*, August 30, 1995; Mary George, "Danger on the Road to Riches: Alcohol-Related Accidents Skyrocket," *DP*, August 30, 1995.

48. Jim Gibney, "Cripple Creek Limpin' in Tunnel Closure," *DP*, December 30, 1993.

49. Alex Berenson, "Gambling Has Seen Both Payoffs and Drawbacks," *DP*, November 5, 1995.

50. Virginia Culver, "Gambling-Town Churches Find Religion Not a Big Draw," *DP*, November 2, 1991; idem, "Churches Struggle with Traffic, Bare Pews," September 13, 1992.

51. Steve Garnaas, "Glitzy Casinos Replace Old Haunts," *DP*, September 27, 1992.

52. Steve Garnaas, "Towns Make Way for Gambling, but Residents Fear the Consequences if Amendment 4 Passes," *DP*, October 28, 1990.

53. Steve Garnaas, "Gilpin Residents Warily View Promise of Tax-Relief," *DP*, October 20, 1992.

54. Joan Wiggs, letter, "Gambling Has Made Government Greedy," *DP*, October 23, 1992.

55. State of Colorado, Department of Legal Affairs, Division of Property Taxes, "Twenty-fifth Annual Report to the Governor and the General Assembly," 1995.

56. Joanne Ditmer, "The Price of Gambling," *DP*, *Contemporary Magazine*, June 7, 1992; idem, "Central City: Gambling and the Opera Can Coexist," *DP*, *Contemporary Magazine*, July 12, 1992.

57. Jack Kisling, "Many Sides of Central City Learn to Coexist," *DP*, July 24, 1994.

58. Alex Berenson, "Gambling Has Seen Both Payoffs and Drawbacks," *DP*, November 5, 1995.

59. Marj Charlier, "The Payoff: Casino Gambling Saves Three Colorado Towns but the Price Is High," *WSJ*, September 23, 1992.

60. Steve Garnaas, "Central City Fires Ex-Clerk Who Became Manager of Casino Town," *DP*, October 22, 1994; idem, "Gambling Calling the Shots," *DP*, November 27, 1994.

61. Steve Garnaas, "Central City, Black Hawk Oust City Managers in Same Week," *DP*, October 23, 1994.

62. Steve Garnaas, "Gambling Calling the Shots," *DP*, November 27, 1994.

63. J. Sebastian Sinisi, "Study: Casinos Changed Lifestyle," *DP*, August 14, 1992.

64. Patrick Long, Jo Clark, and Derek Liston, *Win, Lose, or Draw? Gambling with America's Small Towns* (Washington, D.C.: Aspen Institute, 1994), 41–42.

65. Dan Whipple, "Gambling on the Heat of Central City," *Casper Star-Tribune*, October 22, 1994.

66. Mark Wolfe, director, Deadwood Historic Preservation Commission, personal interview, October 29, 1991.

67. Ibid.

68. Wolfe, interview, November 19, 1993.

69. While not sampling employees who lived elsewhere, Long's study showed that when asked whether they would like to move away from their community, 44 percent of the Cripple Creek residents, 32 percent of Black Hawk residents, 39 percent of Central City residents, and 29 percent of Deadwood residents agreed with the statement "I would like to move away from this town" (Long, Clark, and Liston, *Win, Lose, or Draw?* 54–56).

70. Wolfe, interview, November 19, 1993.

71. Joe Case, "Deadwood Housing Gets Boost," *LCC,* October 15, 1994.

72. George Ledbetter, "Deadwood Okays Apartment Plans," *LCC,* October 22, 1994.

73. George Ledbetter, "Apartment Plan on Burnham Hill Rejected," *LCC,* September 10, 1994. Even the interest on the historic preservation loan to the Gillmore was reduced from 6.4 percent to 2 percent because of the inability of the owners to keep the rent-subsidized apartments fully occupied. George Ledbetter, "Interest Rate Reduced on Gilmore [*sic*] Loan," *LCC,* June 28, 1997.

74. Wolfe, interview, October 29, 1991.

75. In Central City historic trolleys were initially used to transport patrons from the hilltop parking lots to the downtown casinos but were soon replaced with bus shuttles ("Trolley Starts Winter Schedule," *LCC,* November 2, 1994).

76. George Ledbetter, "Lead/Deadwood Shuttle Service to End," *LCC,* May 16, 1992.

77. Char Martin, "Affordable Transportation between Twin Cities?" *LCC,* September 25, 1993.

78. George Ledbetter, "Resort Calls Halt to Trolley Service," *LCC,* November 2, 1994.

79. Wolfe, interview, November 19, 1993.

80. George Ledbetter, "Railroad Plans Move Forward," *LCC,* May 9, 1992; idem, "Deadwood, County Asked to Form Railroad Authority," *LCC,* May 30, 1992. By 1995 early efforts to rebuild old railroad lines to gambling towns had also appeared in Colorado. In Gilpin County narrow-gauge line was proposed for diesel-pulled shuttles for casino employees and tourists linking Black Hawk and the intersection of Colorado 119 and U.S. Highway 6, costing $6 to $8 million. In southern Colorado, the Colorado Springs & Cripple Creek Railway Co. Inc. has plans for a thirty-five-mile route from Colorado Springs west to Woodland Park and Cripple Creek and was trying to secure $2.5 million for a feasibility study and environmental assessment (Associated Press, "Casinos Propose Rail Links," *RCJ,* March 18, 1995).

81. George Ledbetter, "Deadwood Supports RR, Strengthens Noise Ordinance," *LCC,* June 10, 1991.

82. Marian Eatherton, "Rail Authority Corners Whitewood Council," *LCC,* July 8, 1992.

83. George Ledbetter, "Lead Joins Deadwood in Railroad Authority," *LCC,* September 10, 1994; Todd Williams, "Lead Gives Green Light on Railroad Authority," *BHP,* September 7, 1994.

84. Shane Mott, "Highway 85 Construction Begins," *LCC,* January 9, 1993.

85. George Ledbetter, "Dunbar Water Permit Approved," *LCC,* September 3, 1994.

86. Pat Dobbs, "$1 Million Grant for Resort Water," *RCJ,* March 15, 1994; Joe Case, "Bids Awarded on Deadwood Hill Project," *LCC,* August 3, 1994; "Money Continues to Pour in for Dunbar," *BHP,* October 2, 1995; Pat Dobbs, "Dunbar and Public Funds," *RCJ,* October 22, 1995; idem, "Bid near $2 Million for Dunbar The-

ater," *RCJ*, November 9, 1995; idem, "Dunbar Spending $20 Million," *RCJ*, November 28, 1995. Like a chameleon, the projected costs for this resort have varied from $50 to $100 million, and the completion date has likewise varied from 1997 to sometime after 2000.

87. George Ledbetter, "Deadwood Could Have $2 Million Downtown Parking Ramp by May," *LCC*, November 21, 1990.

88. Char Martin, "Deadwood Parking Study Prepares for Phase II," *LCC*, December 9, 1992.

89. Scott Randolph, "Board Votes $2 Million for Ramp," *BHP*, November 3, 1995.

90. George Ledbetter, "Deadwood Ramp Funds OK'd," *RCJ*, November 3, 1995.

91. George Ledbetter, "Preservation Commission Commits $2 Million More to Parking Project," *LCC*, June 28, 1997.

92. George Ledbetter, "Special Hearing Set on Mineral Palace Parking," *LCC*, February 24, 1993.

93. Bloomberg, testimony, September 21, 1994.

Chapter 7. Mining Quarters: Settler Camps to Gambler Traps

1. Peggy Pascoe, "Western Women at the Cultural Crossroads," in Patricia Nelson Limerick, Clyde A. Milner II, and Charles E. Rankin, eds., *Trails: Toward a New Western History* (Lawrence: University Press of Kansas, 1991), 40–58.

2. Donald Worster, "Beyond the Agrarian Myth," in ibid., 3–25.

3. Richard White, "Trashing the Trails," in ibid., 26–39.

4. Vicky Hendrickson, personal interview, October 28, 1995.

5. Donna Franke and Vicky Hendrickson, personal interview, October 28, 1995.

6. Selecting only those establishments with gaming, the members included seventeen male and seventeen female proprietors, including three married couples. Sex was unclear in two additional cases, and two listed no specific person as member.

7. Alex Berenson, "Raising Colorado's Stakes," *DP*, November 5, 1995.

8. Mary Schmit, personal interview, January 27, 1997.

9. Randall Lane, "Success Is the Best Revenge," *Forbes*, May 10, 1993, 182; Penny Parker, "Casino Queen," *Denver Post Magazine*, August 27, 1995.

10. Patricia Stowkowski, *Riches and Regret: Betting on Gambling in Two Colorado Mountain Towns* (Niwot: University Press of Colorado, 1996), 167.

11. Dan Daly, "Golddiggers Sold to Calif. Group," *RCJ*, August 29, 1995.

12. Pat Dobbs, "Full House, Iacocca Merger Still Unfinished," *RCJ*, February 24, 1995; idem, "Full House Selling Deadwood Resort," *RCJ*, January 23, 1996.

13. "Silverado Resort Hearing Delayed," *RCJ*, January 18, 1996.

14. Dan Daly, "Illinois Firm Announces Deadwood Project," *RCJ*, March 15, 1996.

15. Steve Raabe, "Top Casino Operator Sold," *DP*, July 22, 1997; J. Sabastian Sinisi, "Lace House to Stay Put?" *DP*, July 30, 1997; Emily Narvaas, "Gambling Town a Gamble?" *DP*, December 11, 1997.

16. Christopher Goodwin, "Sioux Go on Warpath over Costner," *Sunday Times* (London), February 5, 1995.

17. Avid Little Eagle, "Leaders, Elders Upset over Dunbar Resort," *Indian Country Today*, February 16, 1995.

18. Bill Harlan, "Sioux Buy Hills Land with Profits from Casino," *RCJ*, September 20, 1991.

19. Matt Kelly, "Did Anti-Gambling Vote Reveal Racism?" *RCJ*, September 16, 1993.

20. Kit Miniclier, "Ute Mountain Casino Bustles on First Night," *DP*, September 6, 1992.

21. William Chafe, *Women and Equality: Changing Patterns in American Culture* (New York: Oxford University Press, 1977).

22. Robert Venturi, Denise Scott Brown, and Steven Izenour, *Learning from Las Vegas: The Forgotten Symbolism of Architectural Form* (Cambridge: MIT Press, 1977).

23. A. Alvarez, "Learning from Las Vegas," *New York Review of Books,* January 11, 1996.

24. Robert Goodman, *The Luck Business: The Devastating Consequences and Broken Promises of America's Gambling Explosion* (New York: Free Press, 1995), 15.

25. Stanislaus von Moos, *Venturi, Rauch and Scott Brown: Buildings and Projects* (New York: Rizzoli, 1987), 8.

26. Venturi, Scott Brown, and Izenour, *Learning from Las Vegas,* 153.

27. Ibid., 135.

28. Steve Caulk, "Central City Casino Shut; 32 Lose Jobs," *RMN,* September 2, 1992; Steve Garnaas, "2 Casinos Throw in the Cards," *DP,* November 10, 1992; idem, "Industry Standing Pat as Colo. Casinos Fold," *DP,* November 23, 1993.

29. Steve Garnaas, "Financial Woes Close the Toll Gate Casino," *DP,* July 17, 1993.

30. Goodman, *The Luck Business,* 121–134.

31. Bruce Orwall, "Casinos Aren't for Kids, Many Gambling Firms in Las Vegas Now Say," *WSJ,* December 7, 1995.

32. Ibid.

33. Tom Gorman, "Vegas Light Show Dazzles," *DP,* December 3, 1995.

34. Ann Schrader, "Casinos: Kids Have No Place in Them," *DPM,* September 17, 1995.

35. Steve Lipsher, "Casino Kid Ban Tops List of New Laws," *DP,* June 1, 1996.

36. James Sterngold, "Spread of Gambling Prompts Calls for Federal Study of It," *NYT,* November 24, 1995.

37. Scott Randolph, "Going up? Deadwood Group Seeks to Put $25 Bet Limit on Ballot," *BHP,* January 25, 1996.

38. Berenson, "Cripple Creek Has Its Doubts," *DP,* November 6, 1995.

Chapter 8. Legalized Gambling as a Community Development Quick Fix

1. Our discussion of the history of gambling in the United States is indebted to the detailed analysis provided by John M. Findlay's history, *People of Chance* (New York: Oxford University Press, 1986) and to I. Nelson Rose, "The Legalization and Control of Casino Gambling," *Fordham Urban Law Journal* 8 (1980): 245–300.

2. I. Nelson Rose, "The Future of Indian Gaming," *Journal of Gambling Studies* 8, no. 4 (1992): 383–399.

3. Francis X. Clines, "With Casino Profits, Indian Tribes Thrive," *NYT,* January 31, 1993.

4. Dirk Johnson, "Economies Come to Life on Indian Reservations," *NYT,* July 3, 1994.

5. Pauline Yoshihashi, "As Indian Casinos Spread, Politicians and Rivals Maneuver to Fight the Trend," *WSJ,* May 4, 1993.

6. National Indian Gaming Association, www2.dgsys.com/7Eniga/stat.html, July 16, 1996, 2.

7. William R. Eadington, "The Legalization of Casinos: Policy Objectives, Regulatory Alternatives, and Cost/Benefit Considerations," *Journal of Travel Research* (Winter 1996): 6.

8. Dirk Johnson, "Weicker and Indian Tribe in a Slot Machine Parlay," *NYT,* January 14, 1993.

9. Ibid.

10. Barbara A. Carmichael, Donald M. Peppard Jr., and Frances A. Boudreau, "Megaresort on My Doorstep: Local Resident Attitudes toward Foxwoods Casino and Casino Gambling on Nearby Indian Reservation Land," *Journal of Travel Research* (Winter 1996): 9.

11. "Eyeing Reservations, Arizona Bans Casino Games," *NYT,* March 7, 1993.

12. Tim Korte, "Feds Say Casinos Illegal," *DP,* May 15, 1996.

13. Kit Miniclier, "Feds See Jackpot in Tribal Casinos: Tax, Controls Loom as Indians See Expansion," *DP,* April 11, 1994; Pauline Yoshihashi, "As Indian Casinos Spread," *WSJ,* May 4, 1993; Tracey A. Reeves, "Indian Gaming Crackdown Brews," *DP,* June 24, 1994.

14. Robert Goodman, *The Luck Business* (New York: Free Press, 1995), 96.

15. Francis X. Clines, "As States Rush to Gamble, Experts See Risks," *NYT,* April 26, 1993.

16. Martin Koughan, "Easy Money," *Mother Jones* (July–August 1997): 41.

17. Clines, "As States Rush."

18. Ellen Perlman, "Gambling, Mississippi Style," *Governing* (April 1995): 40–41.

19. Semoon Chang, "The Birth of a New Industry: Casinos in the Coastal Mississippi," *Journal of Business Forecasting* (Fall 1995): 8.

20. Kevin Sack, "Gambling Fuels Louisiana Voter Anger," *NYT,* September 26, 1995.

21. Ellen Perlman, "Gambling Mississippi Style," *Governing* (April 1995): 40, 42.

22. Lawrence J. Truitt, "Casino Gambling in Illinois: Riverboats, Revenues, and Economic Development," *Journal of Travel Research* (Winter 1996): 91.

23. Joseph P. Shapiro, "America's Gambling Fever," *U.S. News & World Report,* January 15, 1996, 58.

24. Peter Eisinger, *Rise of the Entrepreneurial State* (Madison: University of Wisconsin Press, 1988).

25. Goodman, *The Luck Business,* 173–191.

26. Patrick Long, Jo Clark, and Derek Liston, *Win, Lose, or Draw? Gambling with America's Small Towns* (Washington, D.C.: Aspen Institute, 1994), 41–42.

27. Steve Garnaas, "Gaming Towns Doubt Benefits," *DP,* November 6, 1995.

28. Pat Dobbs, "Gambling in a Slump," *RCJ,* June 3, 1996.

29. "Gaming Revenues Fall off Sharply in October," *BHP,* November 28, 1995; "Deadwood's Gambling Revenue Down," *RCJ,* November 28, 1995; South Dakota Gaming Commission, "South Dakota Gaming Statistics."

30. "Casino Cuts Hurt City Hall," *DP,* February 19, 1996; Alex Berenson, "Cold Snap Takes Toll on Casino Revenues," *DP,* February 21, 1996.

31. Eadington, "The Legalization of Casinos," 3; Koughan, "Easy Money," 32.

32. Pauline Yoshihashi, "Survey Reveals a Recent Jump in Casino Goers," *WSJ,* January 8, 1993.

33. "Bible Belt Loosens up Rigid Stance on Gambling," *DP,* August 15, 1993.

34. James Sterngold, "Casinos May Find Adversity a Boon," *NYT,* December 31, 1995.

35. Denise Ross, "Gaming Revenue Dips 8%," *RCJ,* June 26, 1997.

36. Ibid.

37. Colorado Department of Revenue, Division of Gaming, "Gaming Update," May 1997.

38. James Wallace, "Wanna Bet? America's Wager Crazy," *DP,* August 15, 1993.

39. "Wagering Boom May Go Bust," *DP,* August 15, 1993.

INDEX

Numbers in italics refer to the illustrations.

Abt, Vicki, 5

Adams brothers, 31, 111, 113

Adams House, Deadwood, 31, *112;* restoration of, 111–13

Adams Museum, Deadwood, 113–14

adaptive reuse, 7, 75, 116, 122, 191

African-Americans, 36–37, 41, 49, 62

Amendment 4 (Colorado), 24–25, 89. *See also* gambling, impacts of legalization

antigambling campaigns, 11, 18–20, 21–22, 34, 47

anti-immigrant sentiment, 28, 49–50

antiprostitution campaigns, 29, 46–47

Apa, Jerry, 12

architecture, 103, 175–77

Asians, 28–29, 36, 41, 49–50

assessed valuations: Colorado, 151–52; Deadwood, 142

Atlantic City, N.J., 14, 184

Ayres, Agnes, 33

Ayres, Albro, 32

Ayres, George V., 32

Ayres Hardware, Deadwood, 32–33

Belvidere Theater, Central City, 43, 81

bet limits, 3, 13, 26, 185; proposals to increase, 98–101, 174, 181, 192

Black Hawk, Colorado, 3, 16, 22–23, 38–39, 41–42, 44, 55, 67, 85–86, 126, 192; casino architecture, *124,* 177; municipal revenues, 192; National Historic Landmark designation, 68; rehabilitation standards, 124, 126

Black Hills gold rush, 10, 35; as theme of Deadwood tourism, 60–61

blackjack, 95, 102, 135

Blair, Linda, 14, 168

Blair, Tom, 12, 15, 69, 77–78, 172

Blake, Norm, 150–51, 154

Bloomberg, Jeff, 132, 146–47, 164–65, 169

brothels. *See* prostitution

Brown, Lary, 23–24, 89

Bullock Hotel, Deadwood, 32–33, 168–69; restoration of, 114, 170

Bullwhackers, 86, 88, 130, *151,* 206n. 56

businesses: conversion to casinos, 74–75, *140,* 191; impacts of gambling on, 85, 132–34, 139, 149–52, *150, 151*

Calamity Jane, 30

Carnegie Library, Deadwood, 33, 118–19

casinos: architecture, 124; closings, 133, 177–78; live entertainment in, 179; local ownership of, 15, 80, 97; names and success of, 177–78; outside investment in, 171–73; profits, 194; size, 89, 172; themed, 177–78; workers' wages, 153

Central City, Colorado, 3, 39, 55, 64, 79, 82–83, *125, 126;* history, 16–20, 41–44; moratorium on casino development, 87–88; National Historic Landmark designation, 68; opening day of gambling, 83–84

Central City Opera Festival: and gam-

bling, 17–18, 44, 64, 128–29, 152–53, 184; as tourist attraction, 44, 63–64
Central City Opera House, 19, 42–44, 66
Central City Opera House Association, 63, 66–67, 128–29, 152–53
Chandler, Mary, 125
children, 109, 137, 142–44, 156, 179–80, 187, 206n. 56
Christiansen, E. M., 5
churches, views on legalization of gambling, 25
class issues, 48, 50–51, 168, 175, 178
Colorado: gambling legalization campaign, 16–26; gold rush, 16, 38, 41–42, 44–45; opening day of gambling, 78, 83–84; South Dakota impacts reported in, 147–48
Colorado gambling law: and buildings, 86; and gaming device limits, 86; and gaming tax structure, 89, 92–93
Colorado Gaming Commission, 89
Colorado State Historical Association, 128
Community Development Block Grants, 58–59, 70
community impacts of legalized gambling, 132–65, 191–92; on businesses, 133–34, 149–52; on children, 142–45; in Colorado, 147–56; in Deadwood, 132–47, 180–81; on employment, 134–37, 153; on health services, 148; on housing, 158–59; on law enforcement, 145–47; on parking, 163–64; on politics, 154; on social services, 137–41; on tourism, 191–92; on traffic, 148–49; on transportation, 159–61
Connecticut, Indian gaming in, 186
Costner, Dan, 78, 80, 100–101, 115, 173
Costner, Kevin, 78, 97–98, 115, 173; conflicts with Sioux peoples, 174–75
Costner Project, 97–102, 173–74; cost of, 213–14n. 86; public funds used for, 162
crime rates, Lawrence County, 145–47
Cripple Creek, Colorado, 3, 18, 49–51, 55, 60, 64–65, 125, *150*, *167*; history, 45–53; National Historic Landmark designation, 68; opening day of gambling, 84–85
Cripple Creek District gold strike, 16, 45
Cripple Creek Historic Preservation Officer, 125, 127
Crotty, Chuck, 138

Dances with Wolves, 97, 173
day care, 88, 137, 144, 171, 206n. 56. *See also* children
Deadwood, South Dakota, 3, 25–26, 28–29, 34, 55, 74; historic preservation projects, 109–23; history, 10–12, 27–35; impacts of gambling, 74–75, 132–47; infrastructure, 108–9, 156–64; National Historic Landmark designation, 105; opening day of gambling, 3, 15, 74; source of gambling visitors, 77–78; tourism, 60, 62, 109
Deadwood City Hall, 157
Deadwood Community Housing Organization, 158
Deadwood Historic Preservation Commission (DHPC), 32, 75, 78, 105, 107–23, 154, 158–59, 161, 163, 170; funding decisions, 114, 116–17, 118–21; as recipient of gaming tax revenues, 93, 118
Deadwood You Bet Committee, 13–14, 108
"decorated shed," 7, 176–77
Denver, Colorado, 17, 21–22, 44, 63, 67, 81, 84
Dunbar. *See* Costner Project

Eastmo, Virginia and Ron, 143
economic development: model of Peter Eisinger, 7, 58, 76, 90, 130, 190; as rationale for legalizing gambling, 3, 4–5, 8, 14, 190–93
Economic Development Administration, 58
Economic Opportunity Act, 57
Economic Recovery Tax Act, 106
Eisinger, Peter K., 7, 58, 76, 90, 130, 190
employment, 24, 89, 91–92, 134–37, 153
ethnic groups, 36–37, 49, 71–72
Ethnic History Park, Lead, 71

facadism, 108, 116, 118, 122–23, 124–25, *126*, 175
Fairmont Hotel, Deadwood, 33, 103–4
federal policies and programs: historic preservation, 7, 59, 67–68, 106; influence on population redistribution, 56–57; to reverse rural economic decline, 58–59; role of, in states' legalization of gambling, 182
Findlay, John M., 6, 72, 215n. 1
Fish and Hunter Warehouse, Deadwood, 32, 157

foreign investment, 83, 129
Foxwoods, 186
Franke, Donna, 135–36
Franklin Hotel, Deadwood, 33, 111
frontier, gambling and, 6, 10. *See also* West, the American

gambling: for economic development, 3, 4–5, 8, 14, 190–93; as entertainment, 6, 187, 191, 193; expansion proposals, 96–102, 175, 181; and government's evolution from watchdog to partner, 105; history, 11, 17, 22–23, 83–84; impacts of legalization, 74–77, 79, 85, 132–65, 191–92; opening day, 3, 15, 74, 78, 83–85; as painless taxation, 164–65, 195; profits, 91, 193–94; residents' expectations for, 9; residents' views of impacts of, 151–52, 155–56; second thoughts on, 180–81; as vice, 5, 148, 183, 187, 193
gaming devices, 15, 81, 83–84, 99, 130; fees, 22–23, 77, 93–94; limits, 26, 97, 102–4
gaming tax revenues, 48, 114, 164–65, 183, 192–93; distribution of, 92–94
gender, 29–30, 48–49, 168–71, 175, 178. *See also* women
Gillmore Hotel, Deadwood, *110*, 111
Gilpin County, Colorado, 39–44, 82, 87
Goldberg, Jake, 31
Gold Mine casino, Black Hawk, 84, 171
gold mining, 6, 10, 16–17, 27, 38, 45–46, 50, 52, 54, 183; as casino theme, 177–78
Greeley, Horace, 39, 43
Gregory, John, 38–40
Griffith, Lowell, 19–21
Gushurst, P. A., 31
Gustafson, Mike, 99

Harvey's, Central City, *125*, 130
Hawkins, Lora, 137, 143–45
health services, impacts of gambling on, 148
Hearst, George, 35, 38
Hearst, Phoebe Apperson, 36, 38
Hearst Mercantile Company, Lead, 37–38, 70
Hemmeters, 86, 88, 173
Hendrickson, Vicky, 135–36
historic preservation, 4, 12, 24–25, 33, 59, 66–68, 105–32; exterior vs. inte-

rior, 75, 86, 115–16, 122–23; federal programs, 7, 59, 106; and historic integrity, 127–28; ironies of, 180; and private interests, 118–22; state programs, 106–7
historic preservation funds: sources of, 16, 93–94, 105–7; use of, 77, 111, 113, 116–17, 123–30, 157–58
Homestake gold strike, 10, 35
Homestake Mining Company, 31, 35–38, 69–71. *See also* Lead, South Dakota
Horner, Chuck, 137–38
housing, 79–80, 110–11, 139, 141, 158–59
Howe Building, Deadwood, 115
Huxtable, Ada Louise, 122

Illinois, riverboat gambling in, 189–90
Imperial Hotel, Cripple Creek, 65
Indian gaming: 4, 102, 175, 180, 193–94; in Arizona, 186; in Colorado, 175, 186–87; in Connecticut, 186; in Minnesota, 185; outside investment in, 172; revenues from, 186; taxation of, 175
Indian Gaming Regulatory Act, 171, 185
infrastructure: improvement programs, 58, 65, 77, 87, 108–9, 131, 156–64; seasonal use of, 192; use of gambling revenues for, 125, 156–57
interstate highway system, 56–57
Iowa, gambling in, 187–88
Izenour, Steven, 7, 176

Jameson, Betsy, 46, 51
Jandreau, Mike, 174
Jenkins, John C., Jr., 18–19, 63
Joy, JoDean, 101, 168, 173

Keen, Lew, 12–13
Krantz, Terry, 161, 174–75

Lace House, Black Hawk, *67*, 127; restoration of, 67–68
landmark designation program, 106. *See also* National Historic Landmark designation
land speculation: after introduction of gambling, 26, 74–75, 79, 81, 191, 204n. 17; public agencies' involvement in, 82–83
Las Vegas, 22, 176; compared to four towns studied, 179

law enforcement, 145–47; legislation limiting tax revenues for, 147

Lawrence County, South Dakota, 5, 10, 35–36, 38. *See also* Deadwood, South Dakota

Lawrence County Courthouse, Deadwood, 12, 34, 83, 157; restoration of, 108

Lead, South Dakota, 10, 35, 62, 68–72. *See also* Homestake Mining Company

legalization of gambling: in Atlantic City, 184; attempts at, 12–15; in Colorado, 24–25; in Las Vegas, 22; in South Dakota, 77

Levine, Brian, 125, 127

Lewis, Virginia, 168, 171

licensing proposal, 20

Limerick, Patricia, 7

Little Kingdom Historical Foundation, 67–68

Lord's Cupboard (food pantry), Lead, 138–39

Louisiana, gambling in, 189

Lux, Harley, 71

Madden, Michael, 14, 75, 134, 143

Manitou Springs, Colorado, 96–97

Manuel brothers, 31, 35

Marchbanks, Lucretia, 33

Martin, Landis, 128–29

Mattson, Jon, 99–100, 103, 163

McFarlane, Peter, 42–44

Midnight Star, Deadwood, 78, 115, 120

migration, rural to urban, 54, 56–57

mining, decline in, 56. *See also* gold mining

Minnesota, Indian gaming in, 185

Mississippi, gambling in, 188–89

multiple action blackjack, 102

multiple building designation, 102–4

National Historic Landmark designation: Central City, Black Hawk, and Cripple Creek, 68; Deadwood, 74, 105; importance of retaining, 12, 115, 117–18, 123, 125–26

National Historic Preservation Act, 106

National Park Service, 67–68

National Register of Historic Places, 71, 106

National Trust for Historic Preservation, 111, 127

Native Americans, 27–28, 39–41, 102, 174–75, 180, 197n. 1

Neighborhood Reinvestment Corporation, 158

Nelson, Melodee, 13–14, 170–71

Oberlander, Bruce, 15, 98, 134, 146

opening day, 3, 15, 74, 78, 83–85; differences between Colorado and Deadwood, 83

Opitz, George, 145

organized crime, 5, 16, 18–19, 22

outside investment, 80–81, 83, 86–87, 90, 97, 171–73

Parking, 150, 163–64

Phoenix Building, Deadwood, restoration of, 115–16

population decline, in mining towns, 44, 55

population redistribution, rural to urban, 54, 56–57

Poundstone, Freda, 24, 168

primary industries, decline in, 55–56

private homes, loans to, 116–17

private property rights, and historic preservation, 120

property assessments, impacts of gambling on, 9, 26, 74–75, 81, 142, 151–52

property taxes, 79, 100, 132–33, 141–42, 151–52, 191

prostitution, 6, 11–12, 22, 28–30, 34, 40, 42, 45–48, 50, 52, 184; tolerated, 11–12, 34–35, 45–48, 50; as tourist attraction, 60

Public Works and Economic Development Act, 57

Putz, Paul, 12, 106, 118

race, 168, 175, 178. *See also* African-Americans, Asians, Native Americans

racism, 175

railroads, 160–62

Ramstetter, Alice C., 20–21

Randolph, George, 41

Randolph, Harriet, 41

Read, Walter, 14

religion, and opposition to gambling, 25

reservation casinos. *See* Indian gaming

revenues: Colorado, 88, 90–91, 93–94, 193, 194–95; comparison of Deadwood and Colorado, 90–91; Deadwood, 16, 75, 79, 90–91, 192; for

infrastructure improvement, 156–57;
for law enforcement, 147; from pros-
titution, 48
Richards, Clinton, 11
risk taking, 9–10, 57, 72–74, 77, 183–84
riverboat gambling, 4, 187–90, 193
Romer, Roy, 23, 24–25
Rosen, Ruth, 6
Rural Development Act, 57
Russell brothers, 38–40

Salmonson, Dick, 25
Schenkein, Dan, 12–13
Schmit, Mary, 135, 168, 169–70
Scott Brown, Denise, 7, 176–77
seniors, impacts of gambling on, 139, 141
signage, 118–20, 127, 157; Deadwood vs.
Las Vegas, 176–77
Skolnick, Jerome H., 5, 195
slot machines, 21, 23, 89, 94–95, 129,
140, 154. *See also* gaming devices
Smaldone, Clyde, 19
Small Business Administration, 58
Smith, James F., 5
Smith-Rogers, Carol, 113
social change, attitudes toward, 14, 155–
56
social history, western, 168
social services, impacts of gambling on,
137–41, 143–44
South Dakota Gaming Commission, 15–
16, 102
state gaming legislation, 76–77, 129–30;
in Colorado, 25–26, 86, 130, 154, 193;
in South Dakota, 11, 15–16, 130, 147
Street, Julian, 52
Syndicate Building, Deadwood, 121–22

table games, 95. *See also* gaming devices
Tax Increment Financing Districts (TIFD),
Deadwood, 100, 158–59, 162, 173
Tax Reform Act, 106
Teller County, Colorado, 45, 148
Teller Hotel, 42–43, 128
Teller House, 19, 43, 66, 83–84, 128,
152–53
Thomas, Lowell, 52
Ticknor, Mary, 135
tourism, 59–62, 64–65, 72, 77, 148, 183;
and ages of visitors, 179; development
of mining-related, 70; gambling im-
pacts on, 133, 191–92; seasonality of,
61, 63, 82, 131, 191

Tracey, Lucille, 138–39
traffic accidents, 148–49
transients, 138–39
transportation, 159–62, 213n. 80
Treber Ice House, Deadwood, 122
Trucano, Mike, 12–13, 100, 115–16
Tubbs, Poker Alice, 30
Twin City Mall, 69, 139

unions, 48–49, 136
Urban Development Action Grant: in
Deadwood, 69; program, 58

venture capital, 81
Venturi, Robert, 7, 176–77
vice, 45; history of, 183–85; taxation of,
53; tolerance of, 6, 40, 46–67
Victor, Colorado, 45, 47–48, 204n. 7
video lottery, 79

wager totals, 75
wages, 136, 153
Walsh, Bill, 12, 13, 98, 169, 175, 180–81
water and sewage: in Black Hawk, 88; in
Central City, 87. *See also* infrastructure
wealth, turnover in, 156
West, the American: concept of, 168;
gambling in history of, 183; ironies of,
180; mythology of, 7; real vs. imagined, 178–79; theme towns, 168; as
tourist attraction, 60–62, 166–68
Western Federation of Miners, 51
White, Richard, 8, 167
Wild West Winners Club, Deadwood,
172–73
Williams Stables, Central City, restoration of, 66
Wilson, Emily, 19
Wittington, Betty, 13
Wolfe, Mark, 105–9, 112, 116–20,
122–23, 157, 160, 163
Womack, Robert, 45, 51
women, 28, 33, 35, 168–71; in Central
City, 40; in Cripple Creek, 46, 48–49;
in Deadwood, 29–30; employment of,
30, 48–49, 167–68; in Lead, 36; in legalization campaigns, 168–69
Wong Wing Tsu, 28–29
working conditions, 136

Youmans, Russell, 56

ABOUT THE AUTHORS

Audie Blevins, a Texas transplant, has been at the University of Wyoming, Department of Sociology, since 1970, where he is professor and department chair. Since 1981 he has shared both an intellectual life and a familial life with Katherine Jensen. Together they raised four children, Stephanie, Erika, Michael, and Jens. His academic interests intersect the fields of demography, community, and social planning; other interests include backpacking, rafting, fly fishing, and travel. Life in Wyoming has been interrupted by sabbatical stays at the Australian National University, a family round-the-world trip, teaching and research during two springs in London, and other travel in Europe and Egypt. His next research projects involve historical demography and evaluating social policies on the Wind River Indian Reservation. Blevins anticipates additional research and writing as well as more travel adventures with Katherine Jensen.

Katherine Jensen grew up on a cattle ranch in the Northern Black Hills of South Dakota. After educational sojourns in the Midwest and Southwest, she has spent two decades at the University of Wyoming. Primarily using women's oral histories, she has written about uncovering the undocumented lives and unpaid work of rural women in the United States and the Third World. Jensen has served as director of Women's Studies, director of International Studies, and associate dean of the College of Arts and Sciences. As a "regular" professor, she looks forward to additional research in Africa, Asia, and the Rocky Mountains and to scholarship less interrupted by administrative responsibilities.